OUT OF PICTURE

ART FROM THE OUTSIDE LOOKING IN

OUT OF PICTURE

ART FROM THE OUTSIDE LOOKING IN

VOLUME I

VILLARD · NEW YORK

Out of Picture volume 1 is a work of fiction. Names, places, and incidents either are a product of the authors' imaginations or are used fictiously. Any resemblance to actual events, locales, or persons, living or dead, is entirely coincidental.

A Villard Books Trade Paperback Edition

Published in the United States by Villard Books, an imprint of The Random House Publishing Group, a division of Random House, Inc., New York.

VILLARD and "V" CIRCLED Design are registered trademarks of Random House, Inc.

Originally published in hardcover and in different form in 2006 by Editions Paquet

This edition published by arrangement with Out of Picture Press LLC.

ISBN 978-0-345-49872-4

Printed in China

www.villardbooks.com

9 8 7 6 5 4 3 2 1

Masterminds: Daisuke Tsutsumi, Vincent Nguyen
Cover art: Michael Knapp and Daisuke Tsutsumi
Back cover illustration: Daniel López Muñoz
Book design: Michael Knapp

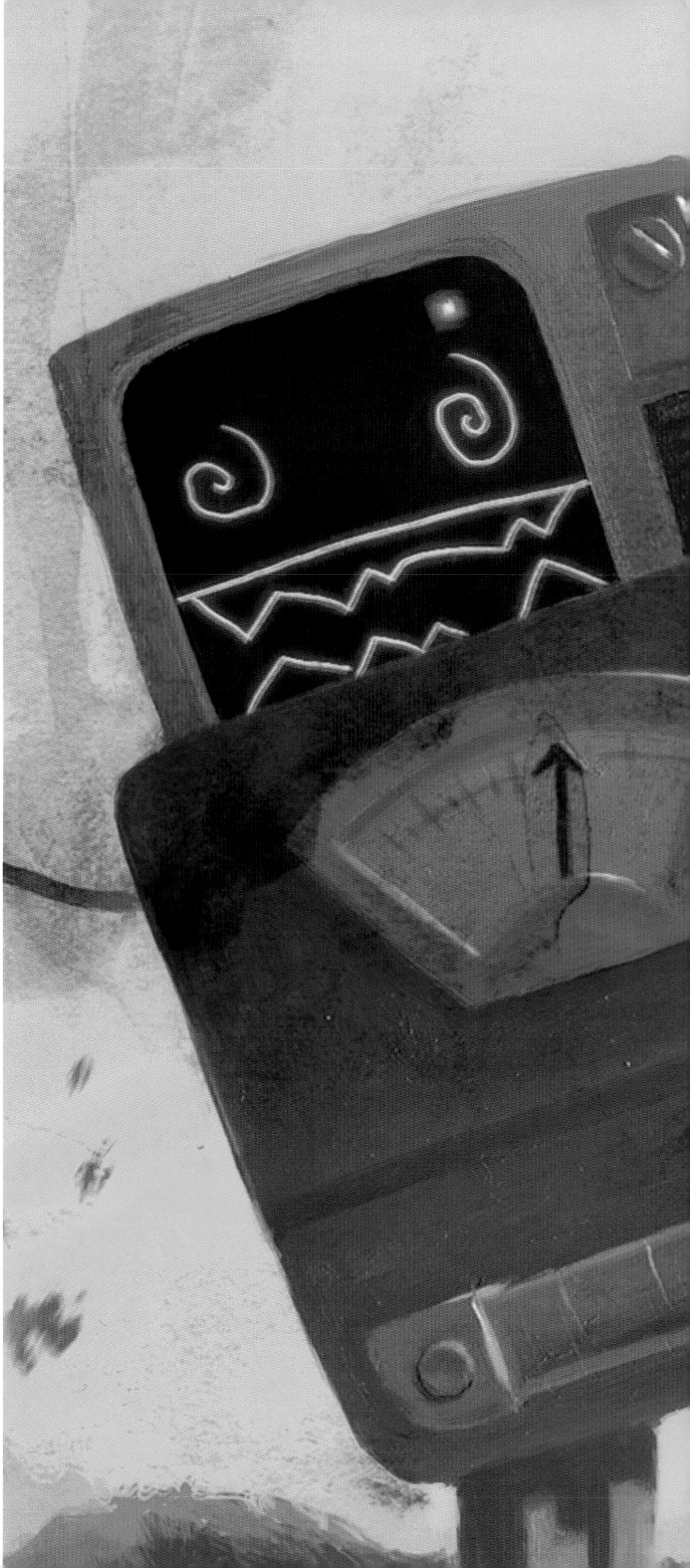

TABLE OF
(MAL)
CONTENTS

FOREWORD by Chris Wedge   7

THE STORIES

1. "Noche y Dia" by Daisuke Tsutsumi   10

2. "Four & Twenty Blackbirds" by Greg Couch   24

3. "Newsbreak" by Michael Knapp   30

4. "Floating Holidays" by Benoit le Pennec   42

5. "Silent Echoes" by Daniel López Muñoz   48

6. "The Mermaid" by Peter de Sève   58

7. "The Wedding Present" by David Gordon   64

8. "Yes, I Can" by Andrea Blasich   76

9. "Domesticity" by Vincent Nguyen   84

10. "Night School" by Nash Dunnigan   94

11. "Around the Corner" by Robert Mackenzie   102

DEVELOPMENT GALLERY   112

Artist Biographies   154

Acknowledgments   156

Illustration by Vincent Nguyen
Drawing on title page by Vincent Nguyen

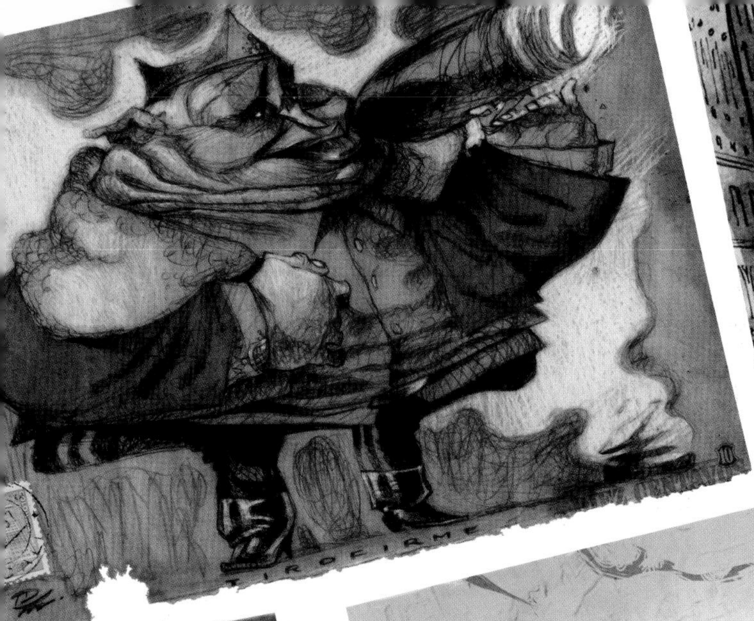

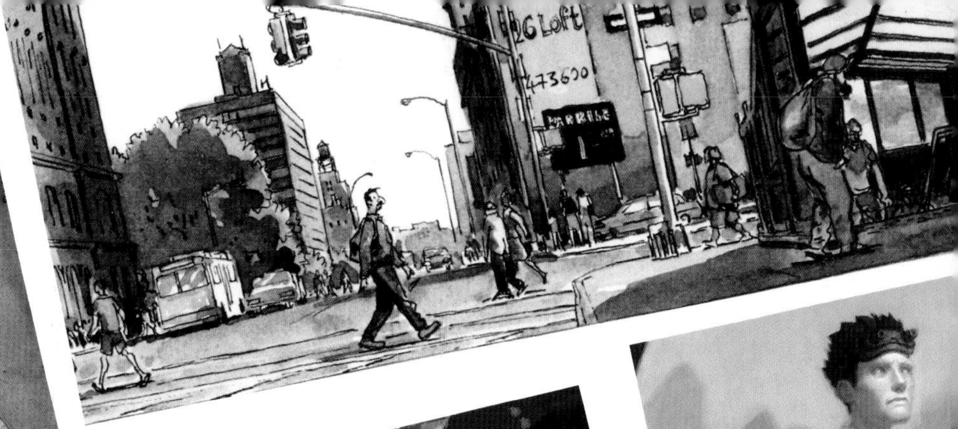

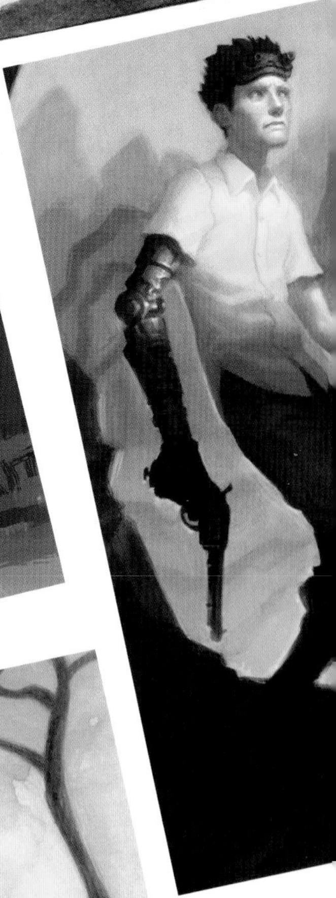

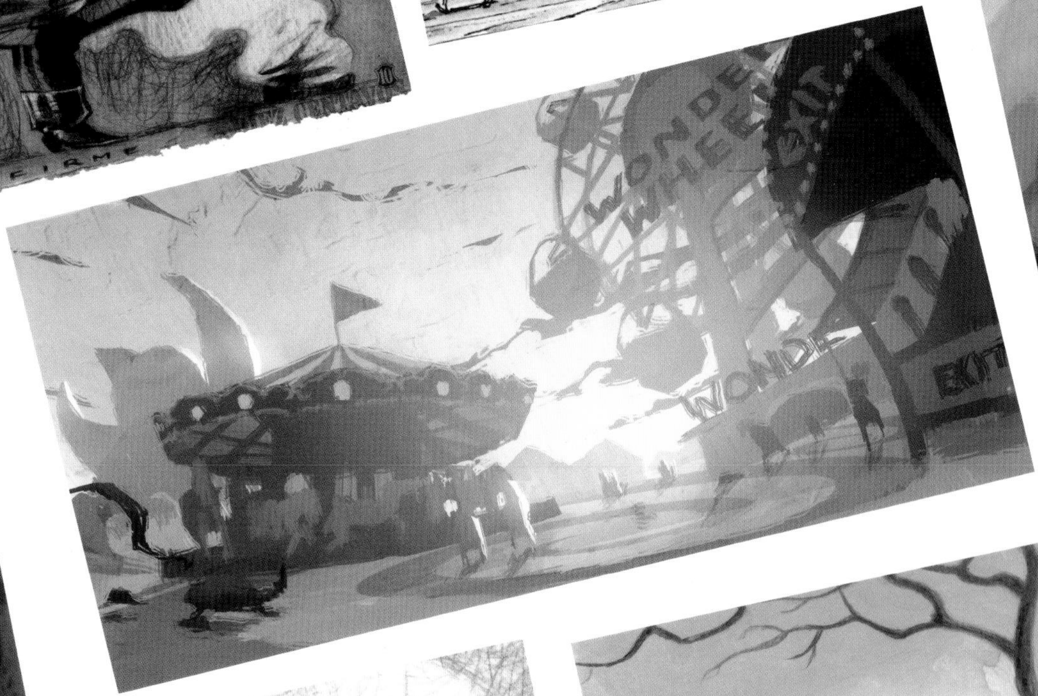
WONDE
EXIT

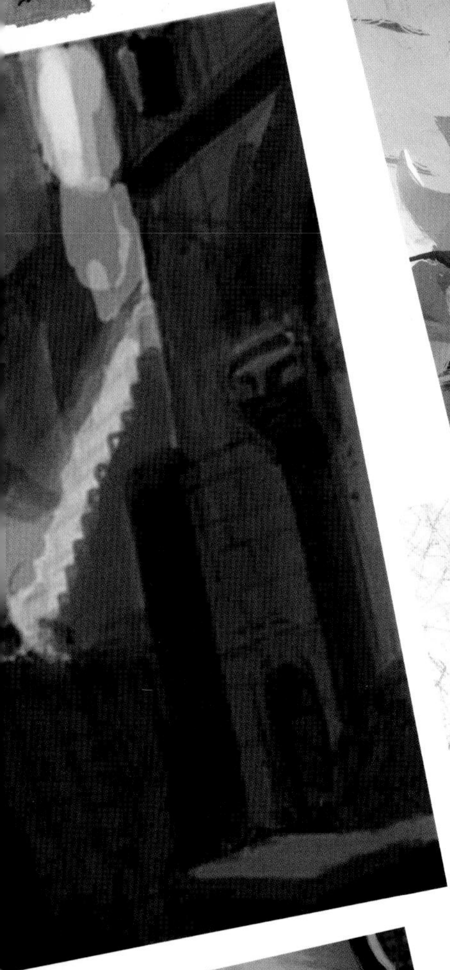

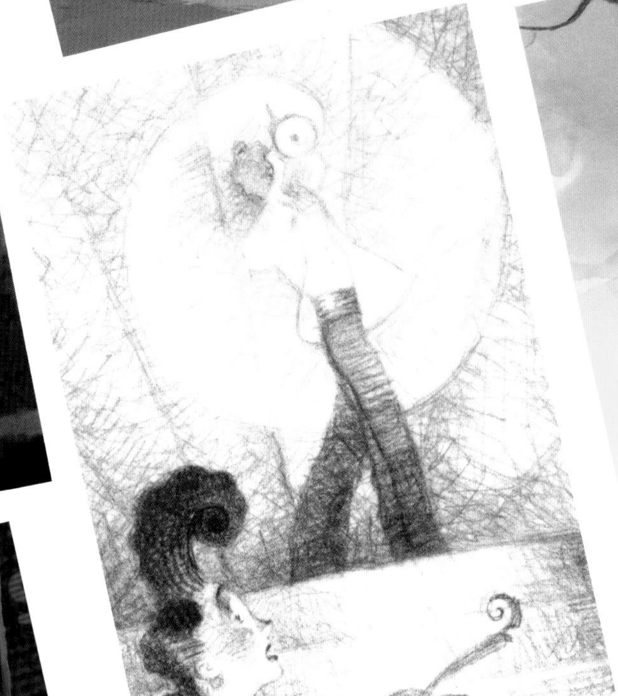

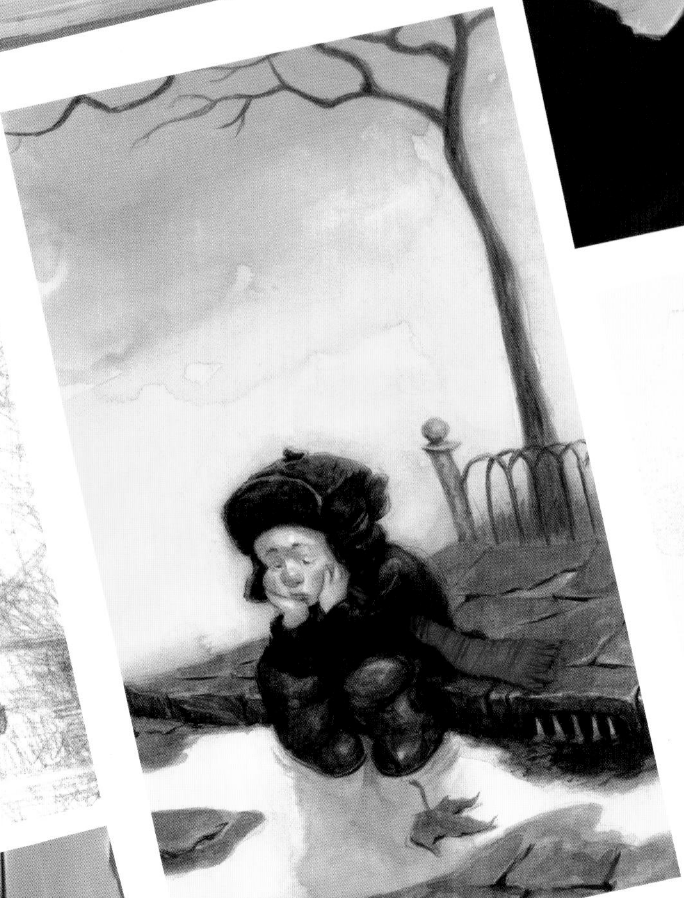

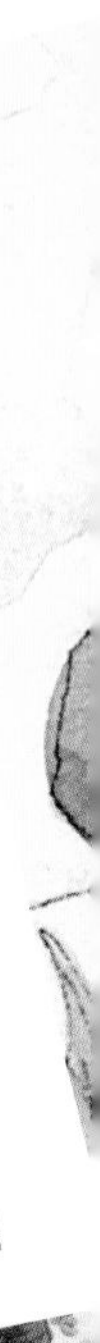

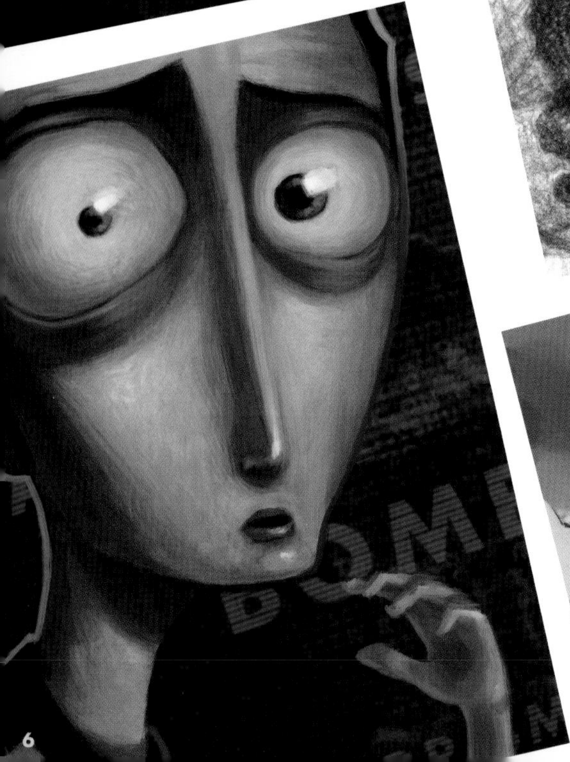

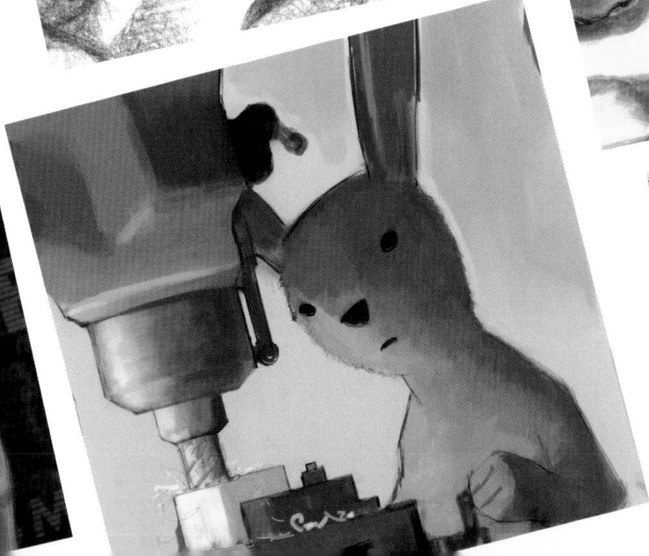

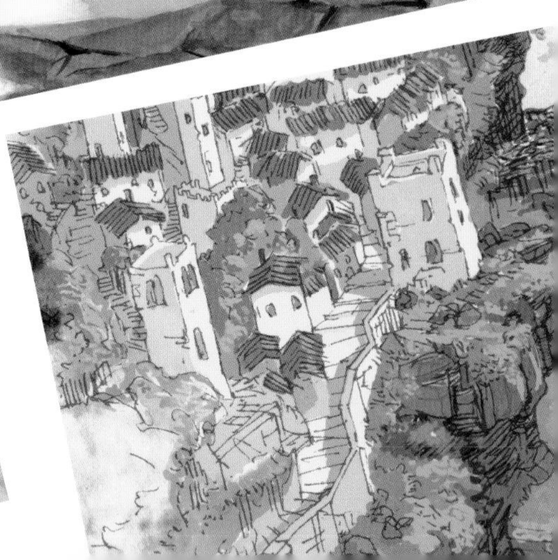

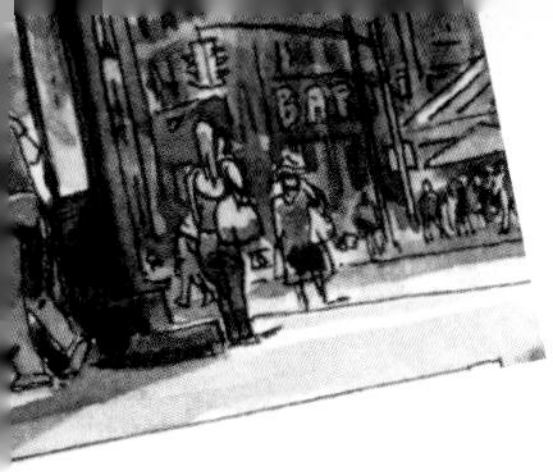

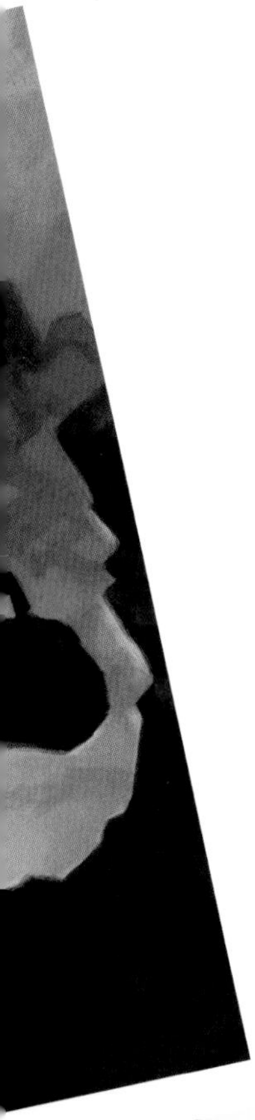

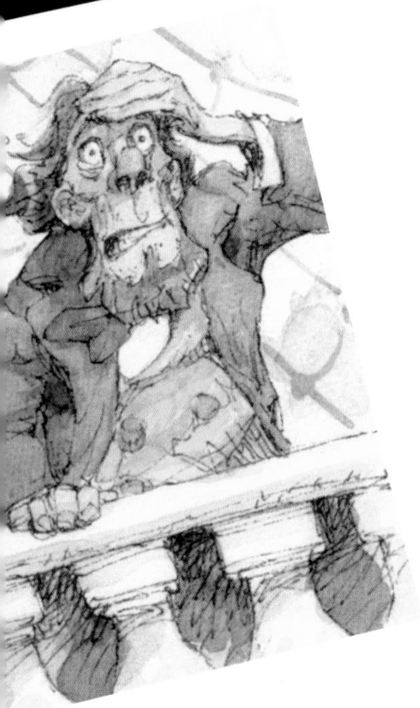

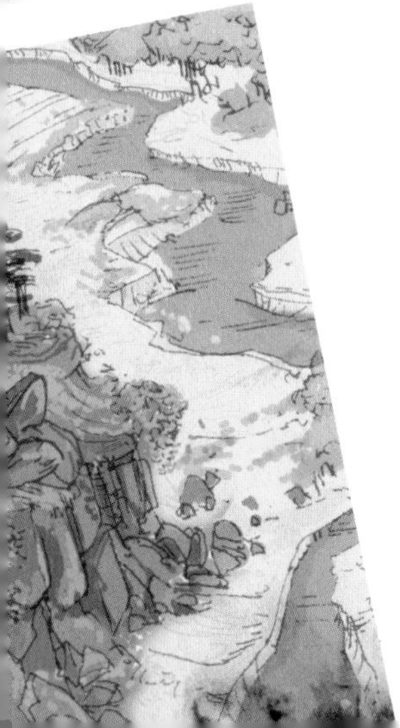

FOREWORD

The artists at Blue Sky exist in a community of collaboration. They dance for years at a time, around a monster called an animated movie. They whisper what it might become into the ether around the operating table. They lay its bones down one by one. They dress it carefully in flesh, and caress the heart of it to bring it to life. Whether it stands and walks or drops in confused convulsions will not be known until they are finished, but it will do so at the feet of these many surrogate parents, entranced at what they have wrought together.

This process by which each contributes a focused ray of his own talent, then steps aside to allow the next the same, is one of measured sacrifice. In giving only what is asked of them, all hold back a reservoir of creative potential that roils, impatient for escape, within their hearts.

Ironically, the worlds that exist within each one of them are as complete as the worlds they create together. This truth I relearn in every interaction in every moment at Blue Sky—that our endeavors together are fed by wells of limitless creativity that exist inside each one of us, and that what forms as complete work outside is a shadow of that potential concealed within.

Here, then, lies a glimpse into the realms which these wizards normally protect for themselves. Released from the laboratory, they have conspired to offer their own stories in their own hands, on their own terms. They have admitted us into a secret circle where each in turn howls at the moon in his own voice.

It is as much a privilege for me to work with these artists as it is to present them to you. They are the means by which our movies are conceived, and by which the future of our medium is undoubtedly assured.

CHRIS WEDGE
DIRECTOR, BLUE SKY STUDIOS
SEPTEMBER 2005

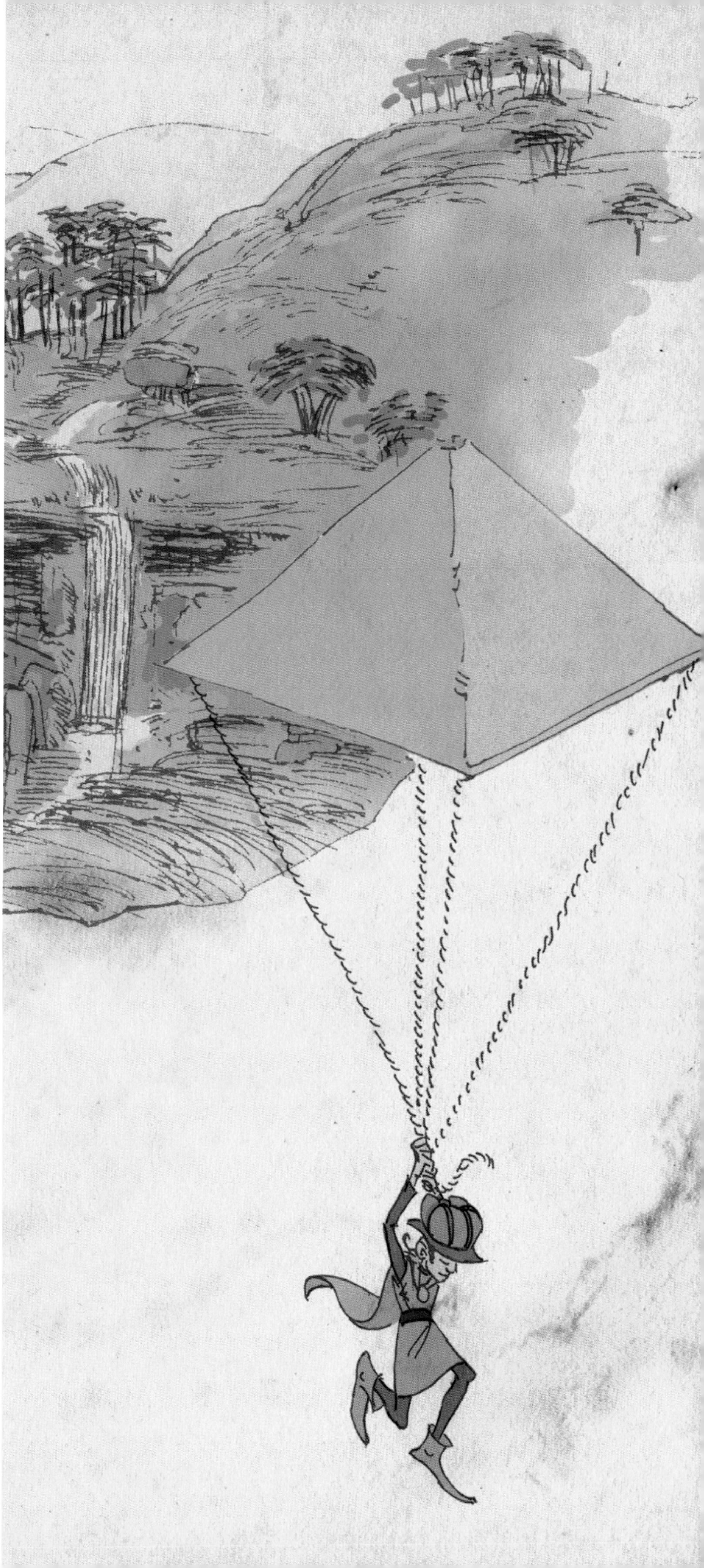

Illustration by Andrea Blasich

Previous spread from left to right, top to bottom: Daniel López Muñoz, Benoît le Pennec, Nash Dunnigan, Daisuke Tsutsumi, Vincent Nguyen, Greg Couch, Robert Mackenzie, Peter de Sève, Michael Knapp, David Gordon, and Andrea Blasich

"Out of picture" is a film term we use whenever something is cut from a movie—or we say "it's OOPed." While it can be frustrating to have to let go of one's ideas, it's the pursuit and exploration of those ideas that can be the most fulfilling. We wanted to share some of our personal ideas outside of our film work with you— out of picture. . . .

We hope you enjoy them.

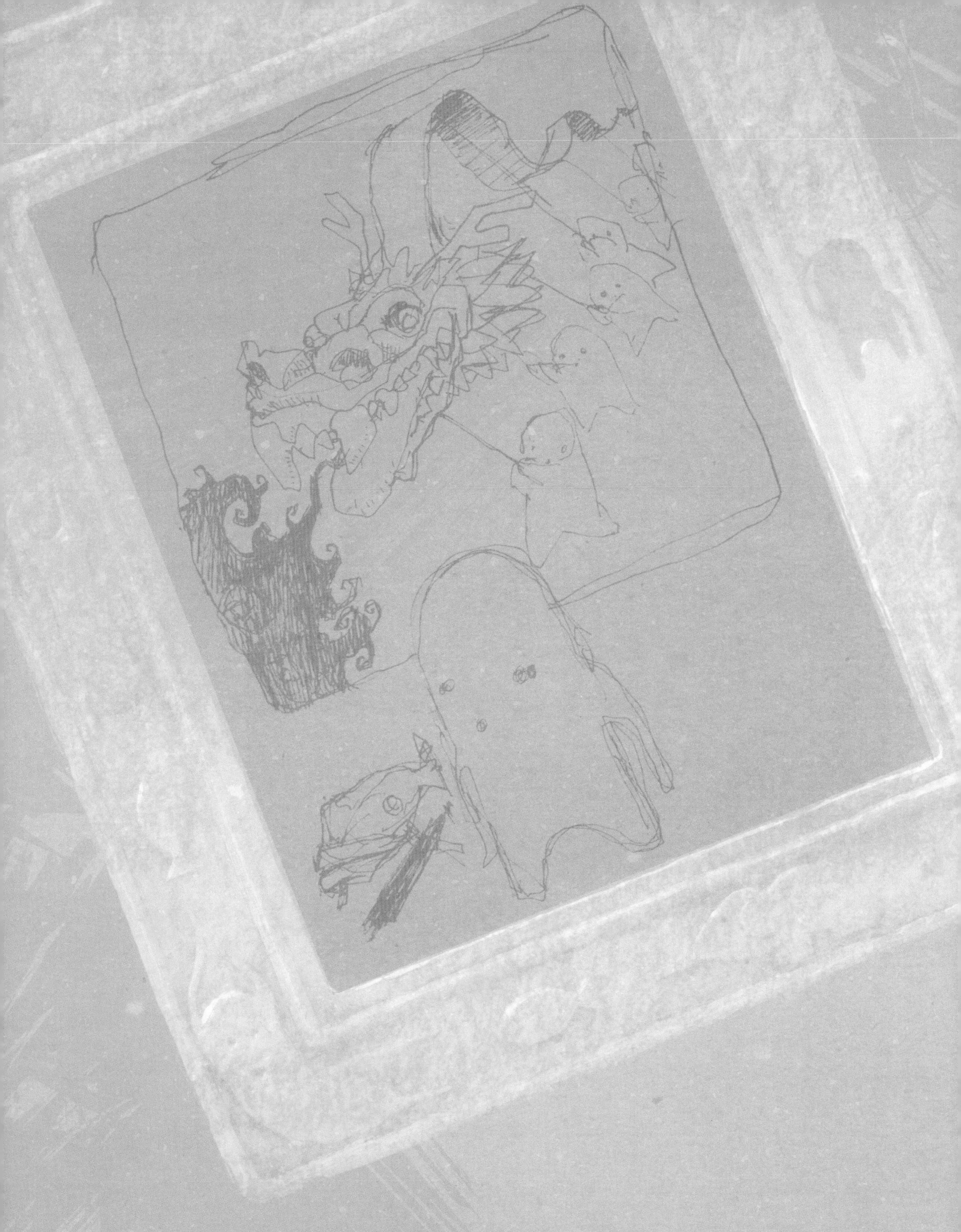

DAISUKE TSUTSUMI

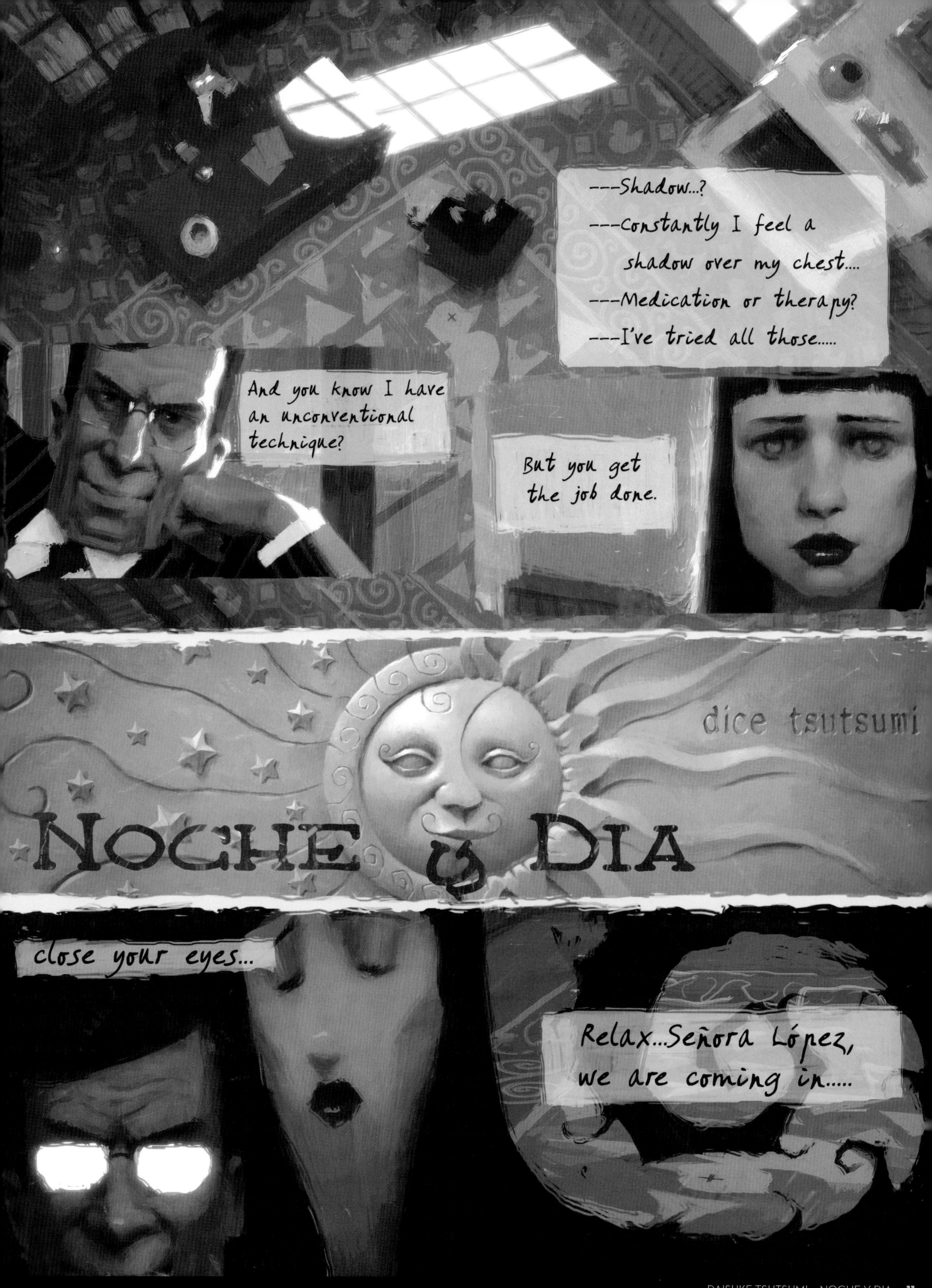
---Shadow...?
---Constantly I feel a shadow over my chest....
---Medication or therapy?
---I've tried all those.....
And you know I have an unconventional technique?
But you get the job done.
dice tsutsumi
NOCHE y DIA
close your eyes...
Relax...Señora López, we are coming in.....

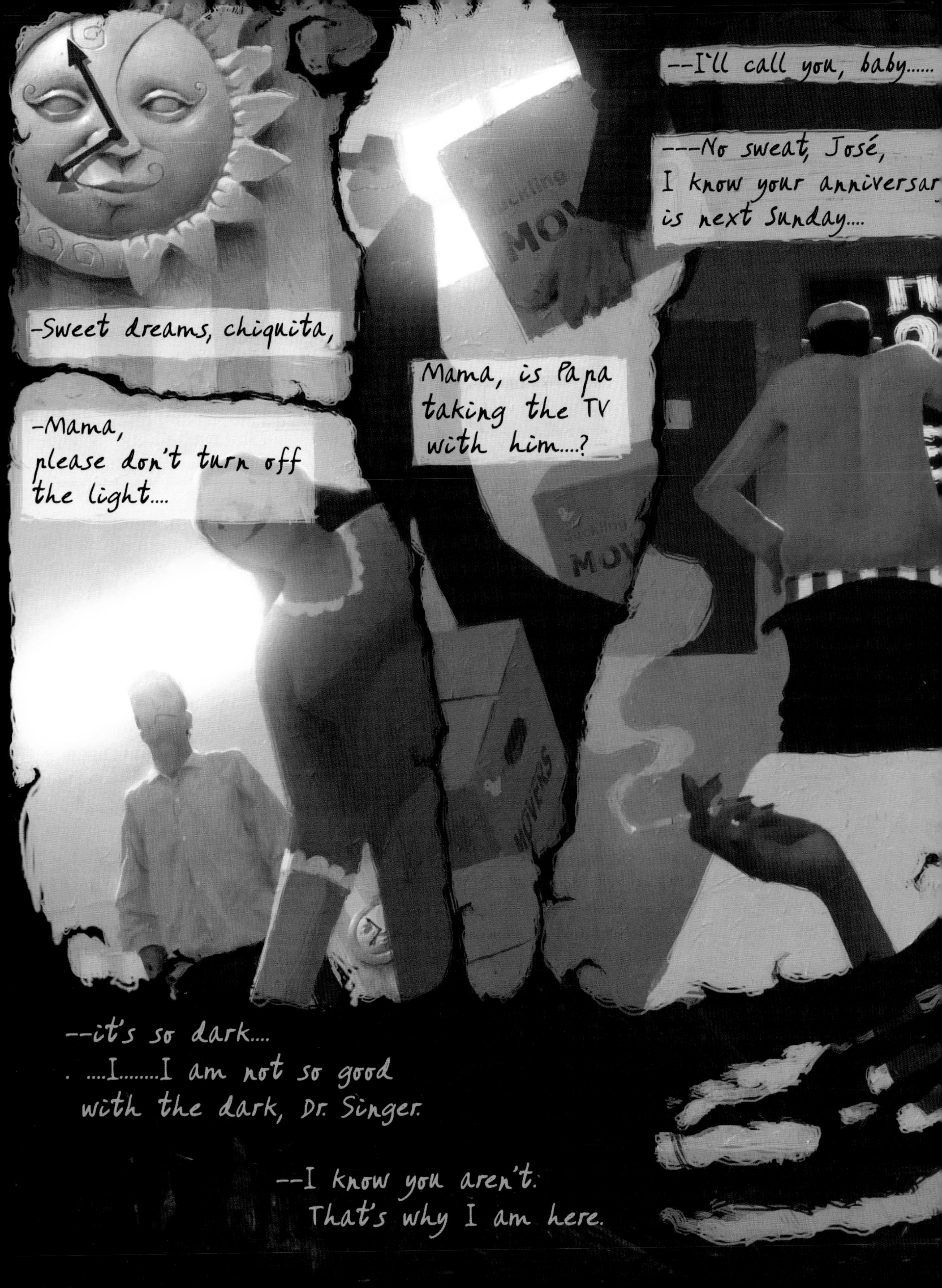
--I'll call you, baby......
---No sweat, José, I know your anniversar is next Sunday....
-Sweet dreams, chiquita,
Mama, is Papa taking the TV with him....?
-Mama, please don't turn off the light....
--it's so dark.... ....I........I am not so good with the dark, Dr. Singer.
--I know you aren't. That's why I am here.

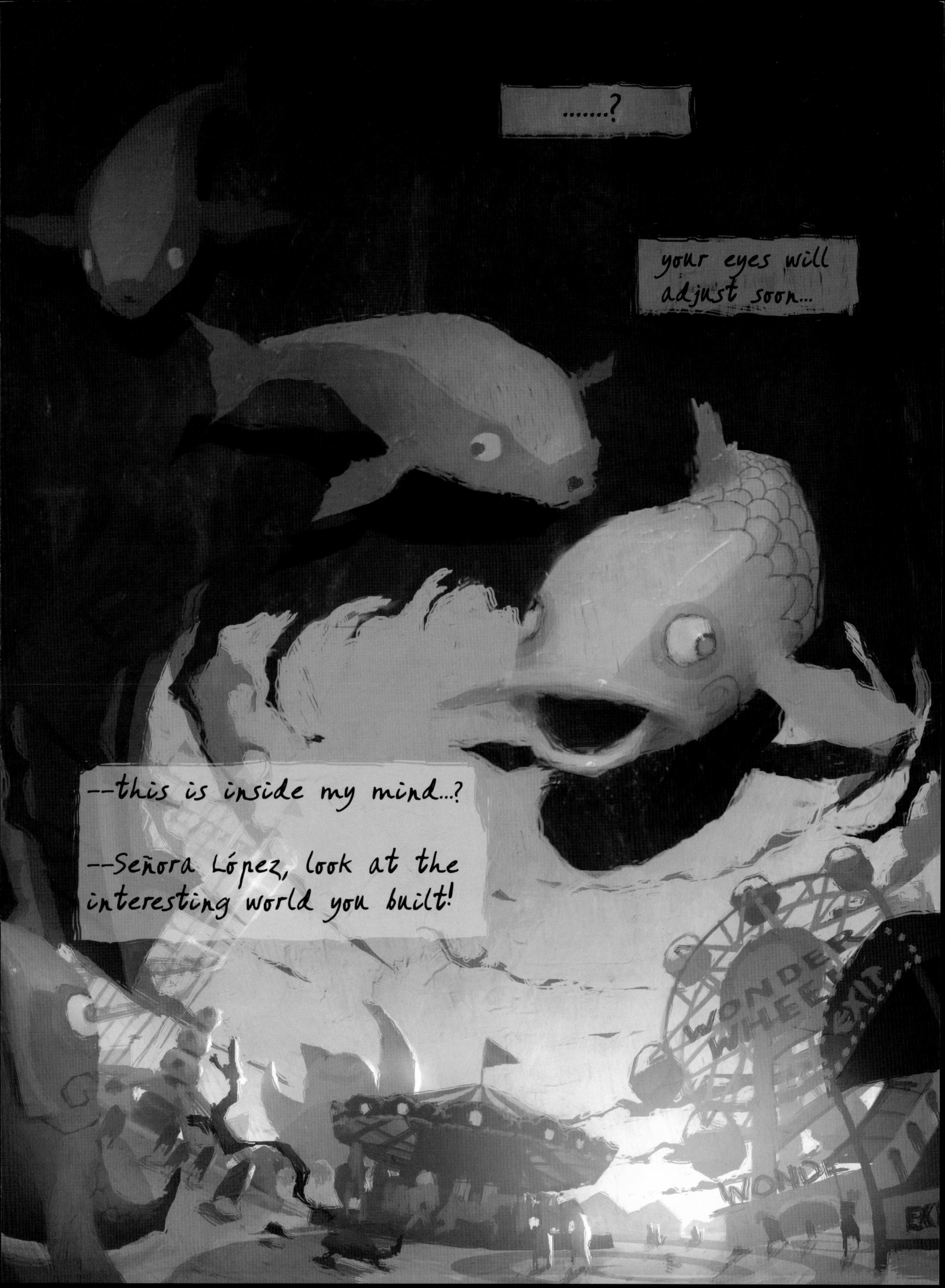

.......?
your eyes will adjust soon...
--this is inside my mind...?
--Señora López, look at the interesting world you built!
WONDER WHEEL
EXIT
WONDE

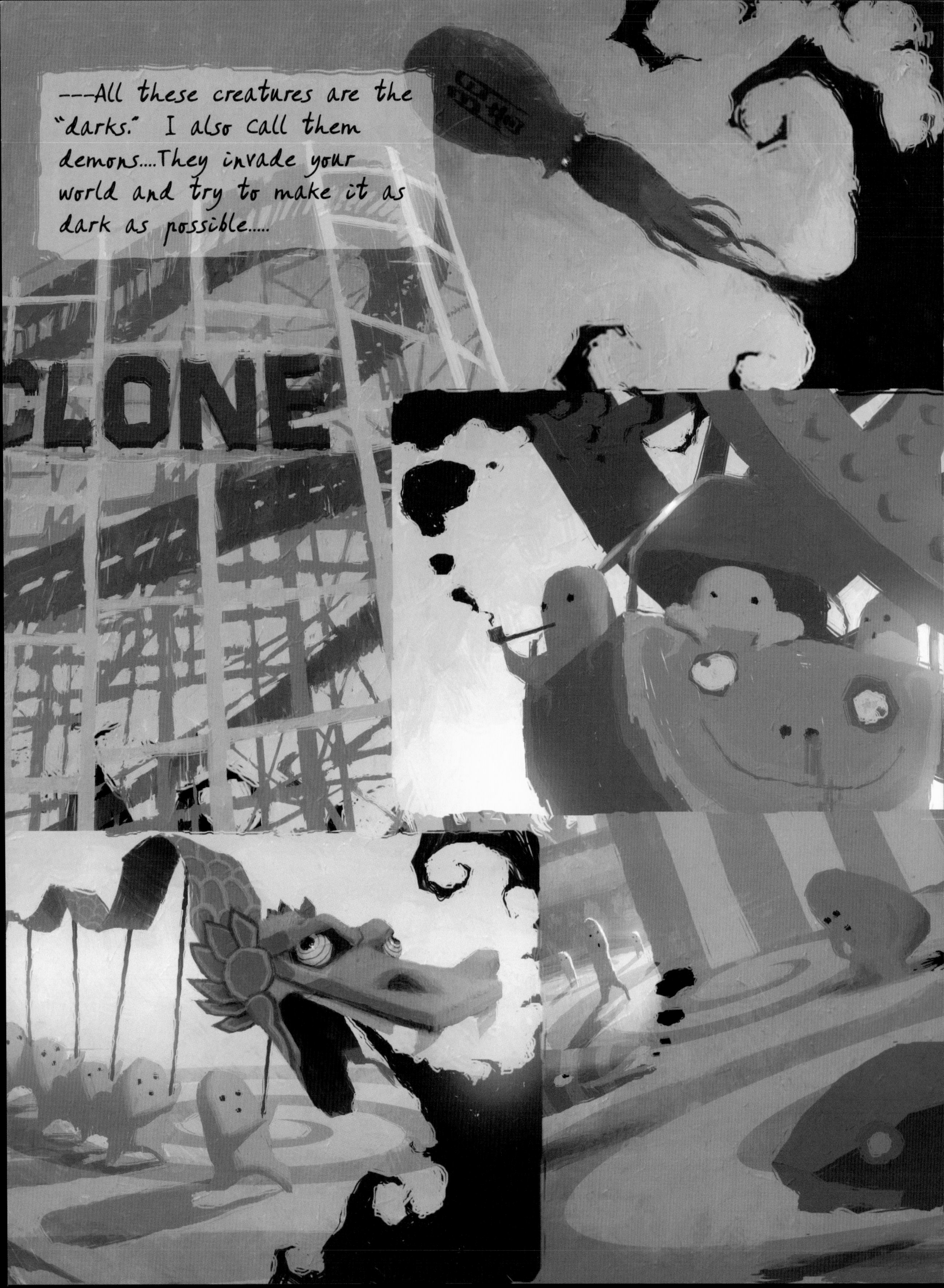
---All these creatures are the "darks." I also call them demons....They invade your world and try to make it as dark as possible.....
CLONE

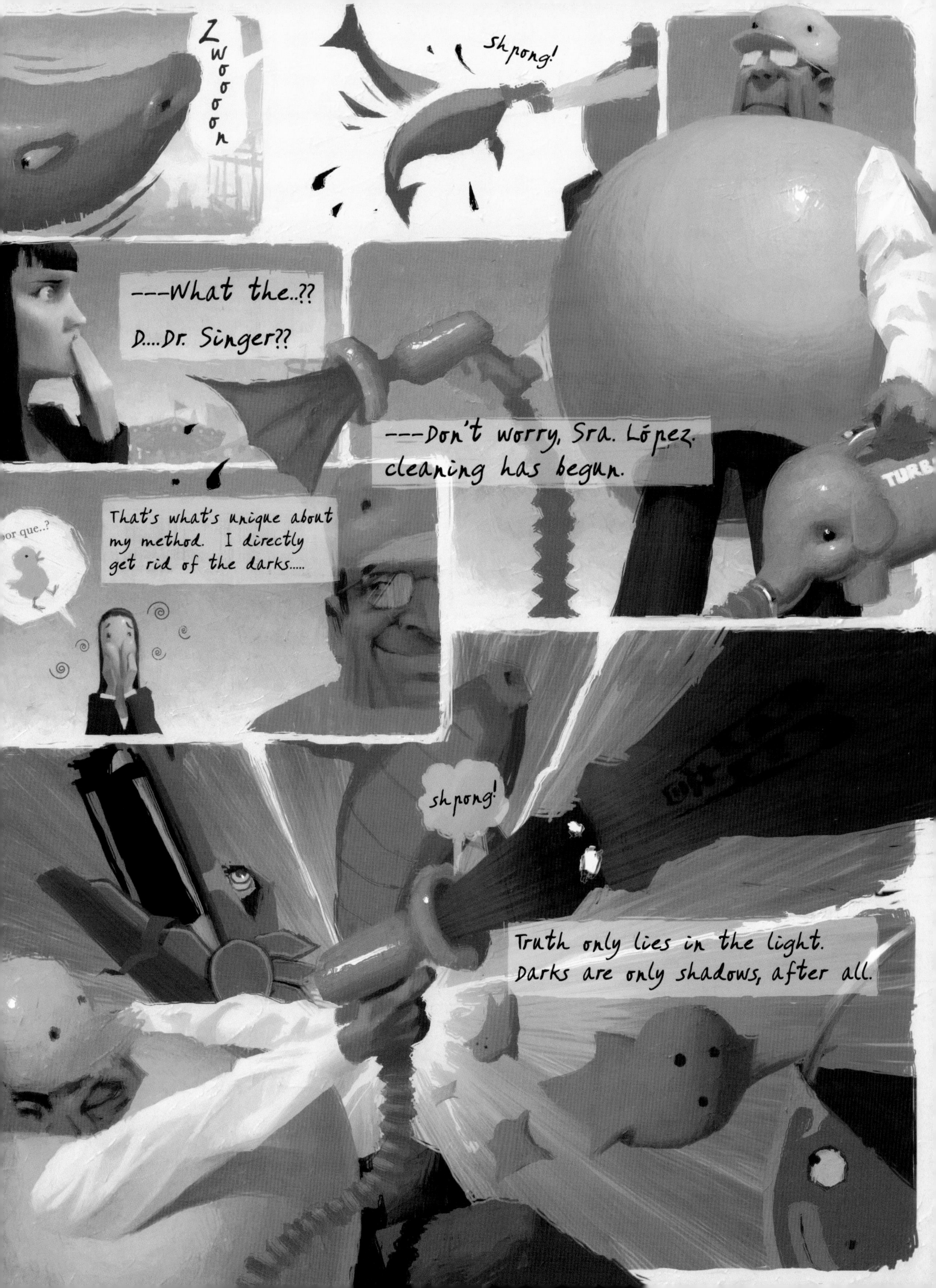
Zwooooon
Shpong!
---What the..??
D....Dr. Singer??
---Don't worry, Sra. López.
cleaning has begun.
That's what's unique about my method. I directly get rid of the darks.....
or que..?
shpong!
Truth only lies in the light.
Darks are only shadows, after all.

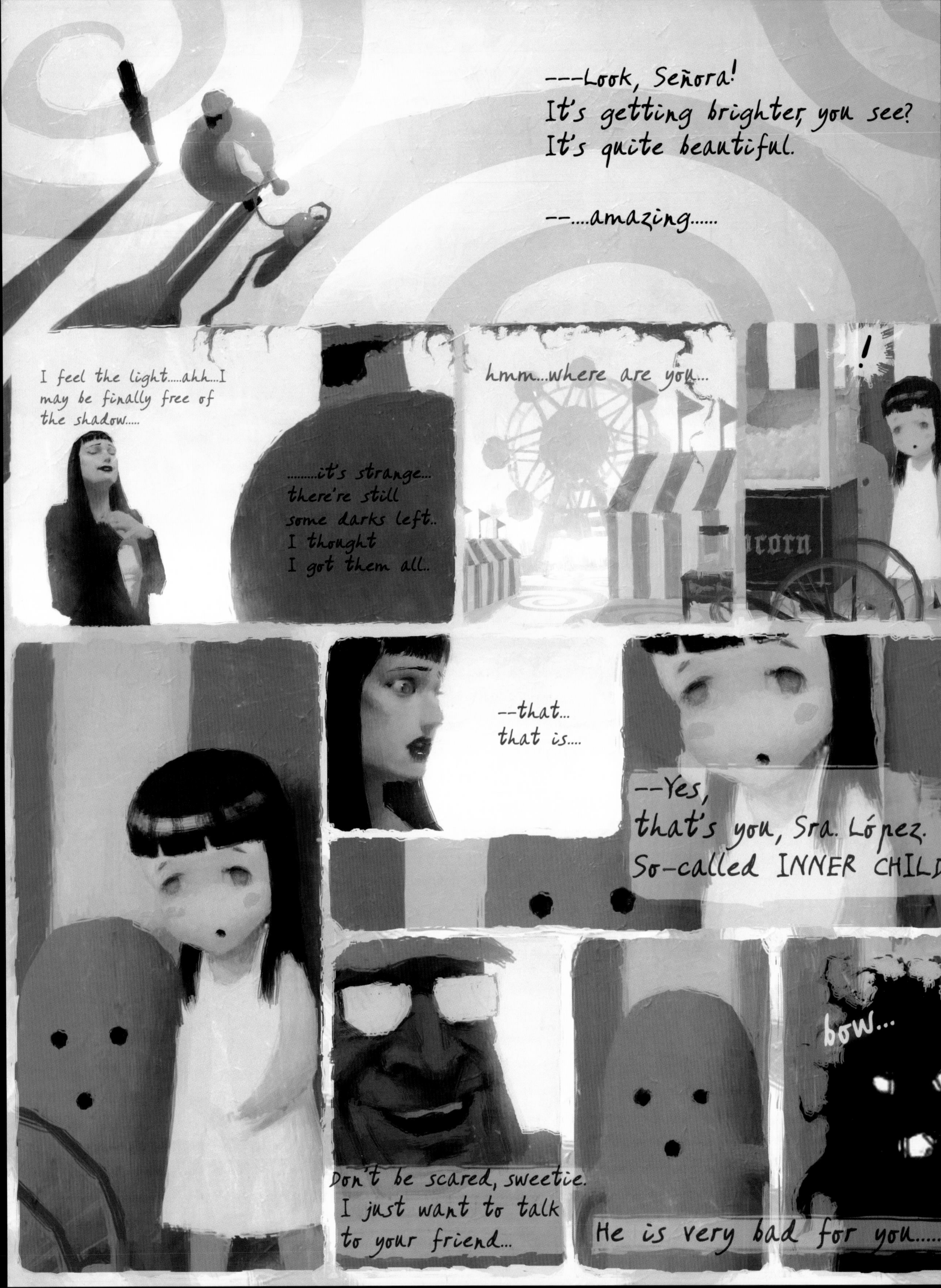
---Look, Señora!
It's getting brighter, you see?
It's quite beautiful.
--....amazing......
I feel the light.....ahh...I may be finally free of the shadow.....
.........it's strange...
there're still some darks left..
I thought I got them all..
hmm...where are you....
!
--that...
that is....
--Yes,
that's you, Sra. López.
So-called INNER CHILD
Don't be scared, sweetie.
I just want to talk to your friend...
He is very bad for you.....
bow...

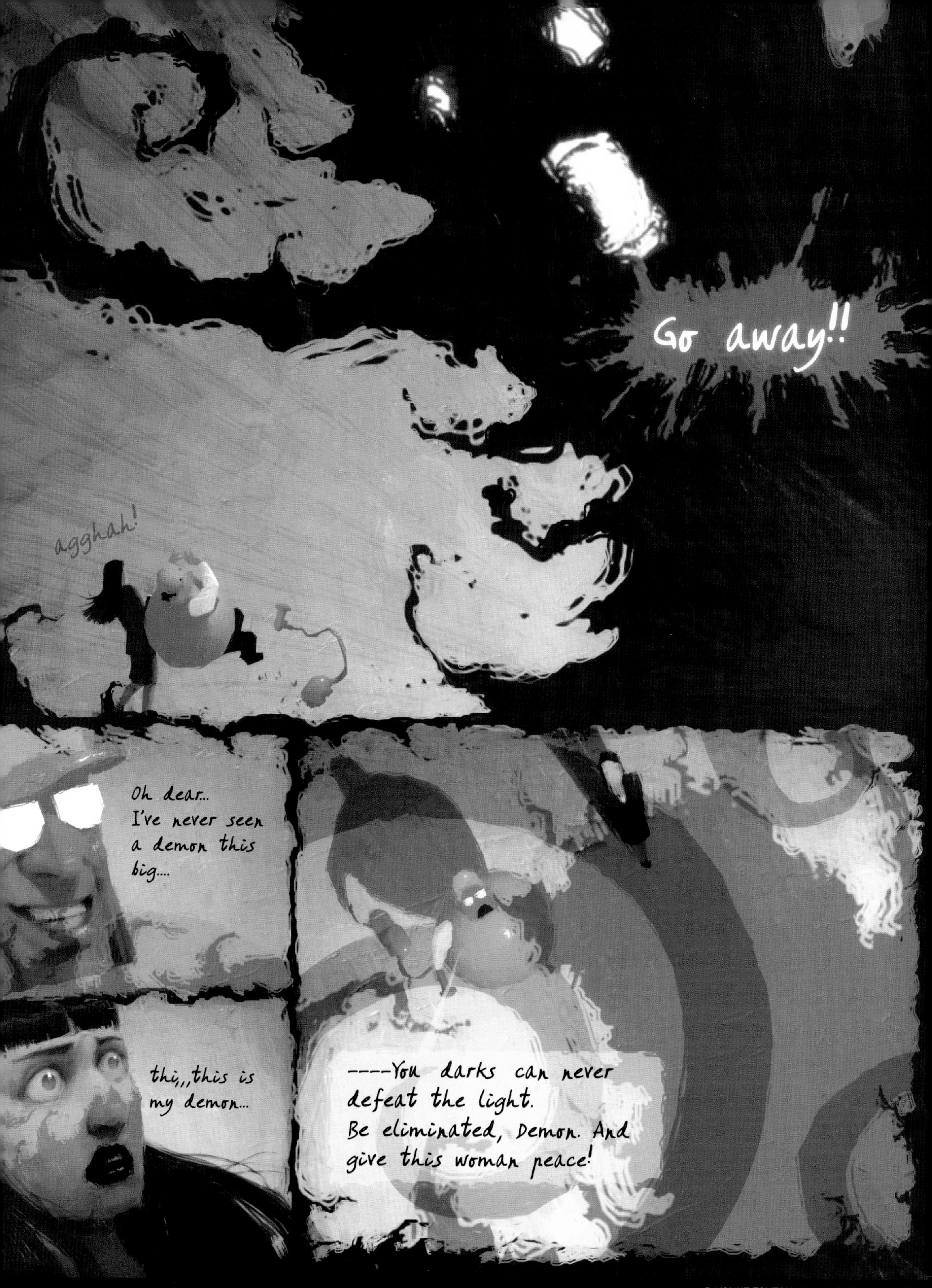
Go away!!
agghah!
Oh dear...
I've never seen
a demon this
big....
thi,,,this is
my demon...
----You darks can never
defeat the light.
Be eliminated, Demon. And
give this woman peace!

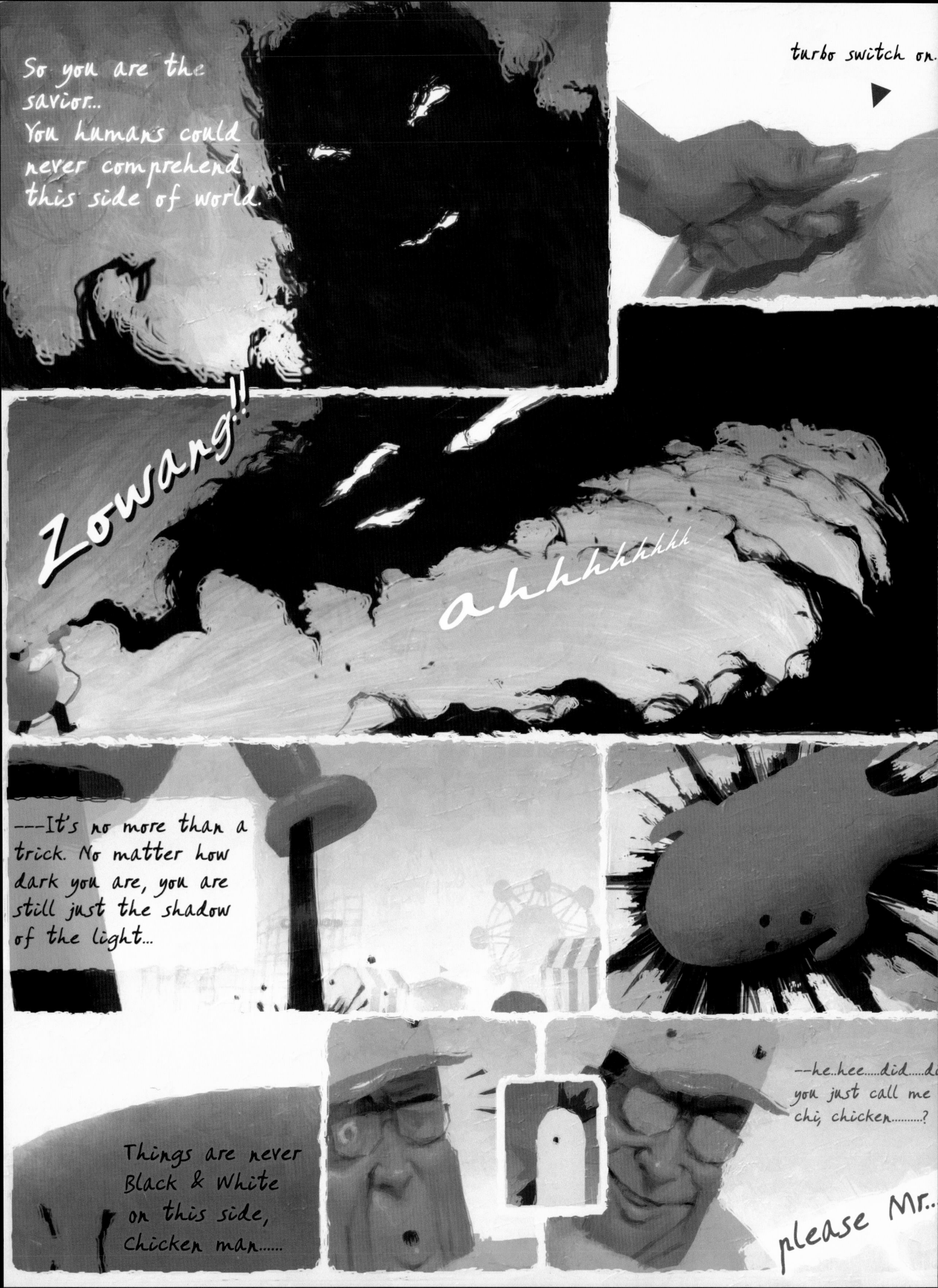
So you are the savior...
You humans could never comprehend this side of world.
turbo switch on.
Zowang!!
ahhhhhhhh
---It's no more than a trick. No matter how dark you are, you are still just the shadow of the light...
Things are never Black & White on this side, Chicken man......
--he..hee.....did.....d
you just call me chi, chicken..........?
please Mr...

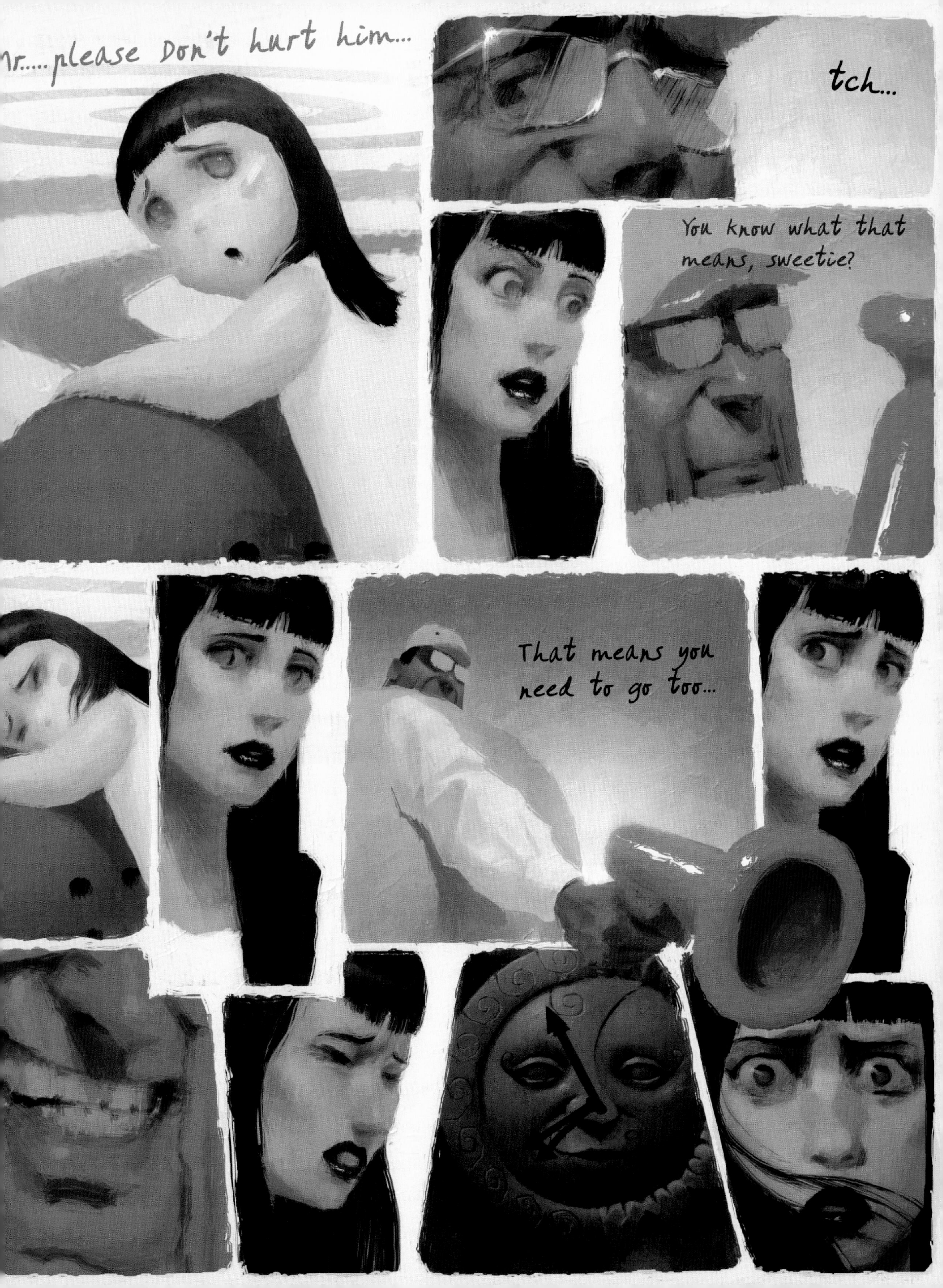
r.....please Don't hurt him...
tch...
You know what that means, sweetie?
That means you need to go too...

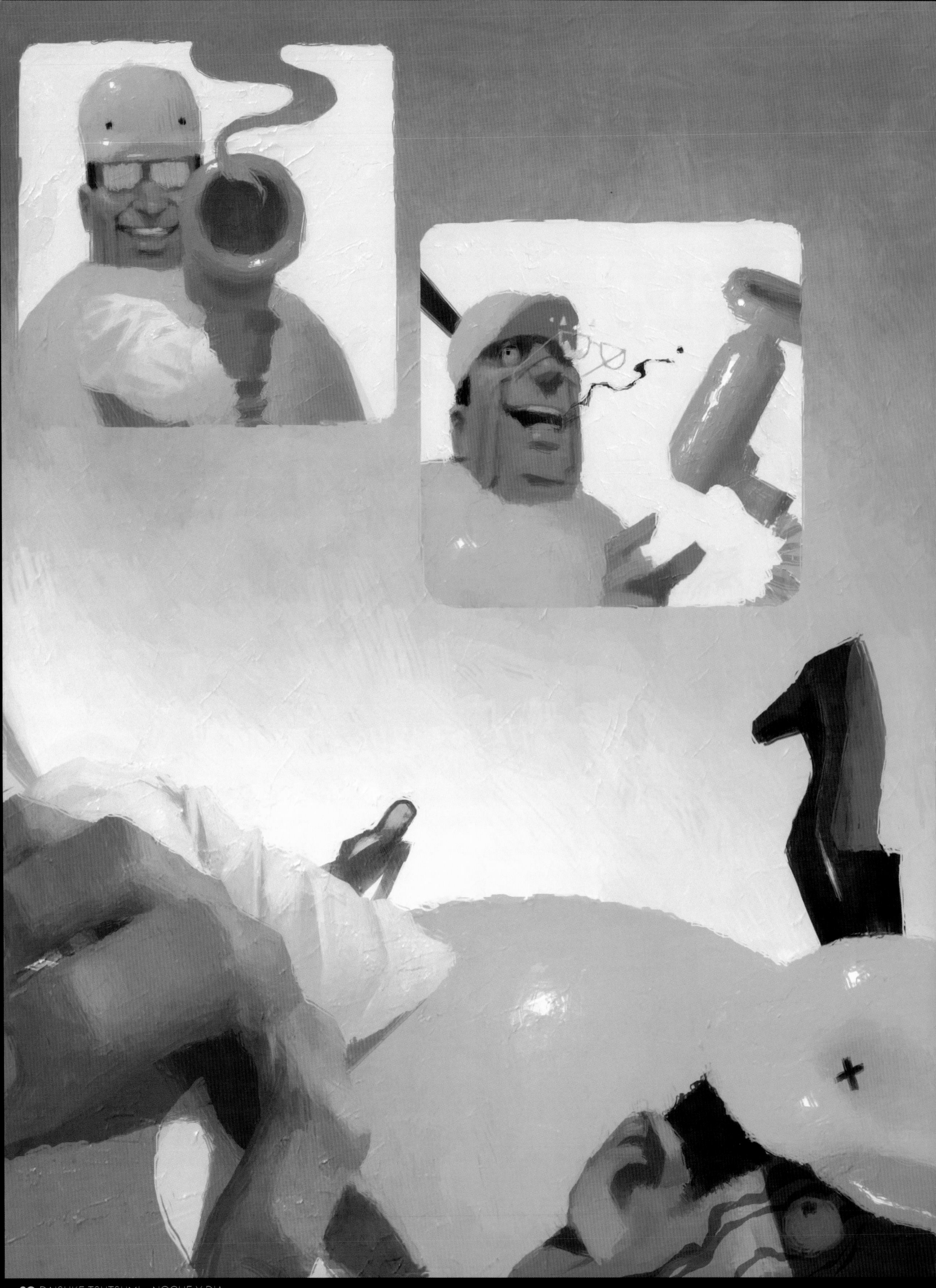

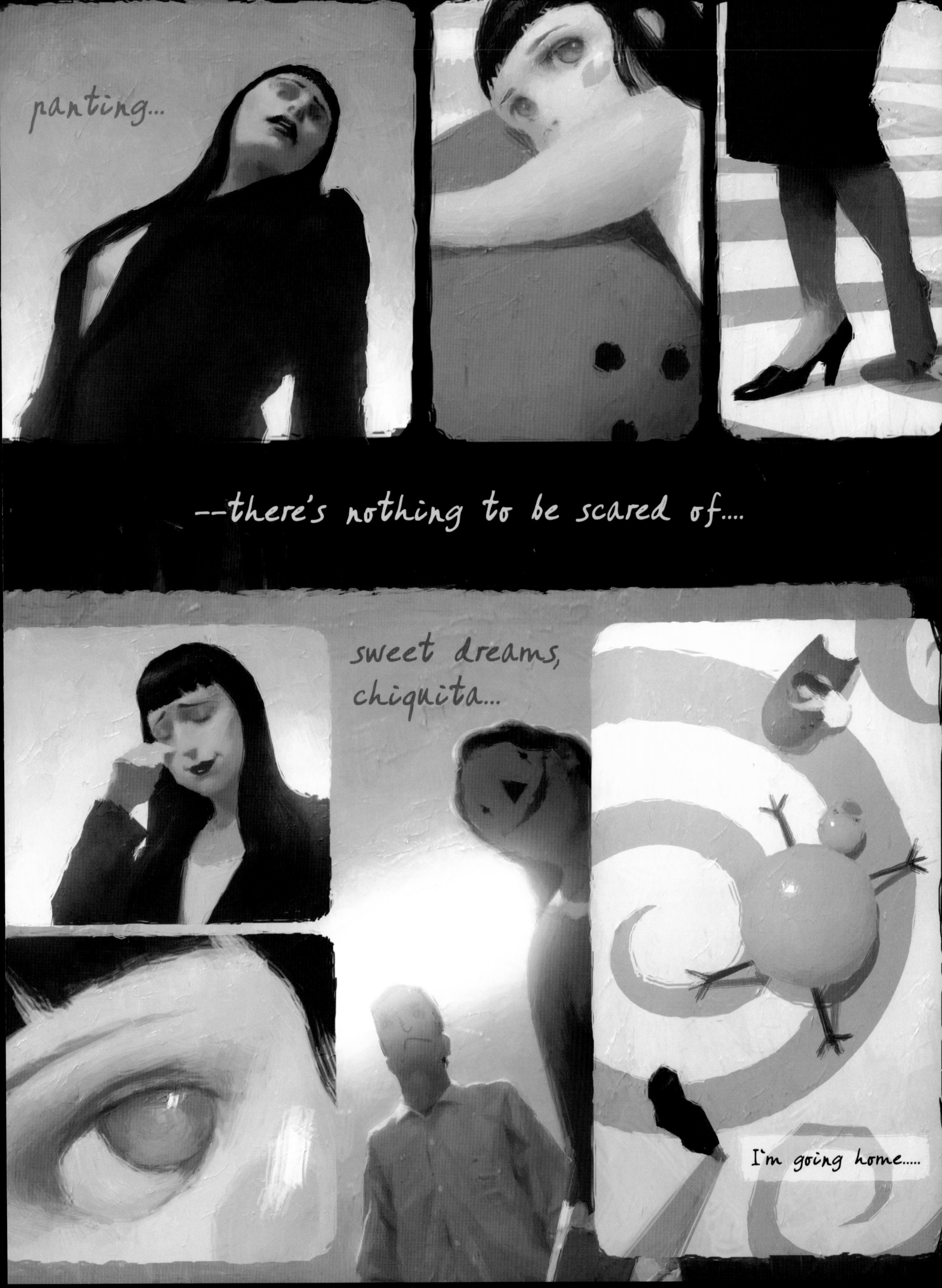
panting...
--there's nothing to be scared of....
sweet dreams, chiquita...
I'm going home.....

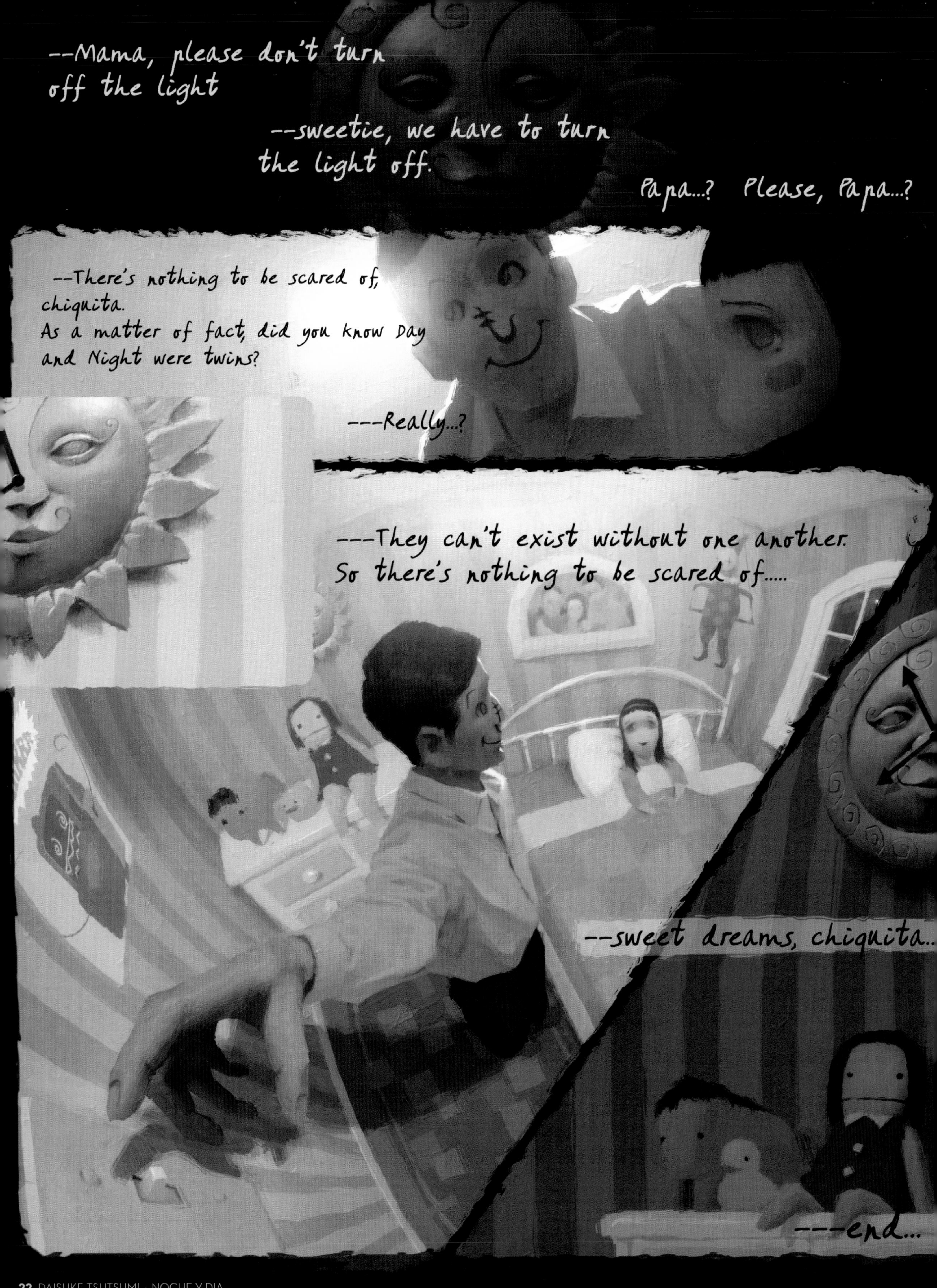

--Mama, please don't turn off the light
--sweetie, we have to turn the light off.
Papa...? Please, Papa...?
--There's nothing to be scared of, chiquita.
As a matter of fact, did you know Day and Night were twins?
---Really...?
---They can't exist without one another.
So there's nothing to be scared of.....
--sweet dreams, chiquita...
---end...

HEY, DIDDLE, DIDDLE

Hey, diddle, diddle!
The cat and the fiddle.

LITTLE BO-PEEP

Little Bo-Peep has lost her sheep,
And can't tell where to find
them;
Leave them a...

HUMPTY

Humpty Dumpty sat o...
...umpty Dumpty had a...
...the King's horse...
...ing's men...
...out Humpty D...

Sing a song of sixpence,
A pocket full of rye;
Four-and-twenty blackbirds
Baked in a pie!

When the pie was opened
The birds began to sing;
Was not that a dainty dish
...before the king?

...was in his counting-house,
...ing out his money;
...een was in the parlor,
...ing bread and honey.

...maid was in the garden,
Hanging out the clothes;
When down came a blackbird
And snapped off her nose.

LITTLE JACK HORNER

Little Jack Horner
Sat in the corner,
Eating of Christmas pie;
...e put in his thumb,
...d pulled out a...
And s...

GREG COUCH

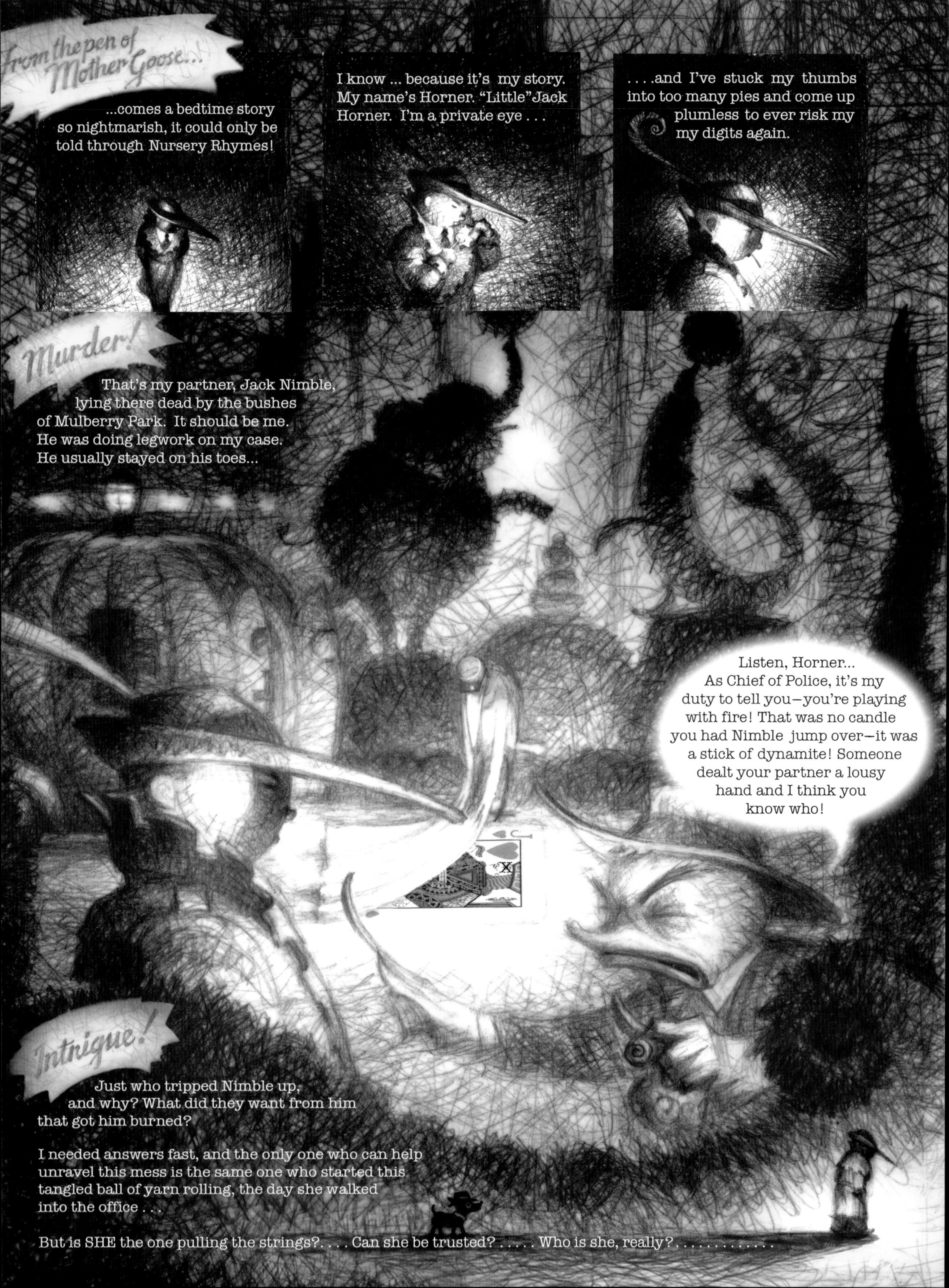
From the pen of Mother Goose...!
...comes a bedtime story so nightmarish, it could only be told through Nursery Rhymes!
I know ... because it's my story. My name's Horner. "Little" Jack Horner. I'm a private eye . . .
. . . .and I've stuck my thumbs into too many pies and come up plumless to ever risk my my digits again.
Murder!
That's my partner, Jack Nimble, lying there dead by the bushes of Mulberry Park. It should be me. He was doing legwork on my case. He usually stayed on his toes...
Listen, Horner... As Chief of Police, it's my duty to tell you—you're playing with fire! That was no candle you had Nimble jump over—it was a stick of dynamite! Someone dealt your partner a lousy hand and I think you know who!
Intrigue!
Just who tripped Nimble up, and why? What did they want from him that got him burned?
I needed answers fast, and the only one who can help unravel this mess is the same one who started this tangled ball of yarn rolling, the day she walked into the office . . .
But is SHE the one pulling the strings?. . . . Can she be trusted? . . . . . Who is she, really? . . . .

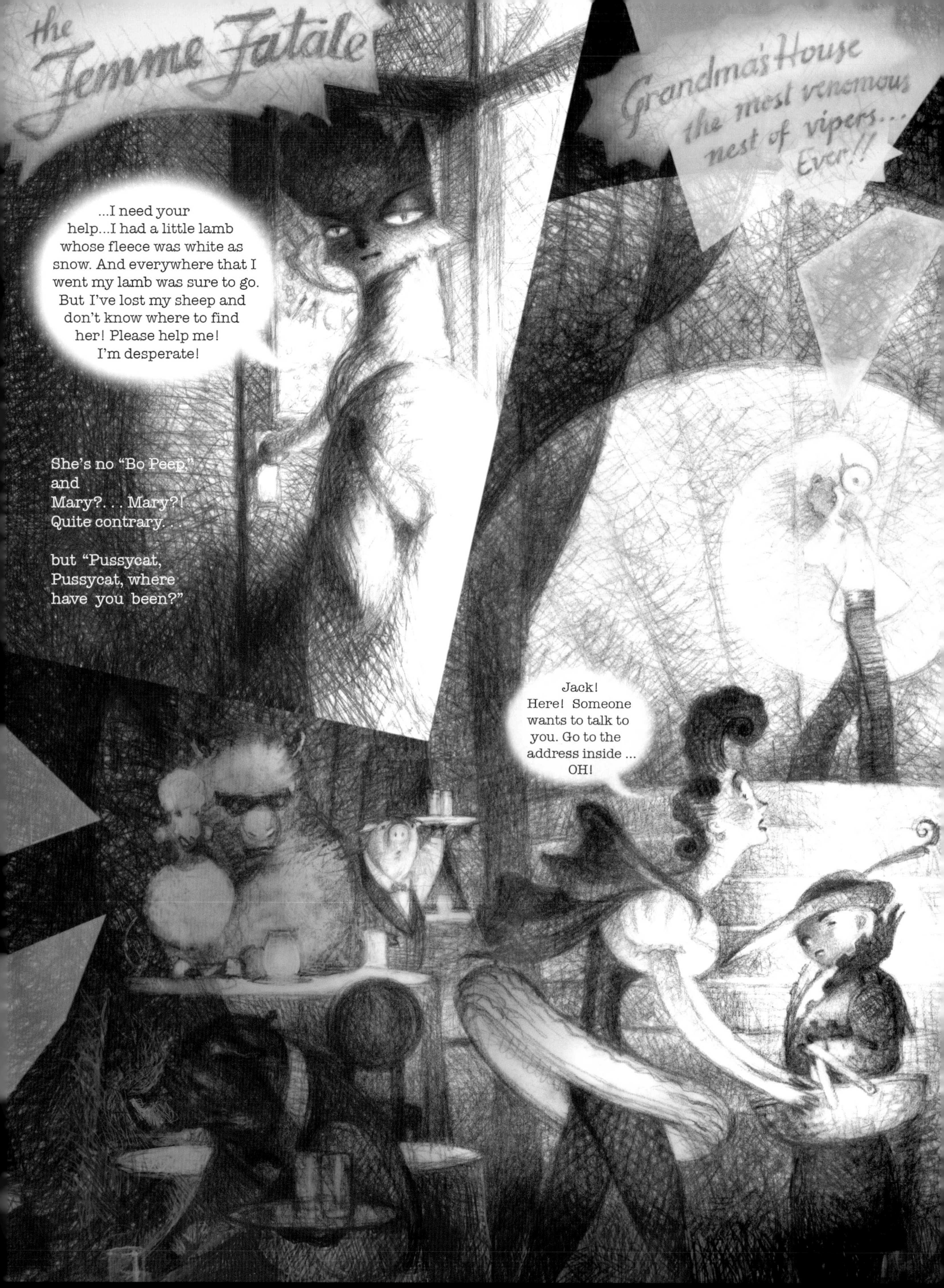
the Femme Fatale
...I need your help...I had a little lamb whose fleece was white as snow. And everywhere that I went my lamb was sure to go. But I've lost my sheep and don't know where to find her! Please help me! I'm desperate!
She's no "Bo Peep." and Mary?. . . Mary?! Quite contrary. . .
but "Pussycat, Pussycat, where have you been?"
Grandma's House the most venomous nest of vipers... Ever!!
Jack! Here! Someone wants to talk to you. Go to the address inside ... OH!

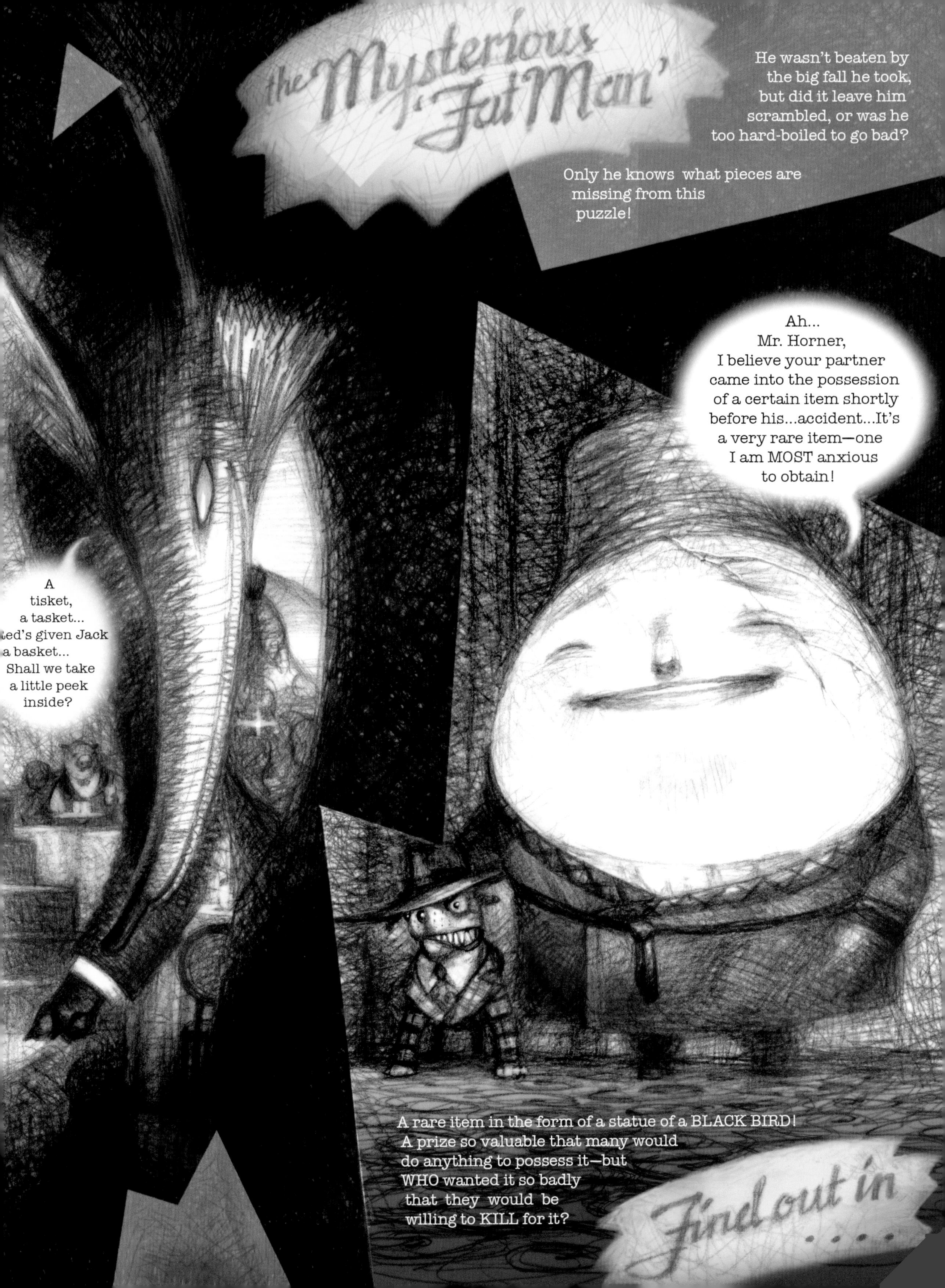

the 'Mysterious Fat Man'
He wasn't beaten by the big fall he took, but did it leave him scrambled, or was he too hard-boiled to go bad?
Only he knows what pieces are missing from this puzzle!
Ah... Mr. Horner, I believe your partner came into the possession of a certain item shortly before his...accident...It's a very rare item—one I am MOST anxious to obtain!
A tisket, a tasket... ed's given Jack a basket... Shall we take a little peek inside?
A rare item in the form of a statue of a BLACK BIRD! A prize so valuable that many would do anything to possess it—but WHO wanted it so badly that they would be willing to KILL for it?
Find out in . . .

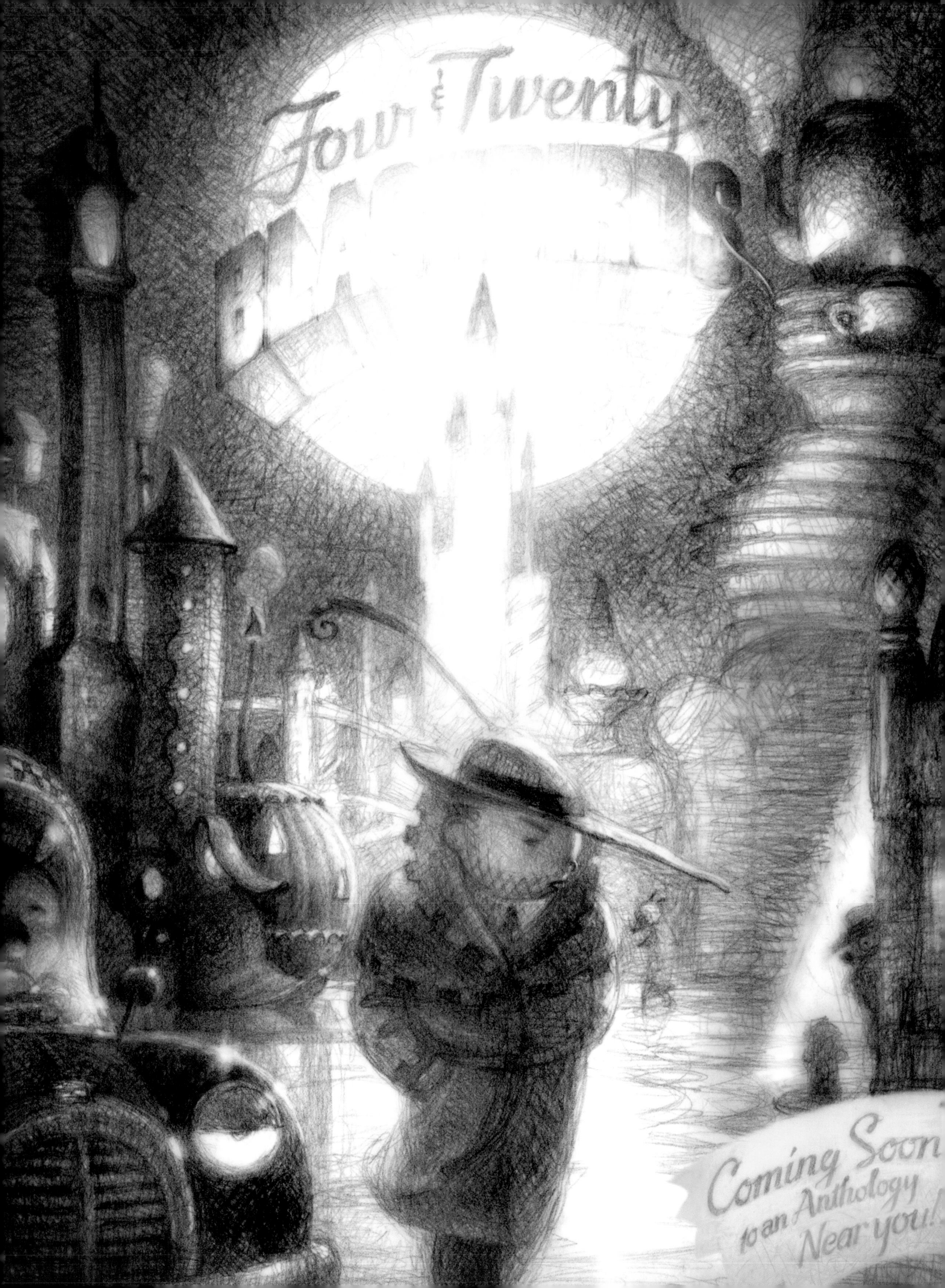
Four & Twenty
Coming Soon
to an Anthology
Near you!

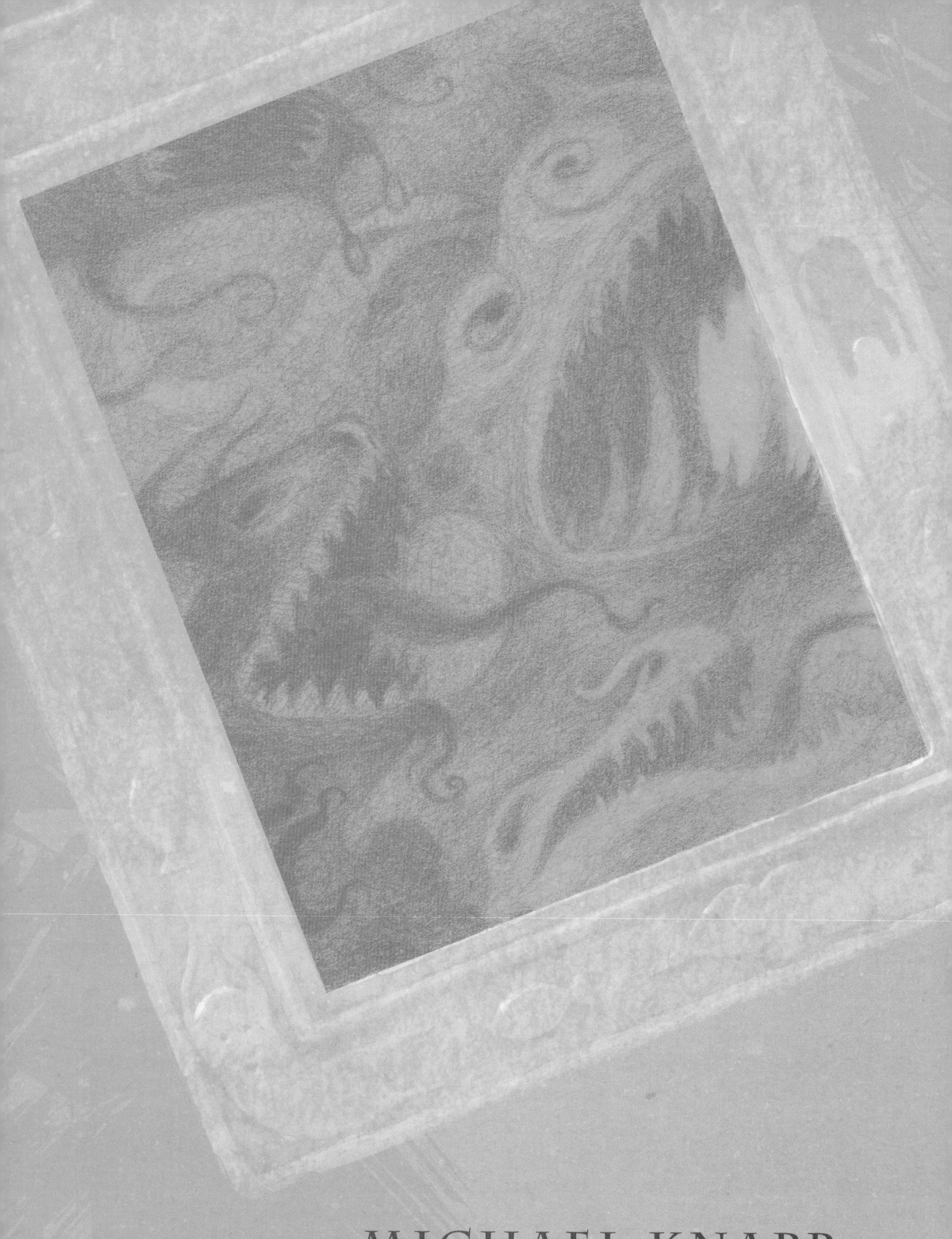

MICHAEL KNAPP

.NEWSBREAK..

by Michael Knapp

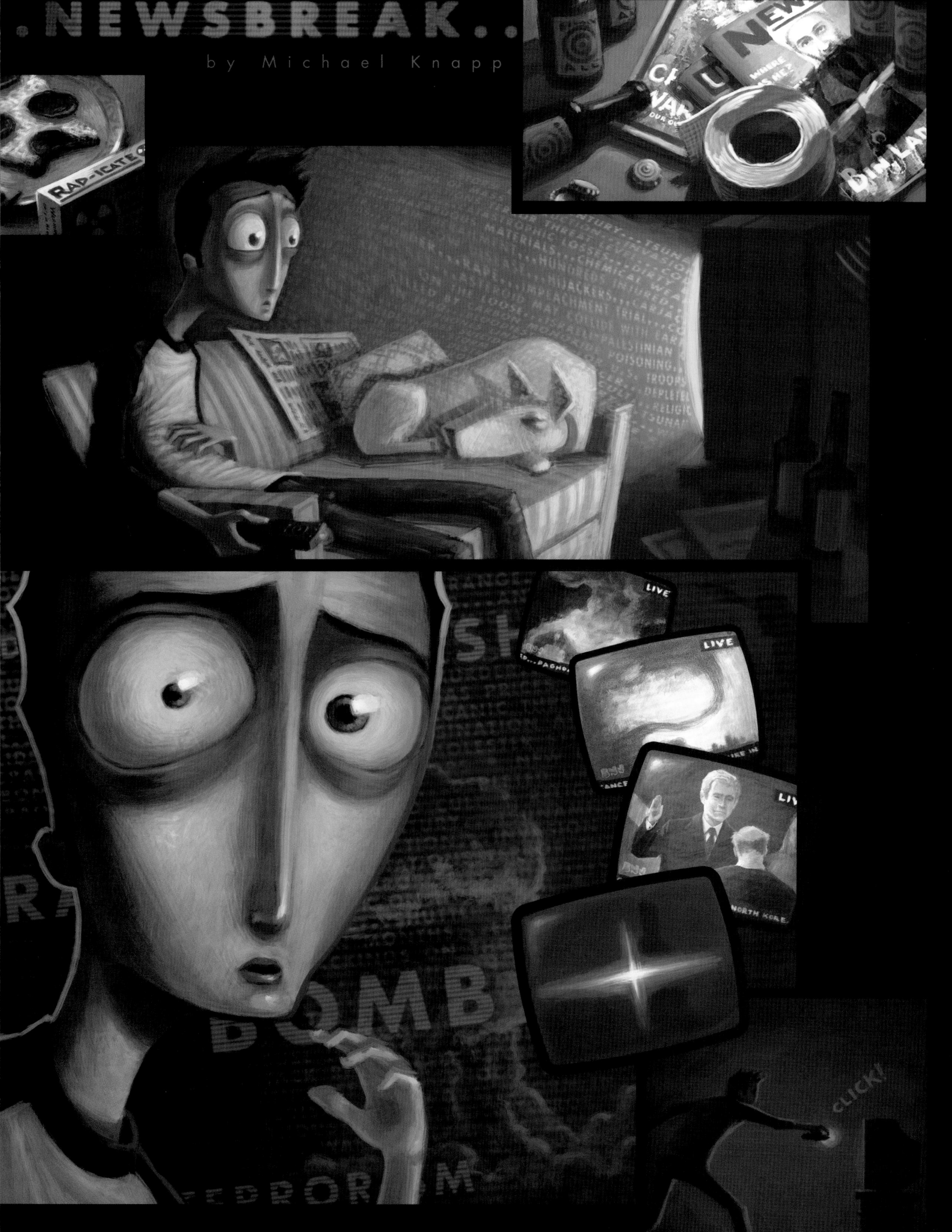
RAD-ICATE
LIVE
LIVE
LIVE
NORTH KOREA
BOMB
CLICK!

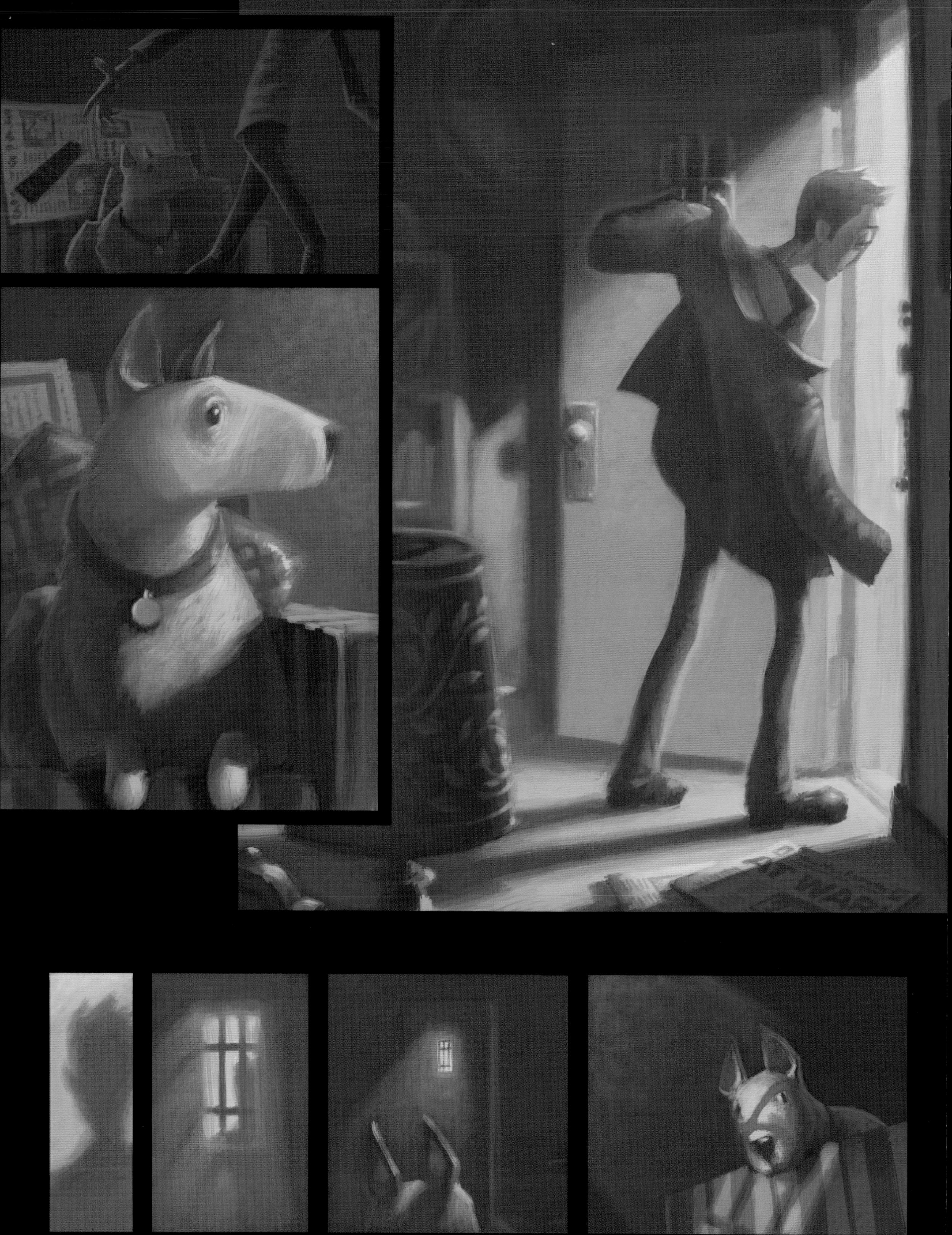
AT WAR!

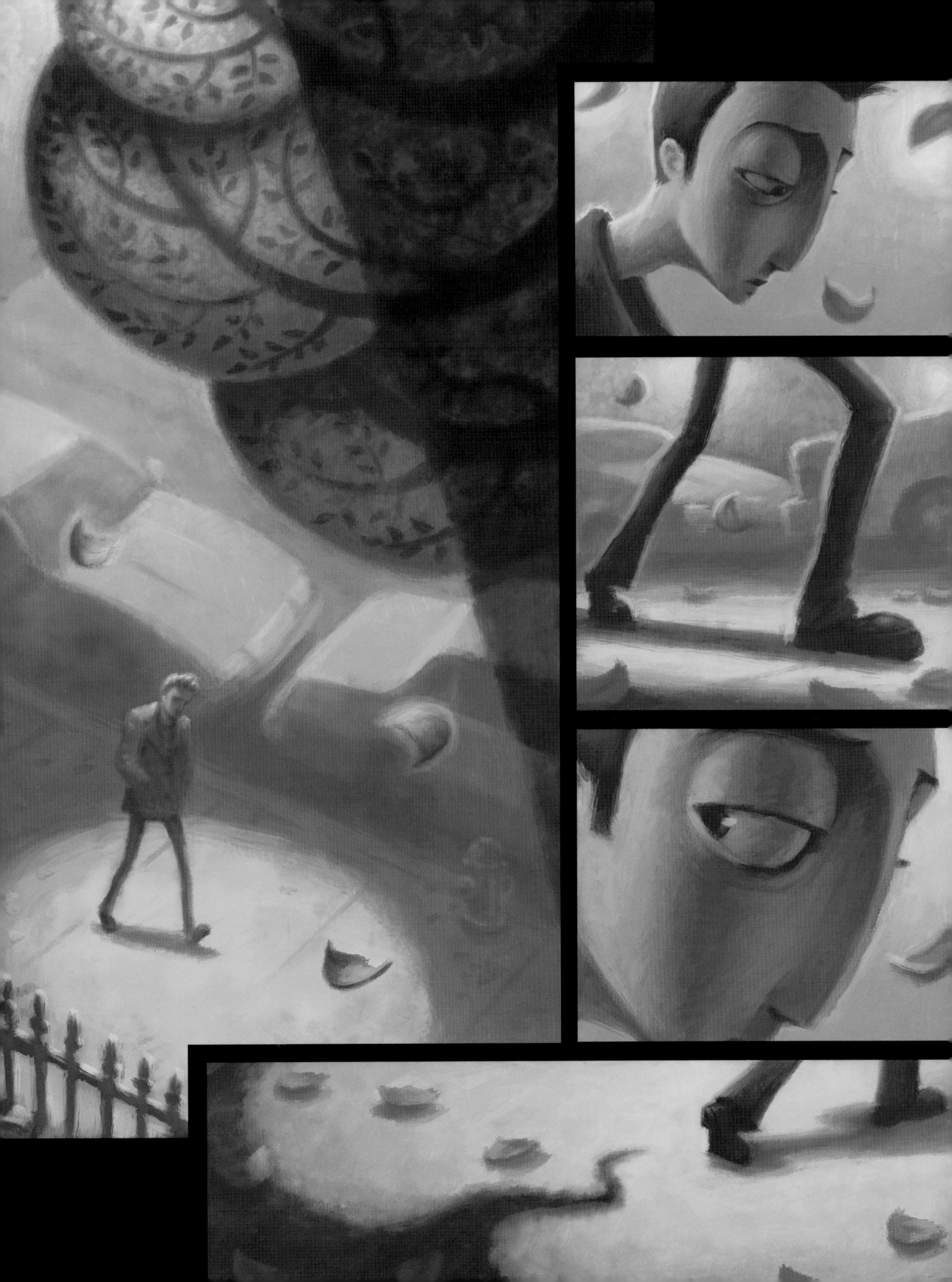

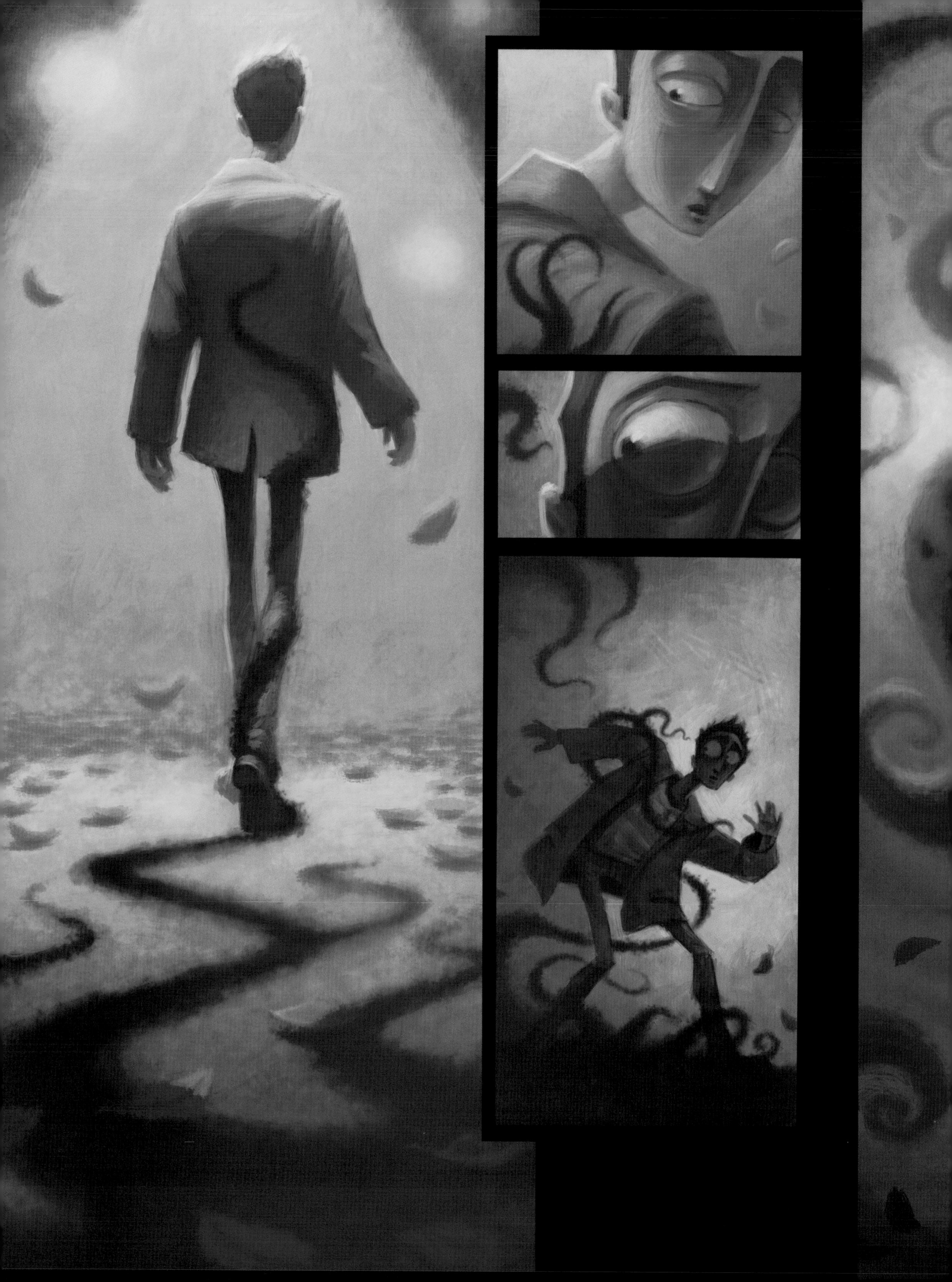

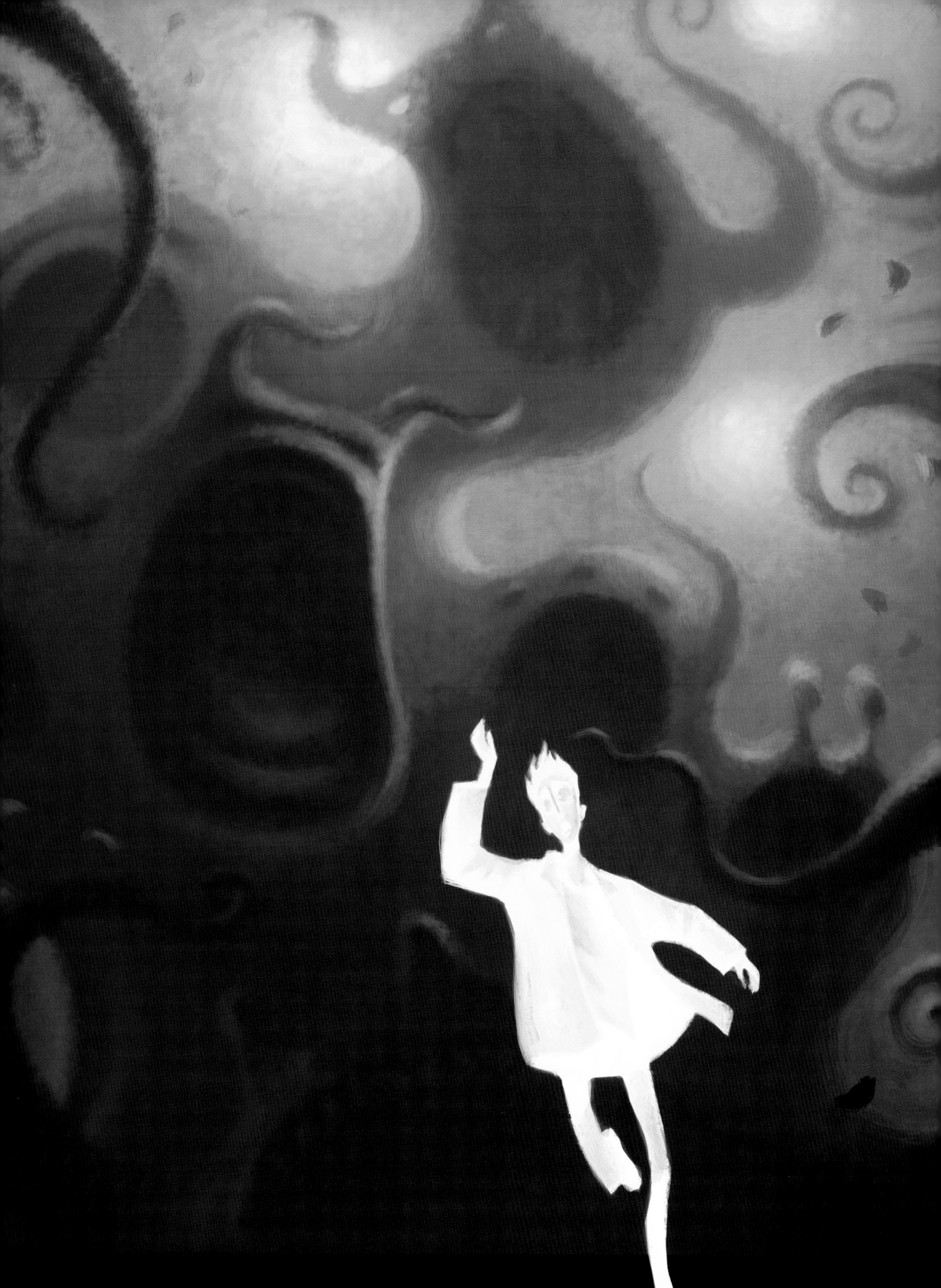

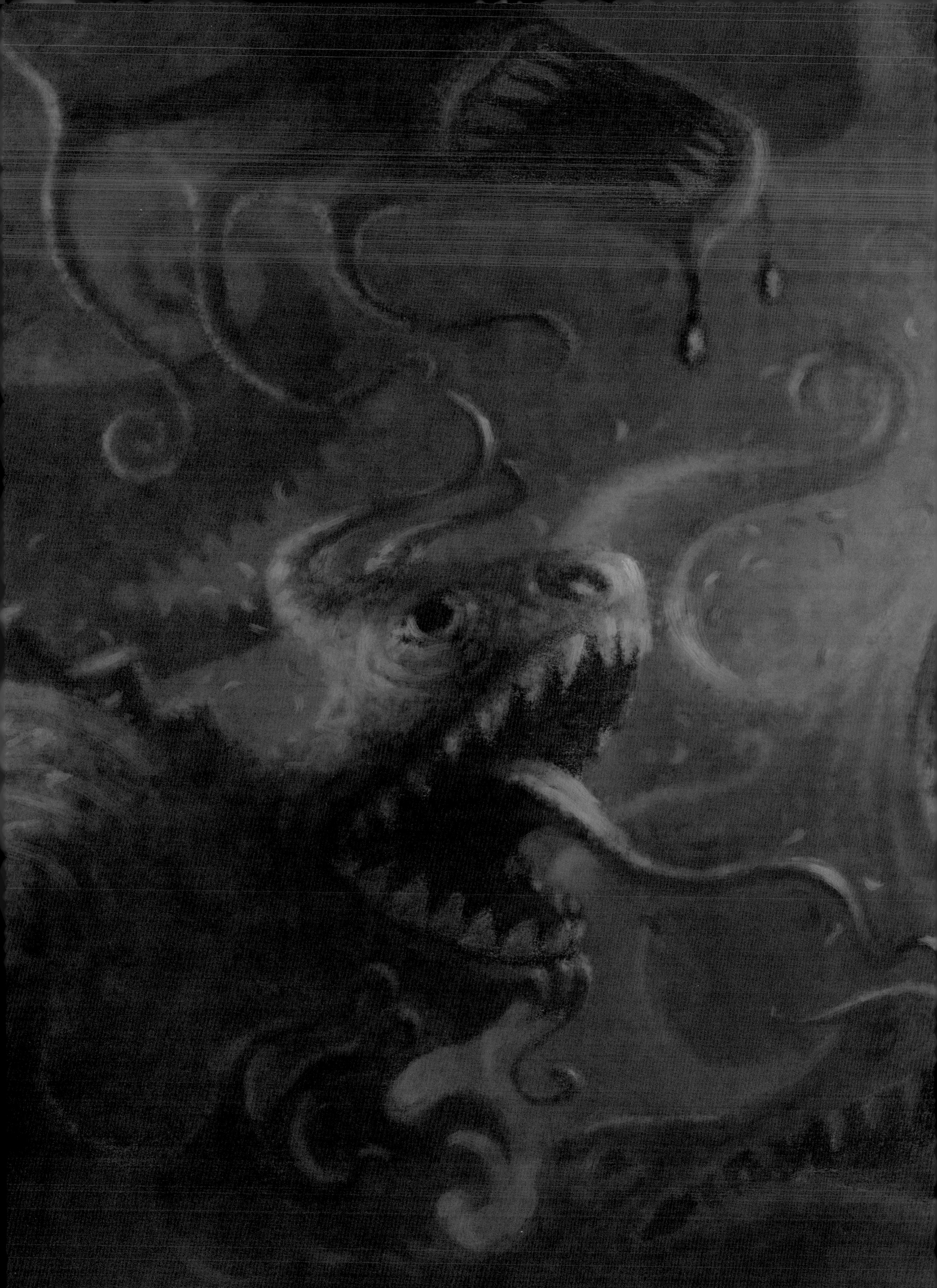

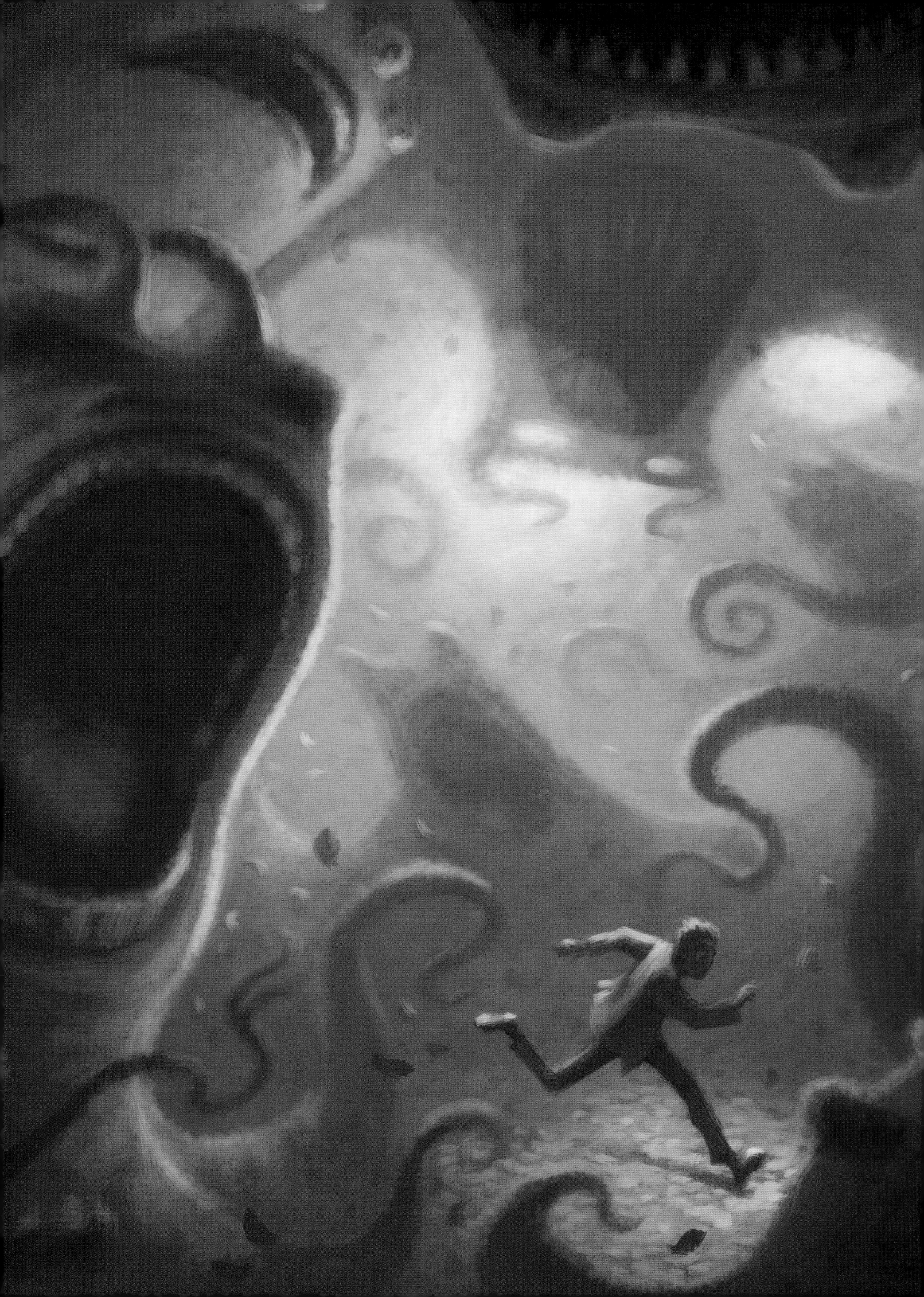

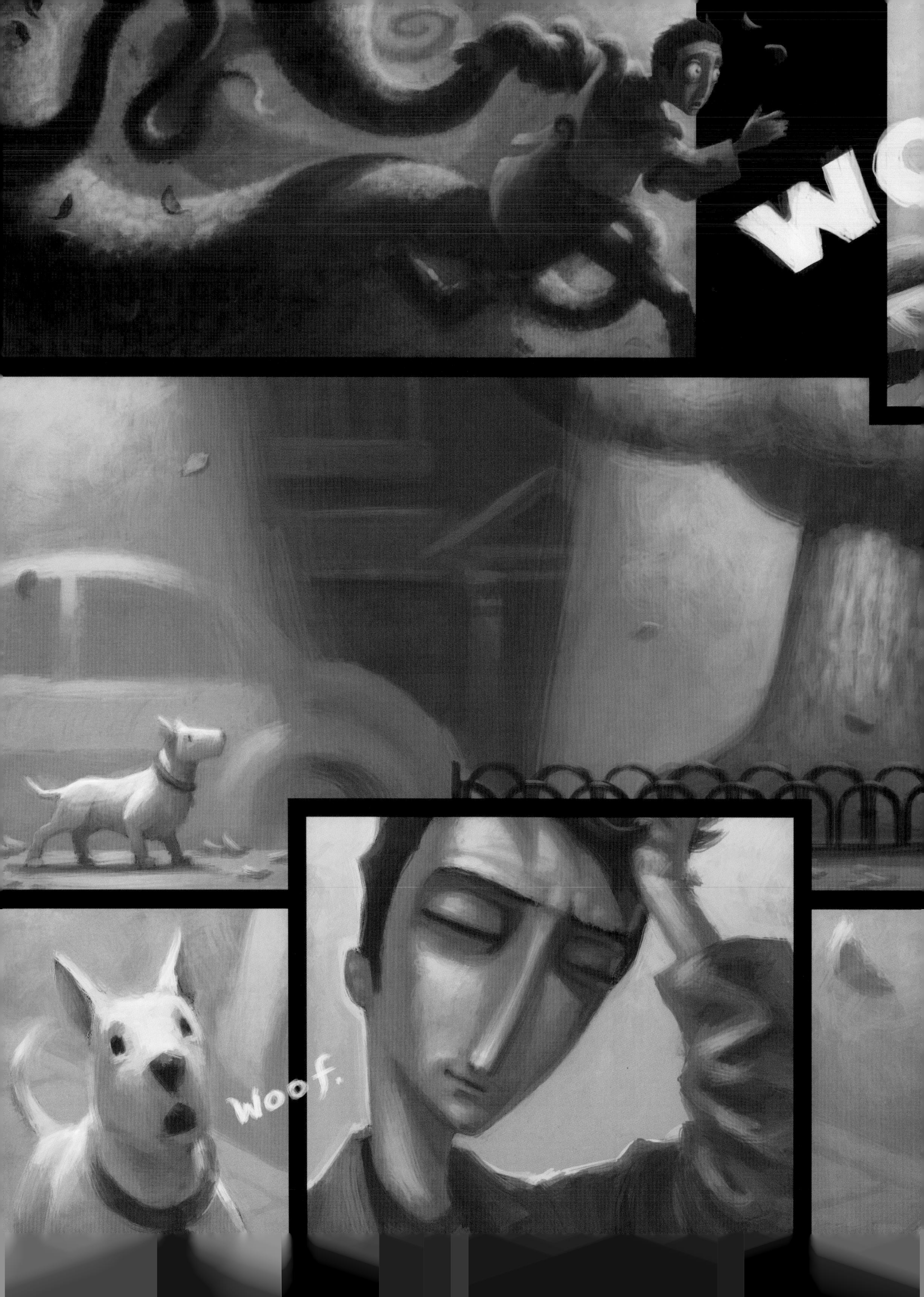
WO
woof.

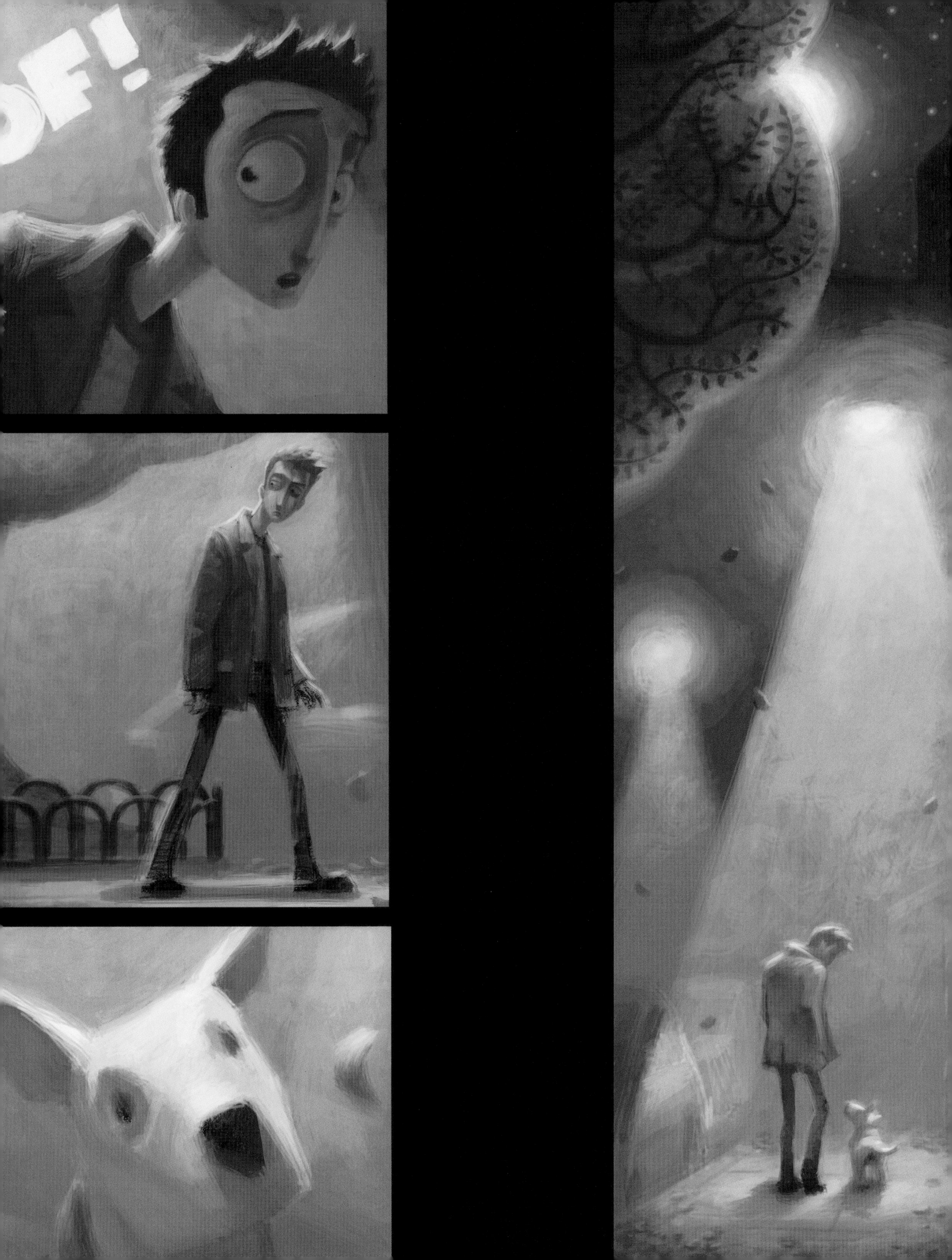
OF!

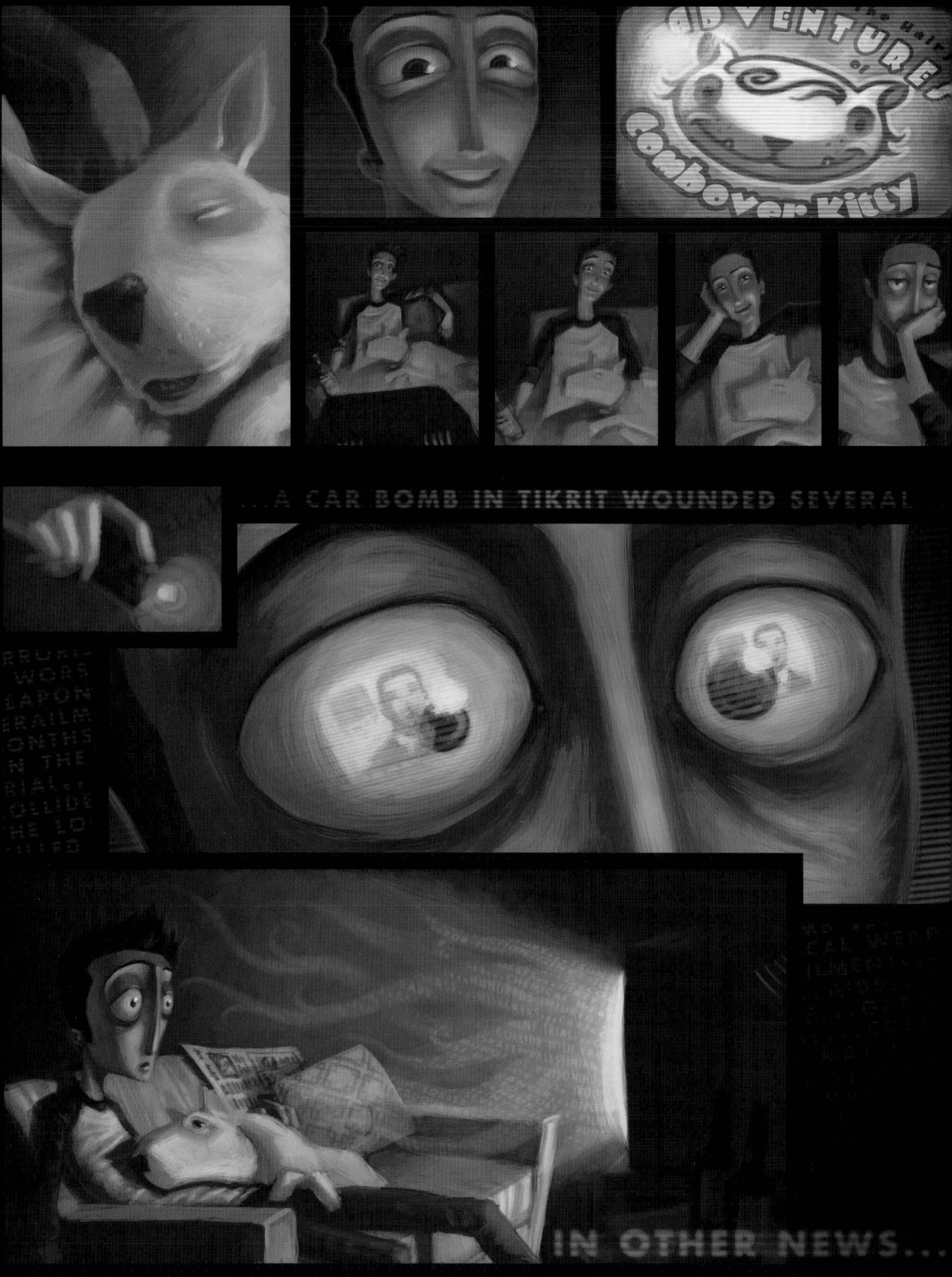
Adventures of Combover Kitty
...A CAR BOMB IN TIKRIT WOUNDED SEVERAL
IN OTHER NEWS...

OUT OF PICTURE

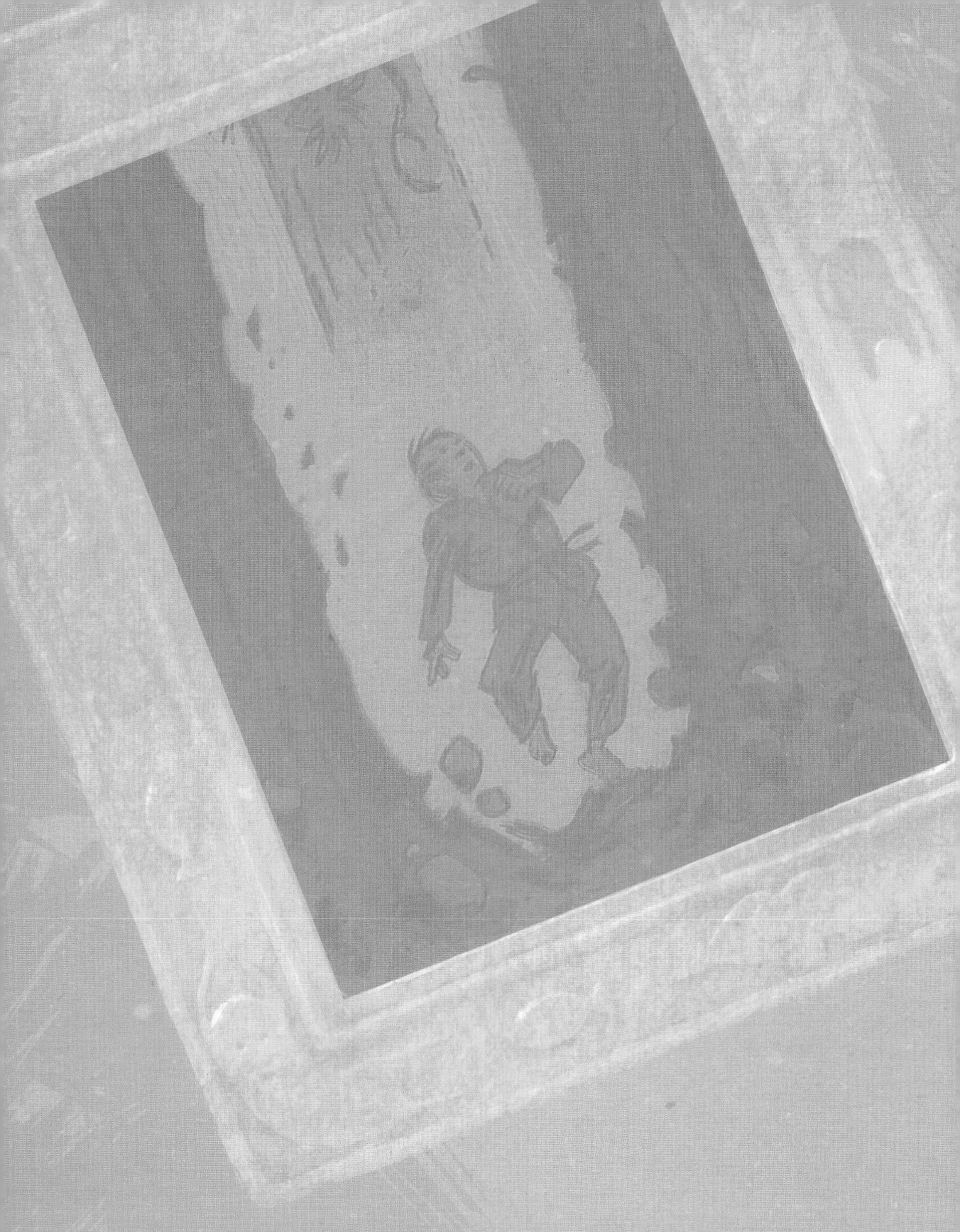

BENOIT LE PENNEC

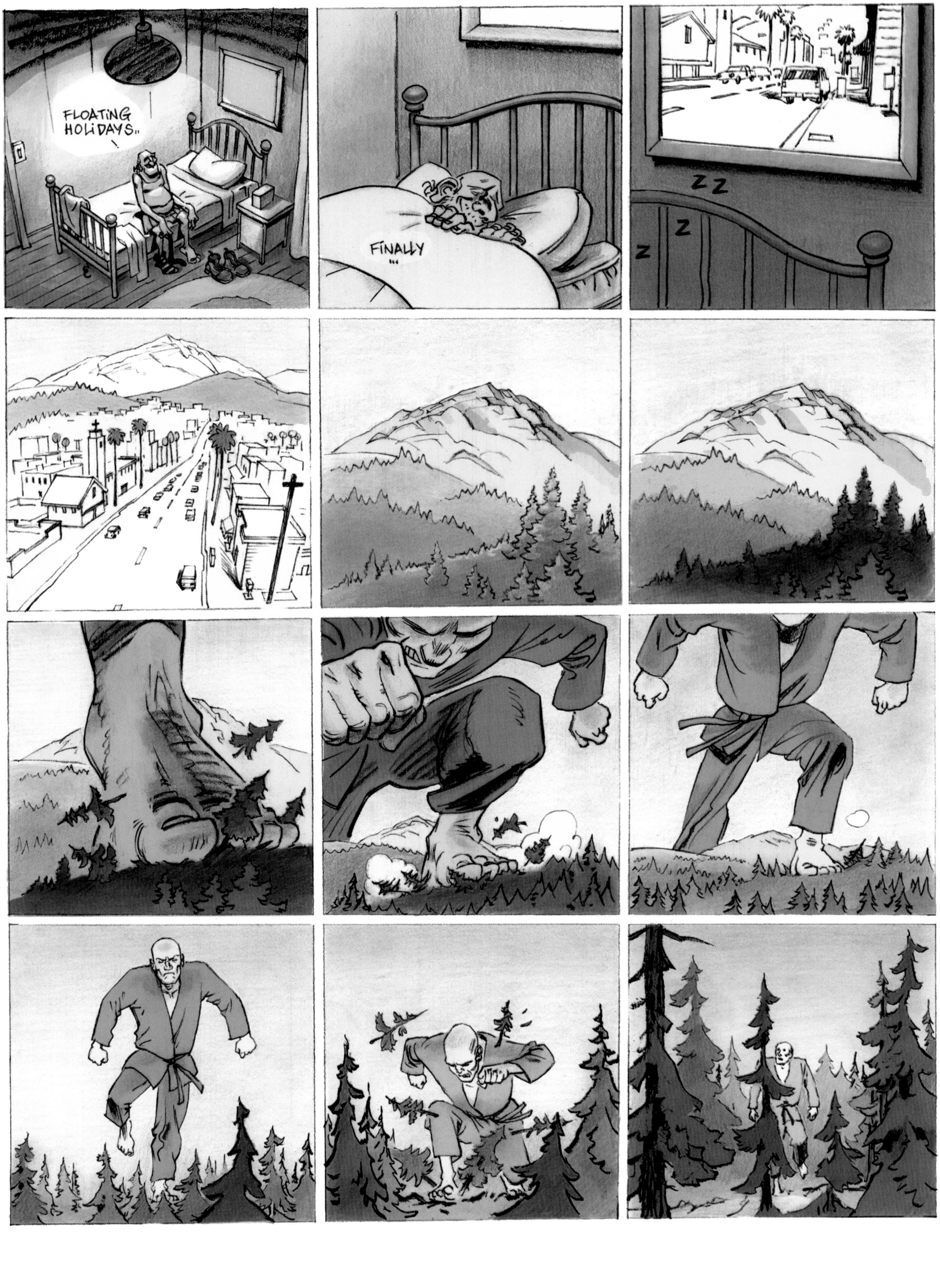
FLOATING HOLIDAYS..
FINALLY ...
Z Z
Z
Z

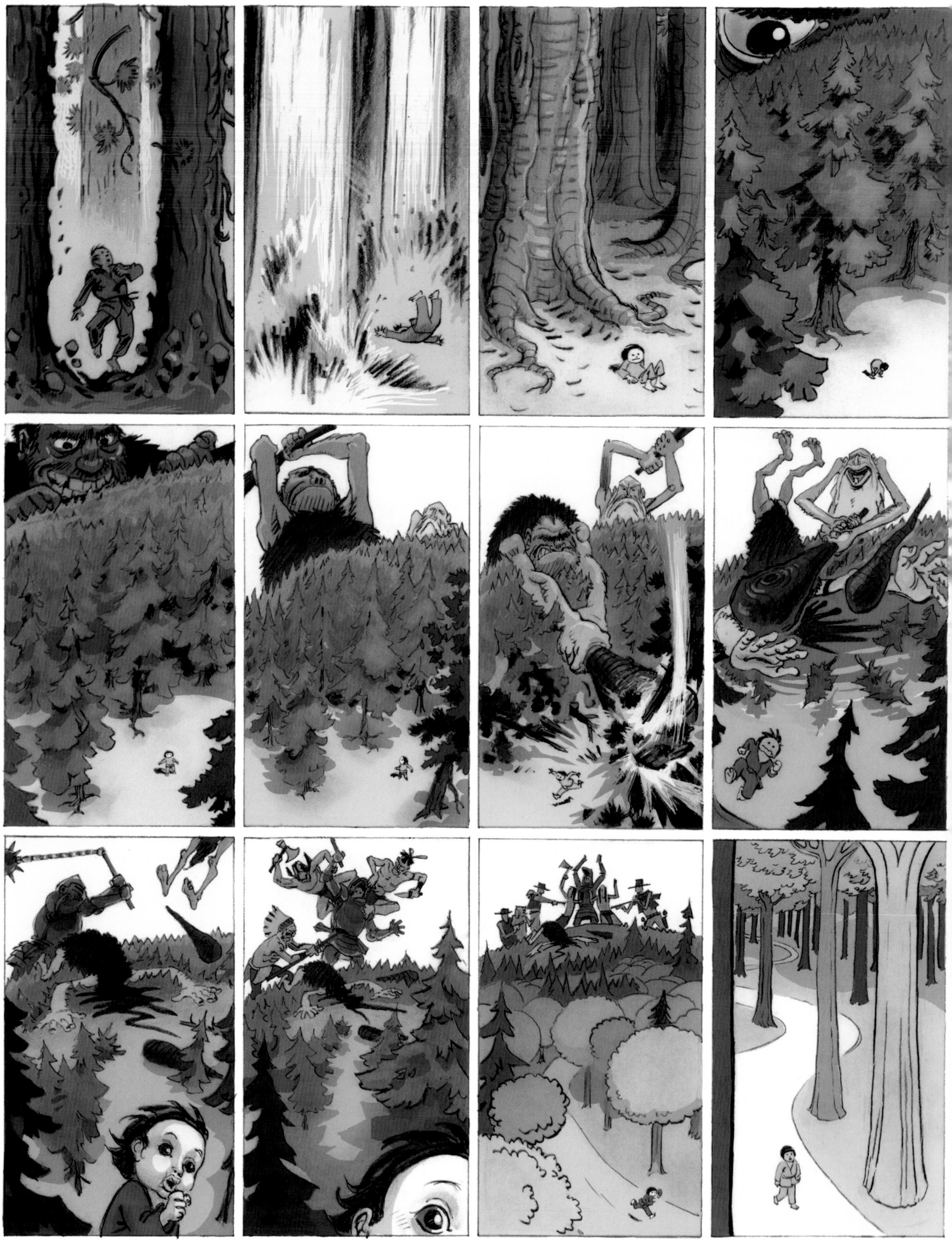

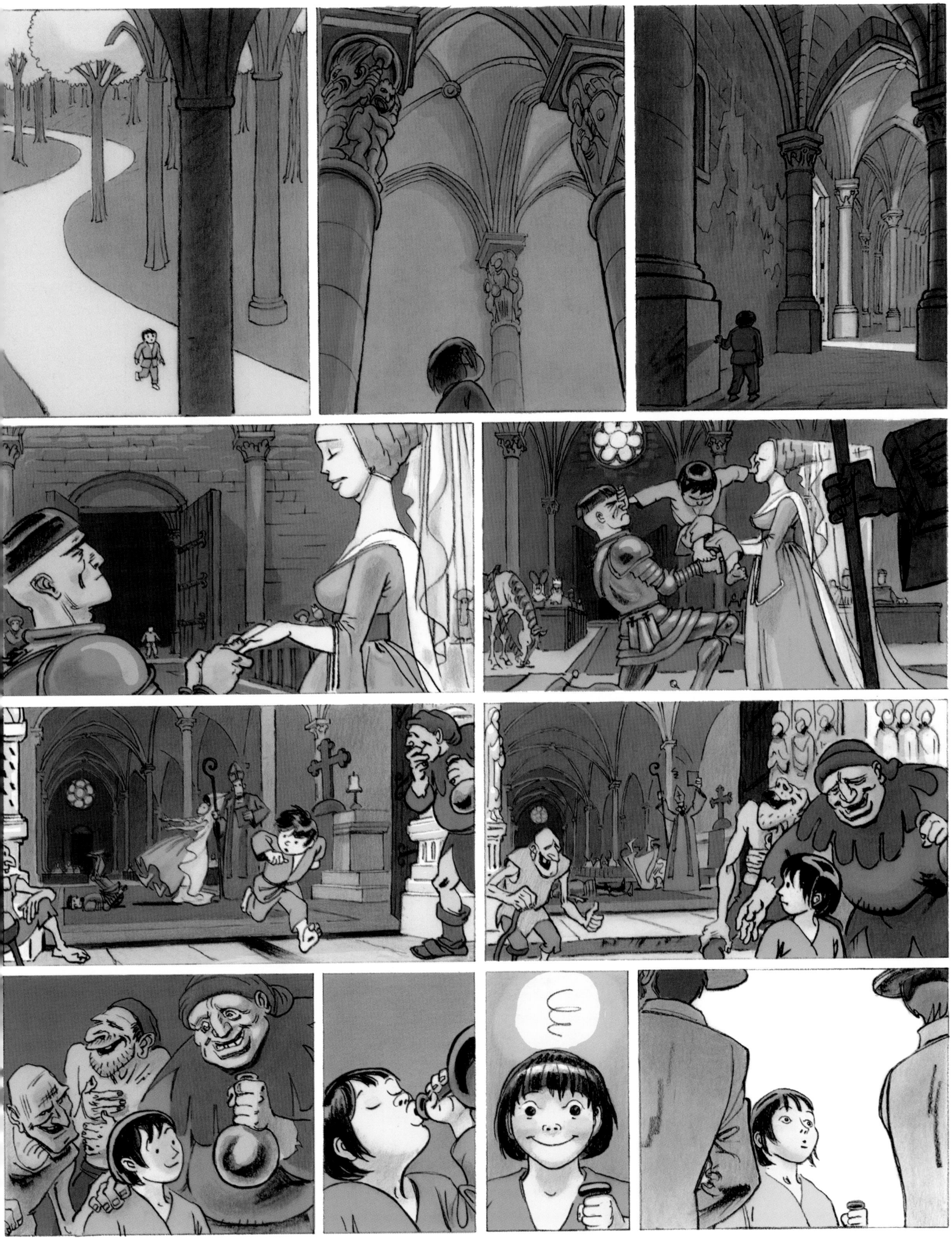

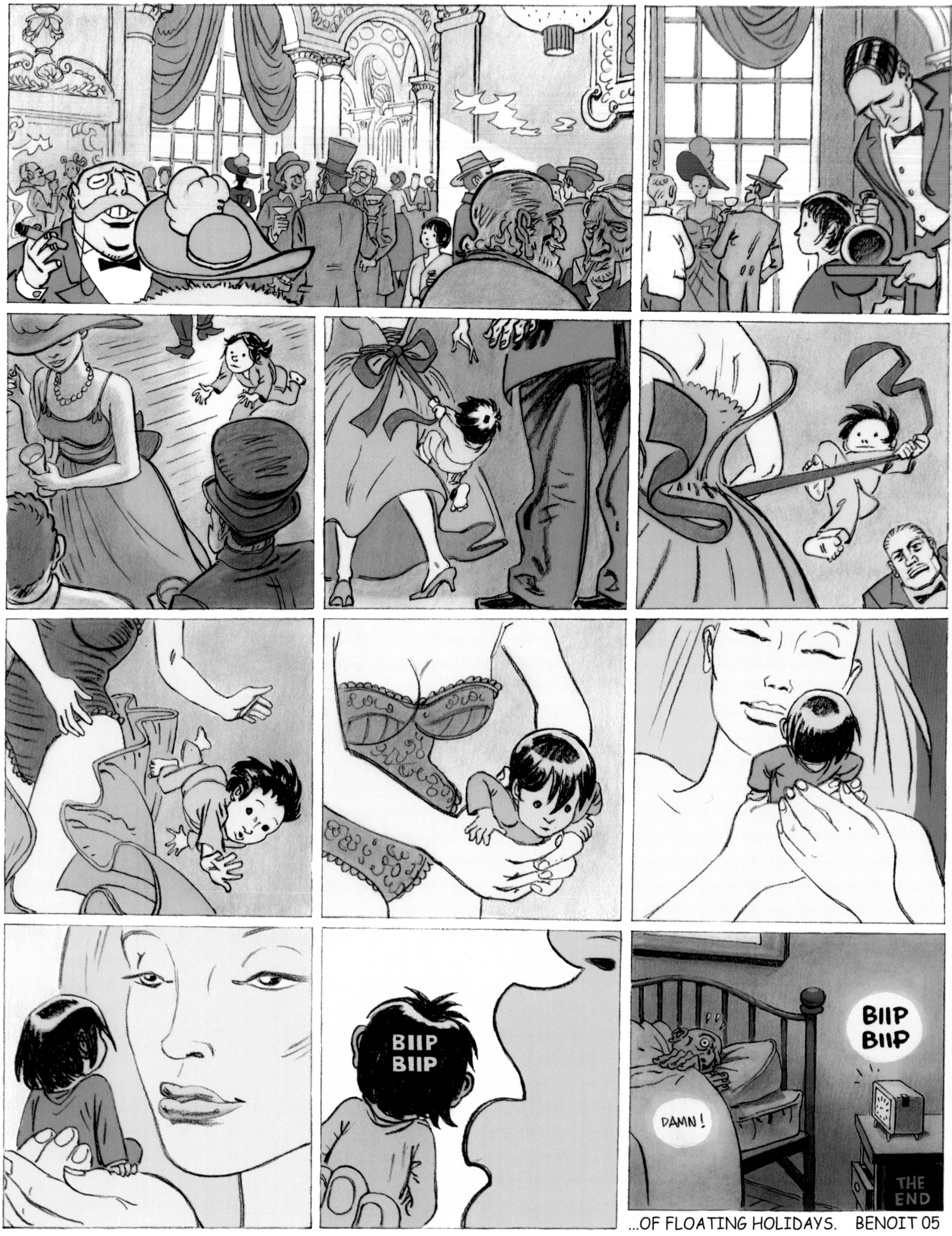
BIIP
BIIP
BIIP
BIIP
DAMN!
THE
END

...OF FLOATING HOLIDAYS. BENOIT 05

OUT OF PICTURE

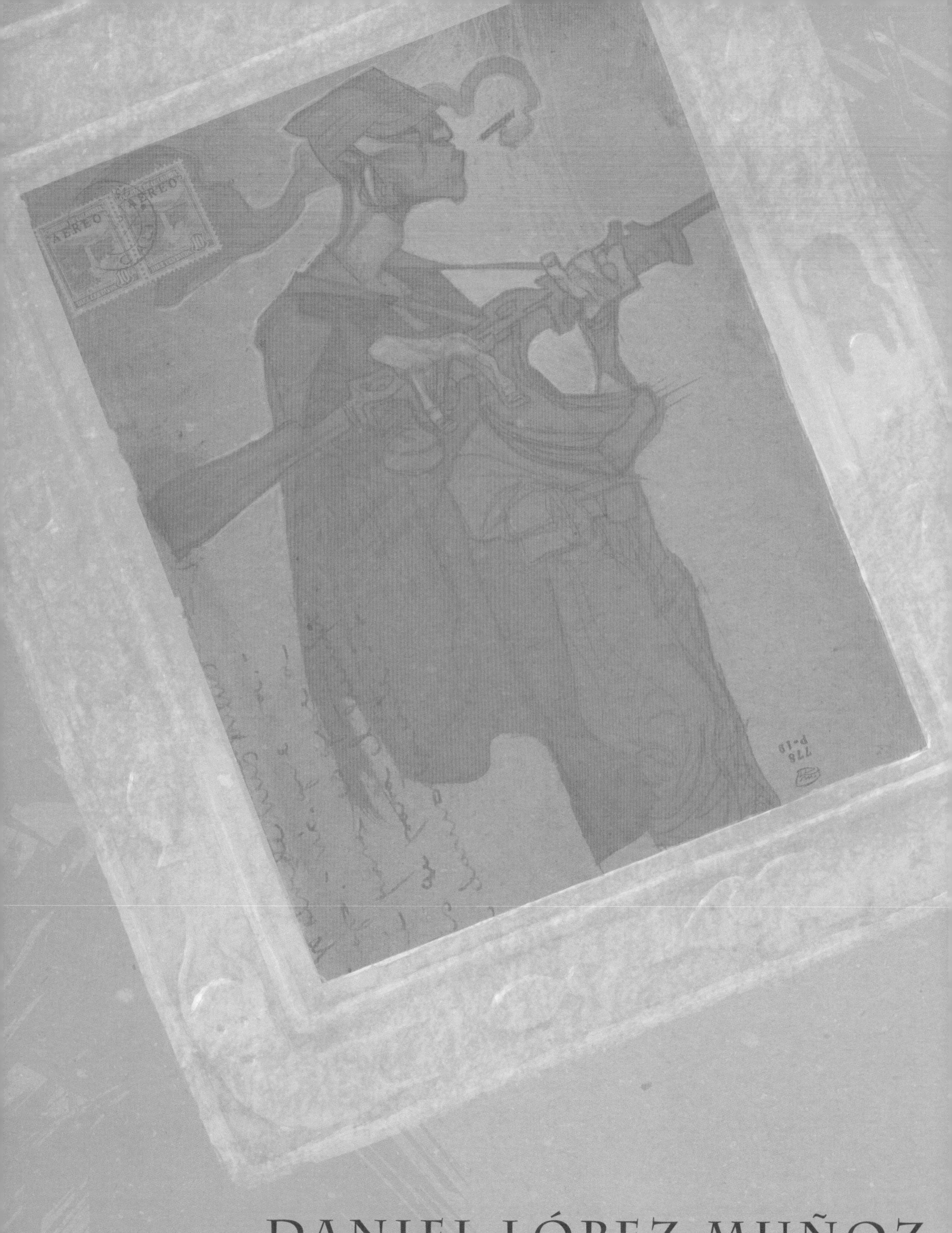
AEREO
AEREO

DANIEL LÓPEZ MUÑOZ

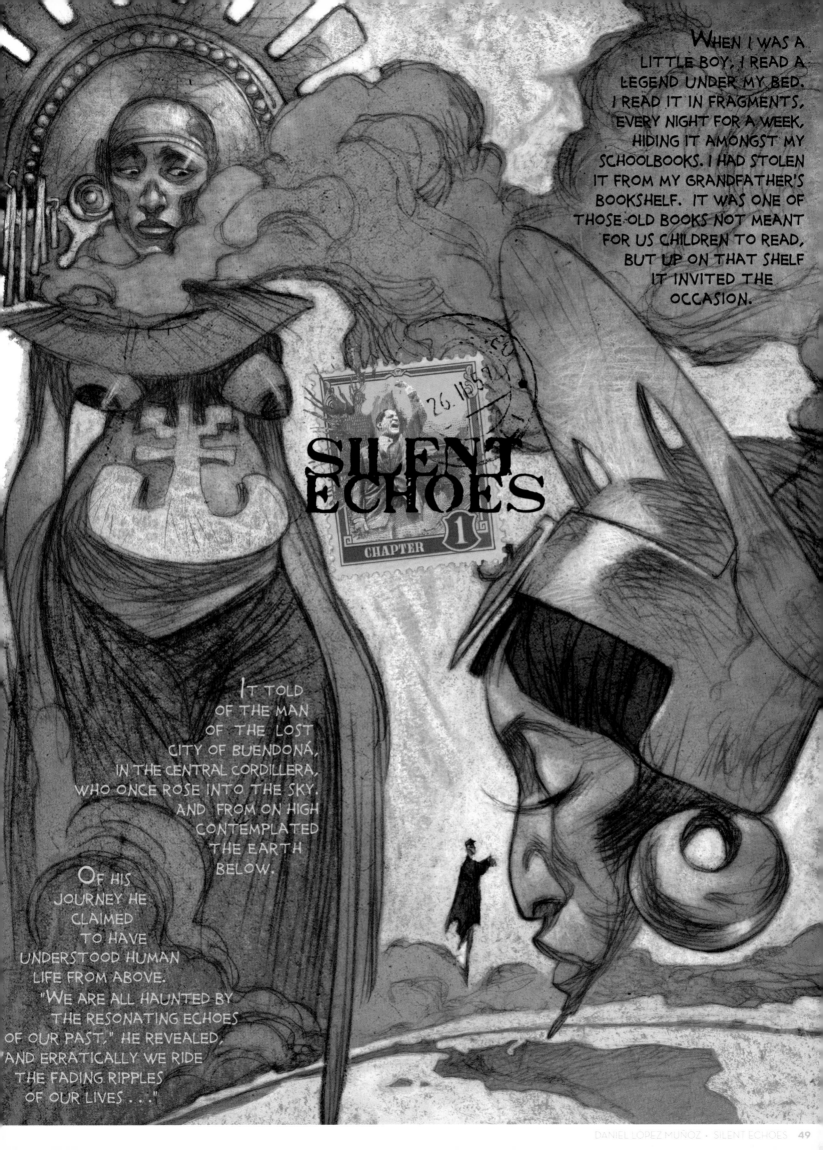

WHEN I WAS A LITTLE BOY, I READ A LEGEND UNDER MY BED. I READ IT IN FRAGMENTS, EVERY NIGHT FOR A WEEK, HIDING IT AMONGST MY SCHOOLBOOKS. I HAD STOLEN IT FROM MY GRANDFATHER'S BOOKSHELF. IT WAS ONE OF THOSE OLD BOOKS NOT MEANT FOR US CHILDREN TO READ, BUT UP ON THAT SHELF IT INVITED THE OCCASION.

SILENT ECHOES

CHAPTER 1

IT TOLD OF THE MAN OF THE LOST CITY OF BUENDONÁ, IN THE CENTRAL CORDILLERA, WHO ONCE ROSE INTO THE SKY, AND FROM ON HIGH CONTEMPLATED THE EARTH BELOW.

OF HIS JOURNEY HE CLAIMED TO HAVE UNDERSTOOD HUMAN LIFE FROM ABOVE. "WE ARE ALL HAUNTED BY THE RESONATING ECHOES OF OUR PAST," HE REVEALED, "AND ERRATICALLY WE RIDE THE FADING RIPPLES OF OUR LIVES . . ."

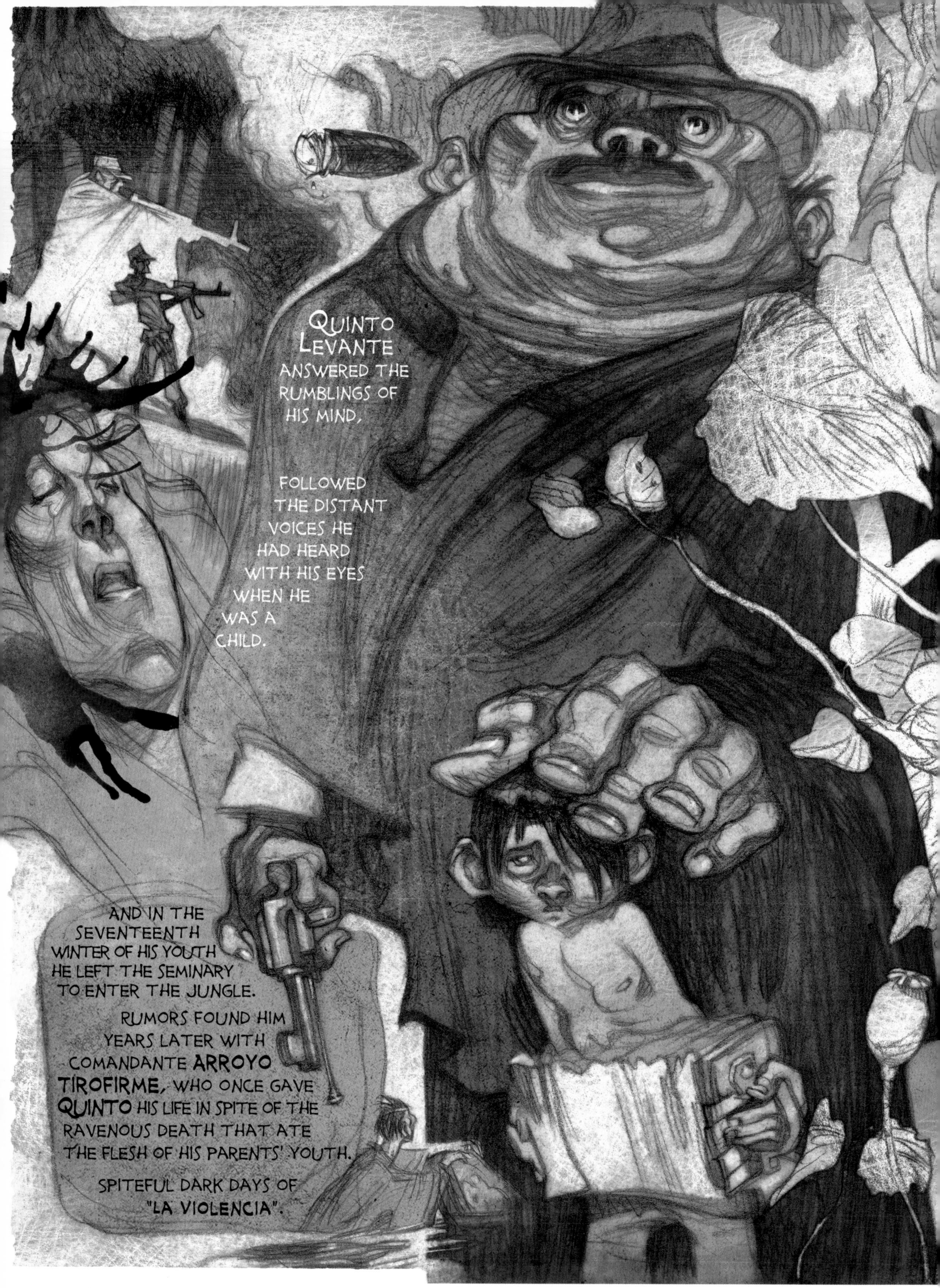
QUINTO LEVANTE ANSWERED THE RUMBLINGS OF HIS MIND,
FOLLOWED THE DISTANT VOICES HE HAD HEARD WITH HIS EYES WHEN HE WAS A CHILD.
AND IN THE SEVENTEENTH WINTER OF HIS YOUTH HE LEFT THE SEMINARY TO ENTER THE JUNGLE.
RUMORS FOUND HIM YEARS LATER WITH COMANDANTE ARROYO TIROFIRME, WHO ONCE GAVE QUINTO HIS LIFE IN SPITE OF THE RAVENOUS DEATH THAT ATE THE FLESH OF HIS PARENTS' YOUTH.
SPITEFUL DARK DAYS OF "LA VIOLENCIA".

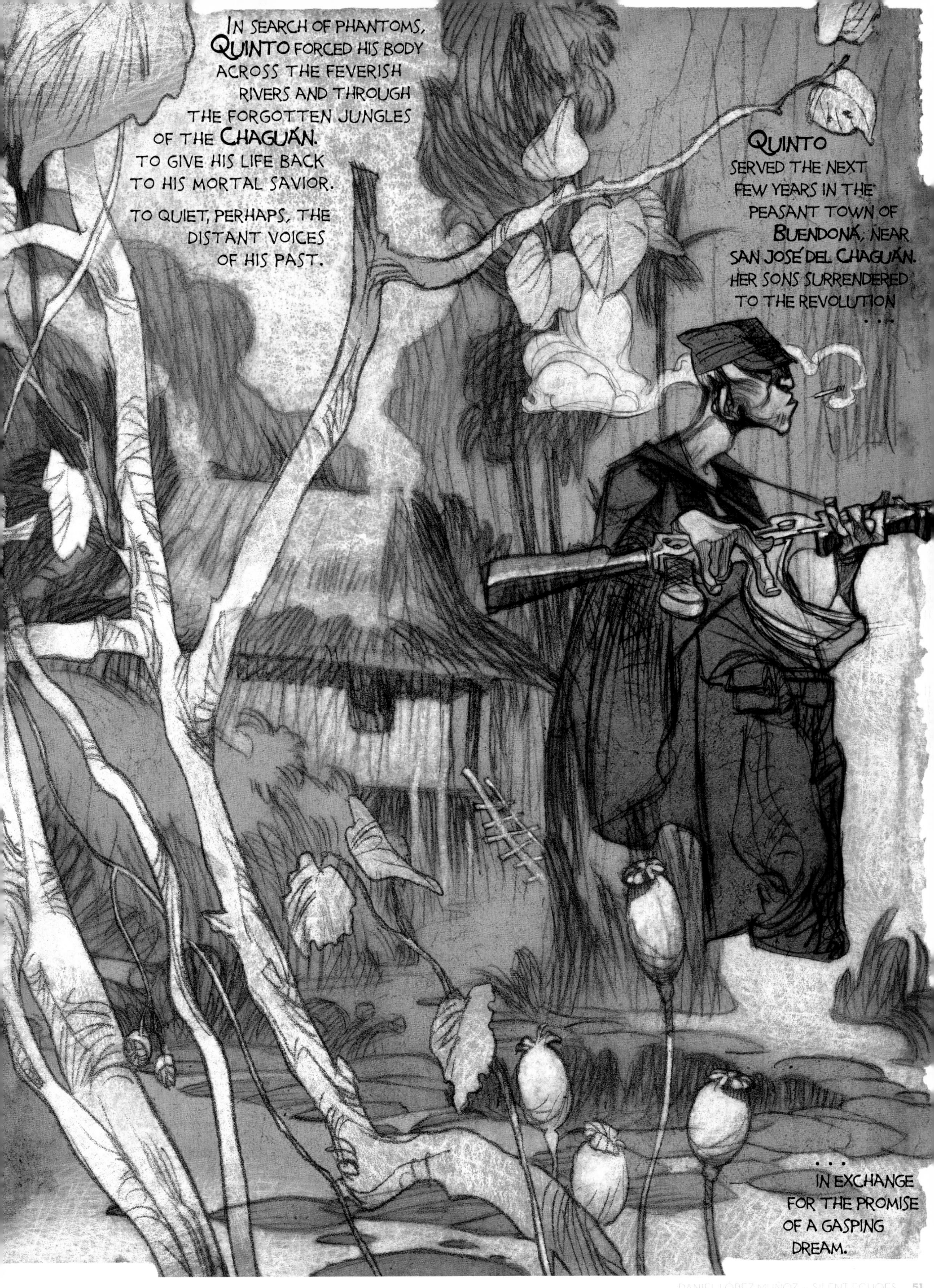
IN SEARCH OF PHANTOMS, QUINTO FORCED HIS BODY ACROSS THE FEVERISH RIVERS AND THROUGH THE FORGOTTEN JUNGLES OF THE CHAGUÁN.
TO GIVE HIS LIFE BACK TO HIS MORTAL SAVIOR.
TO QUIET, PERHAPS, THE DISTANT VOICES OF HIS PAST.
QUINTO SERVED THE NEXT FEW YEARS IN THE PEASANT TOWN OF BUENDONÁ, NEAR SAN JOSÉ DEL CHAGUÁN. HER SONS SURRENDERED TO THE REVOLUTION . . .
. . . IN EXCHANGE FOR THE PROMISE OF A GASPING DREAM.

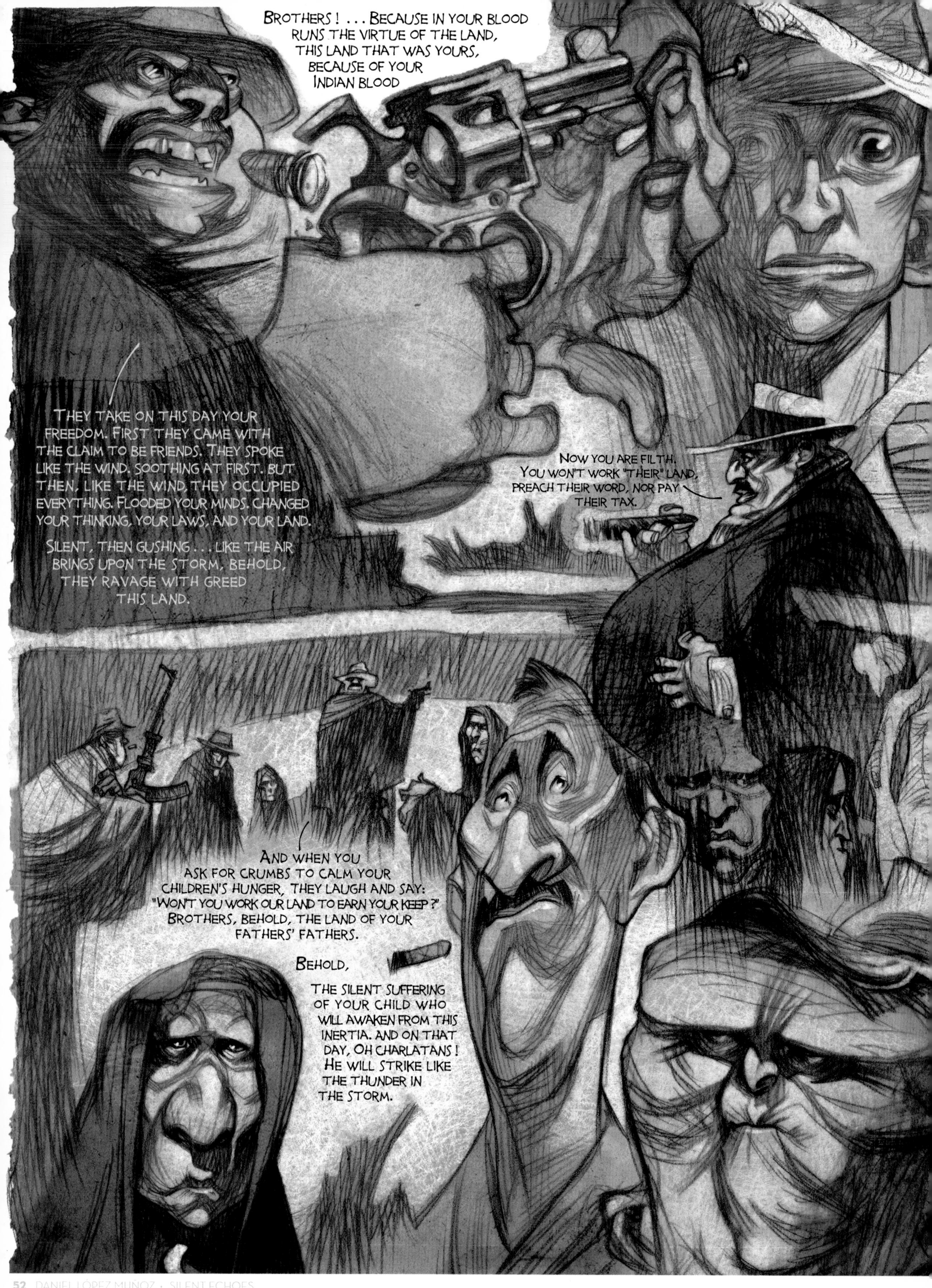
BROTHERS ! . . . BECAUSE IN YOUR BLOOD RUNS THE VIRTUE OF THE LAND, THIS LAND THAT WAS YOURS, BECAUSE OF YOUR INDIAN BLOOD
THEY TAKE ON THIS DAY YOUR FREEDOM. FIRST THEY CAME WITH THE CLAIM TO BE FRIENDS. THEY SPOKE LIKE THE WIND. SOOTHING AT FIRST. BUT THEN, LIKE THE WIND, THEY OCCUPIED EVERYTHING. FLOODED YOUR MINDS. CHANGED YOUR THINKING, YOUR LAWS, AND YOUR LAND.
SILENT, THEN GUSHING . . . LIKE THE AIR BRINGS UPON THE STORM, BEHOLD, THEY RAVAGE WITH GREED THIS LAND.
NOW YOU ARE FILTH. YOU WON'T WORK "THEIR" LAND, PREACH THEIR WORD, NOR PAY THEIR TAX.
AND WHEN YOU ASK FOR CRUMBS TO CALM YOUR CHILDREN'S HUNGER, THEY LAUGH AND SAY: "WON'T YOU WORK OUR LAND TO EARN YOUR KEEP ?" BROTHERS, BEHOLD, THE LAND OF YOUR FATHERS' FATHERS.
BEHOLD,
THE SILENT SUFFERING OF YOUR CHILD WHO WILL AWAKEN FROM THIS INERTIA. AND ON THAT DAY, OH CHARLATANS ! HE WILL STRIKE LIKE THE THUNDER IN THE STORM.

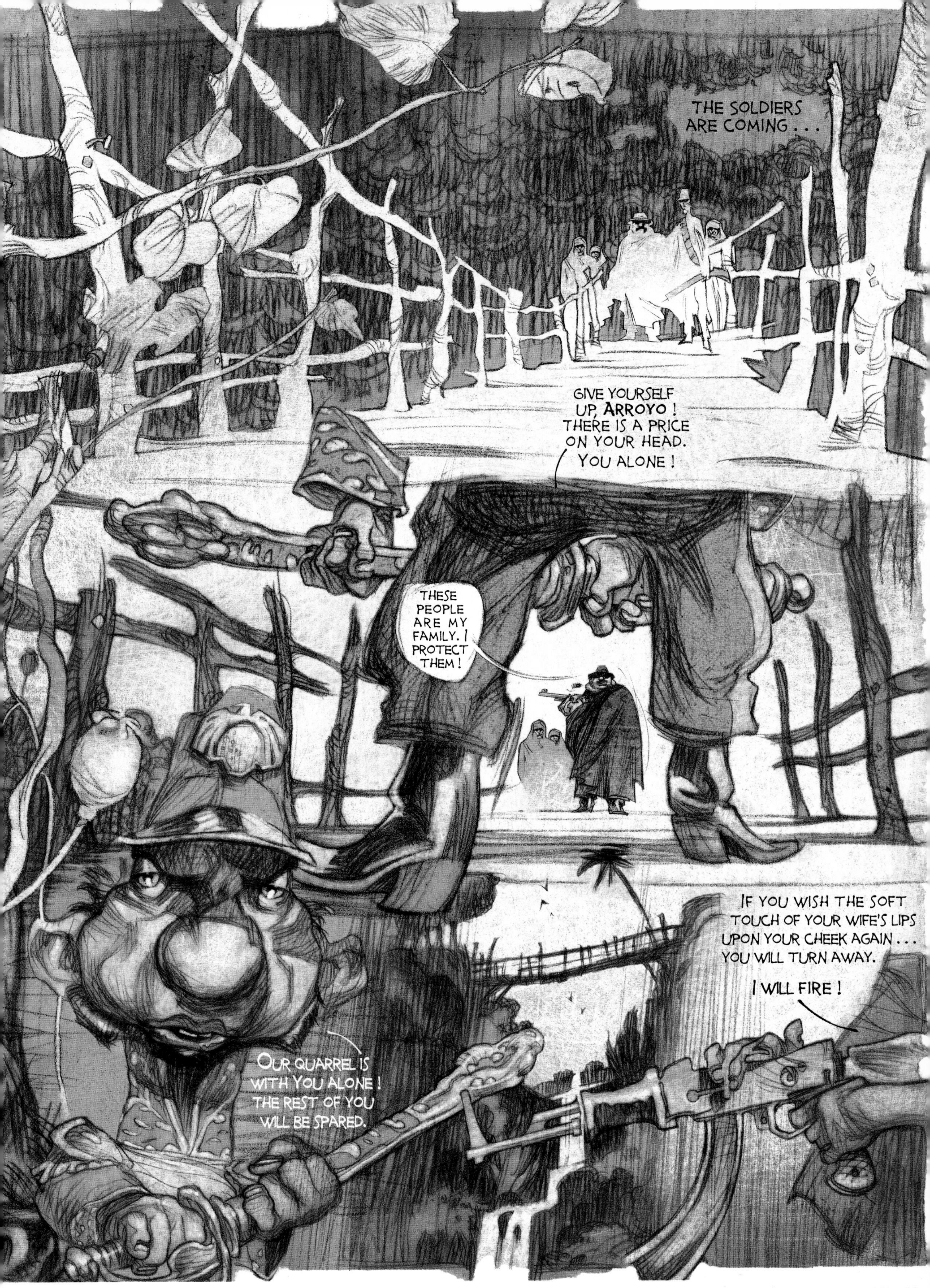
THE SOLDIERS ARE COMING . . .
GIVE YOURSELF UP, ARROYO ! THERE IS A PRICE ON YOUR HEAD. YOU ALONE !
THESE PEOPLE ARE MY FAMILY. I PROTECT THEM !
IF YOU WISH THE SOFT TOUCH OF YOUR WIFE'S LIPS UPON YOUR CHEEK AGAIN . . . YOU WILL TURN AWAY.
I WILL FIRE !
OUR QUARREL IS WITH YOU ALONE ! THE REST OF YOU WILL BE SPARED.

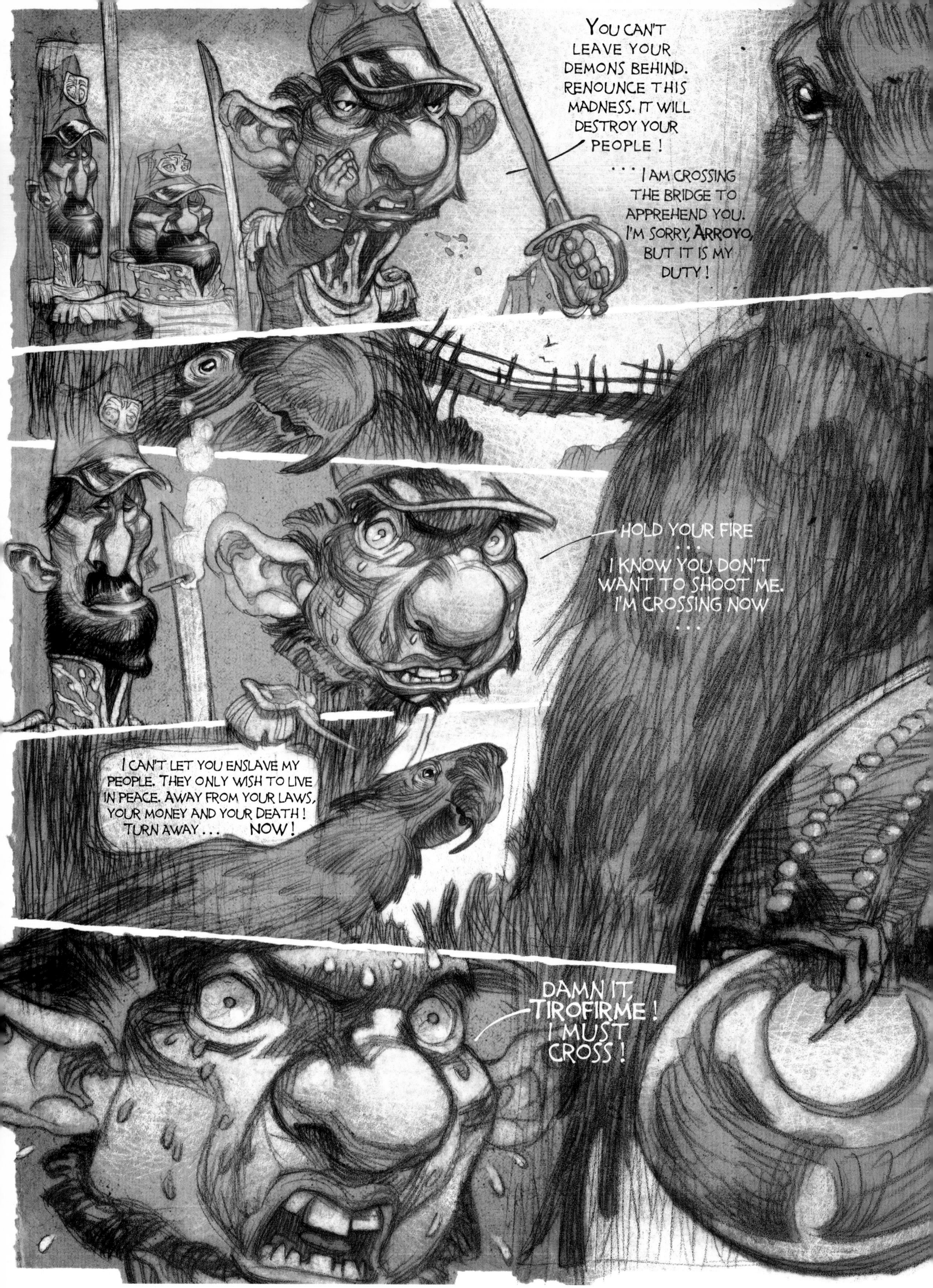
YOU CAN'T LEAVE YOUR DEMONS BEHIND. RENOUNCE THIS MADNESS. IT WILL DESTROY YOUR PEOPLE !
. . . I AM CROSSING THE BRIDGE TO APPREHEND YOU. I'M SORRY, ARROYO, BUT IT IS MY DUTY !
HOLD YOUR FIRE . . . I KNOW YOU DON'T WANT TO SHOOT ME. I'M CROSSING NOW . . .
I CAN'T LET YOU ENSLAVE MY PEOPLE. THEY ONLY WISH TO LIVE IN PEACE. AWAY FROM YOUR LAWS, YOUR MONEY AND YOUR DEATH ! TURN AWAY . . . NOW !
DAMN IT, TIROFIRME ! I MUST CROSS !

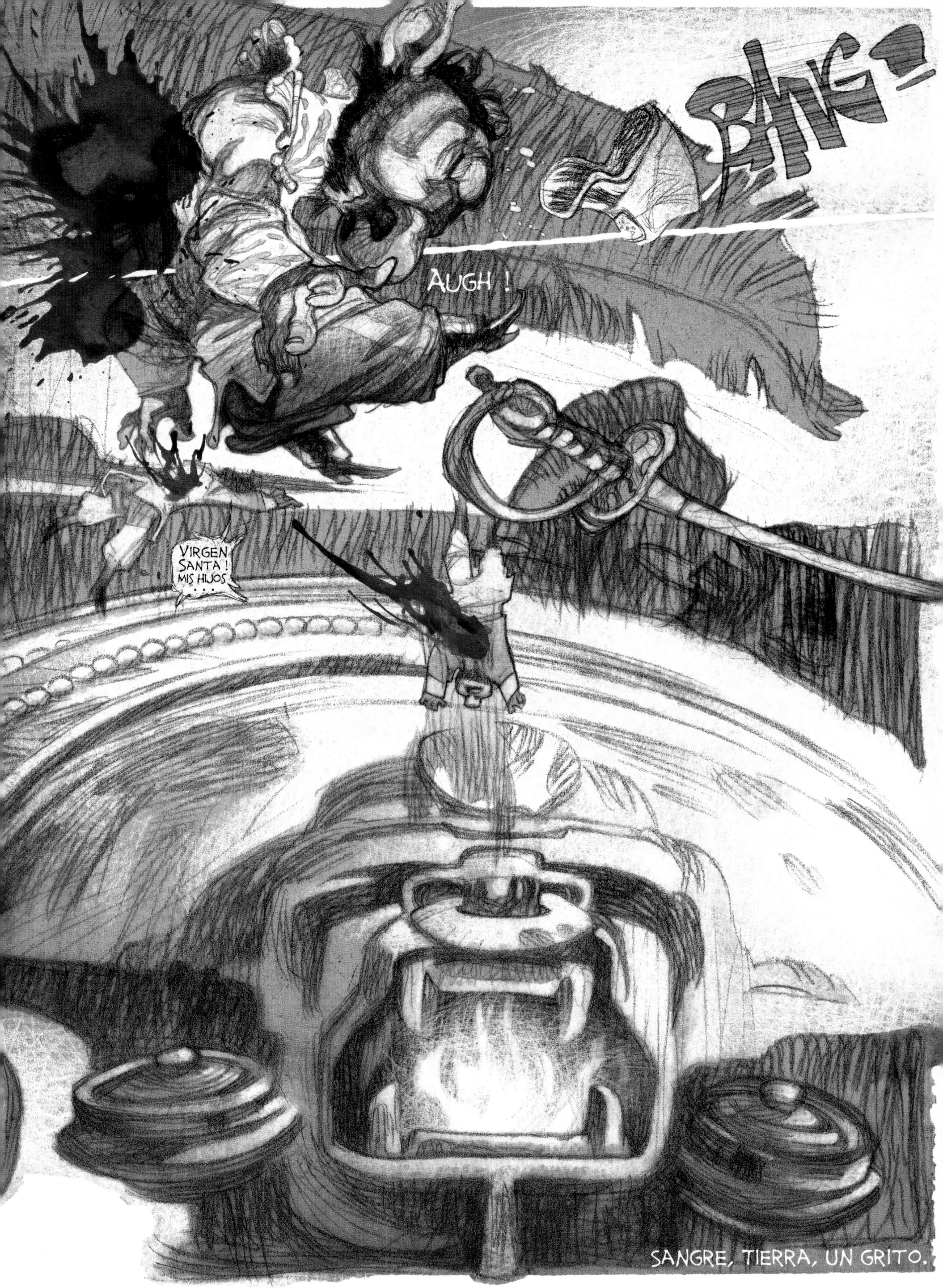
BANG!
AUGH!
VIRGEN SANTA! MIS HIJOS...
SANGRE, TIERRA, UN GRITO.

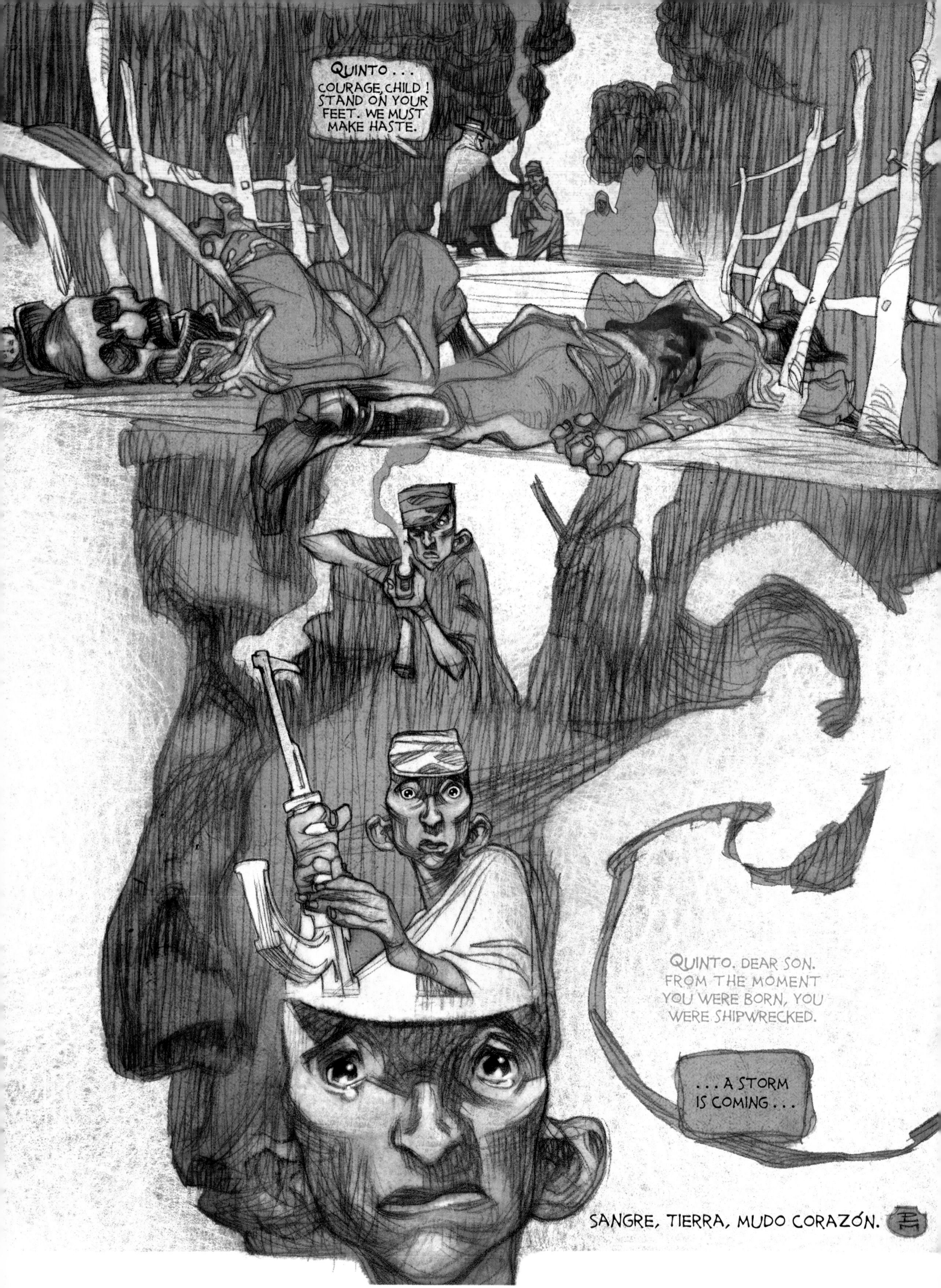
QUINTO . . . COURAGE, CHILD ! STAND ON YOUR FEET. WE MUST MAKE HASTE.
QUINTO, DEAR SON. FROM THE MOMENT YOU WERE BORN, YOU WERE SHIPWRECKED.
. . . A STORM IS COMING . . .
SANGRE, TIERRA, MUDO CORAZÓN.

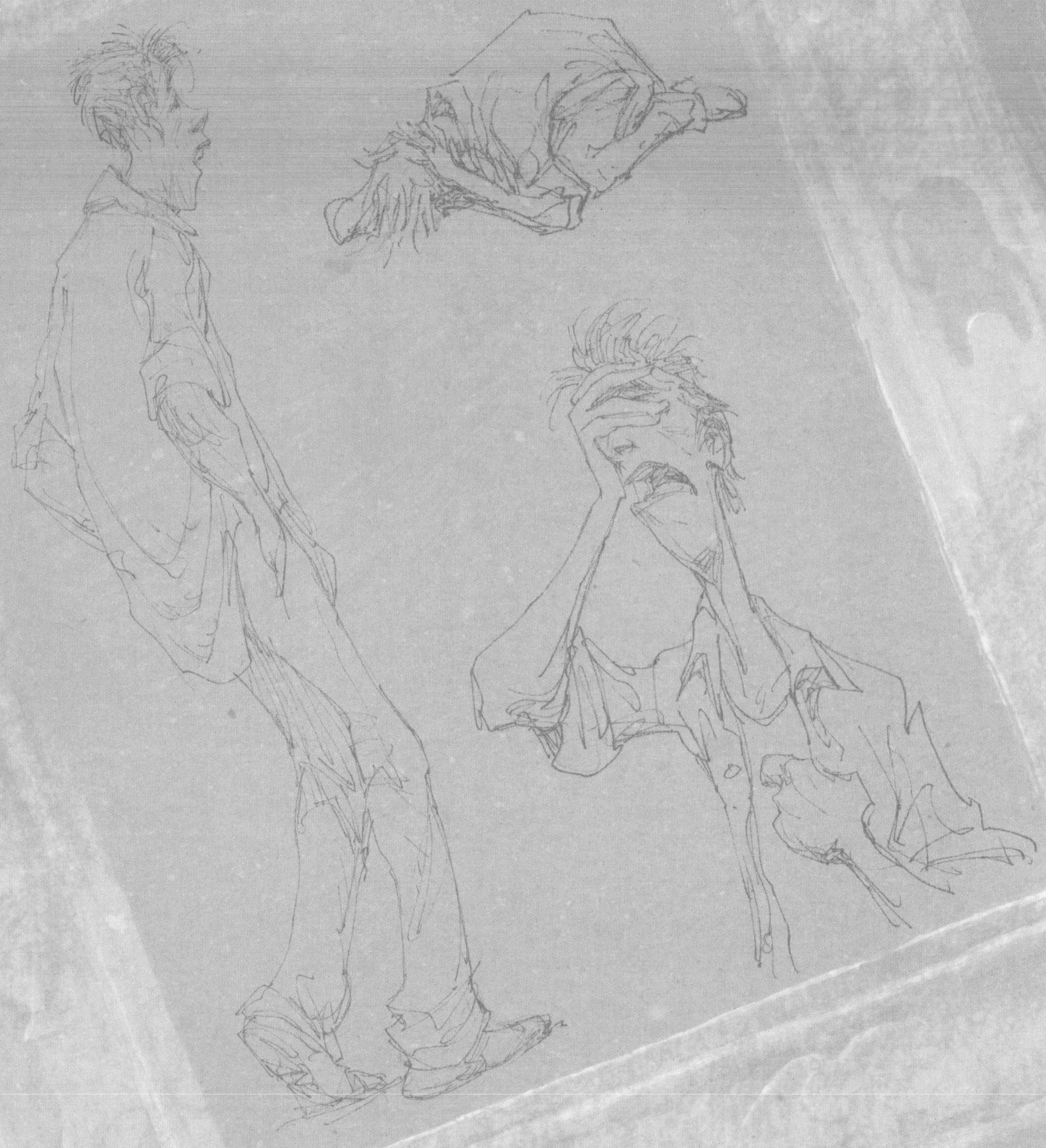

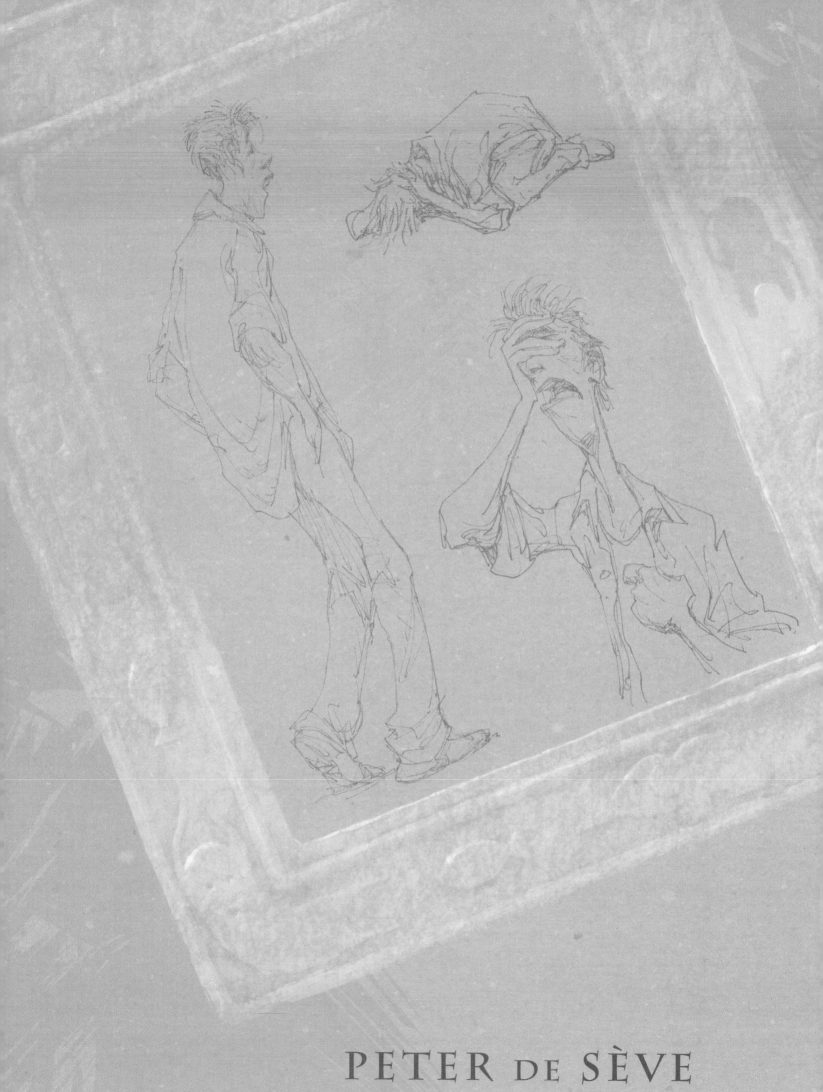

PETER DE SÈVE

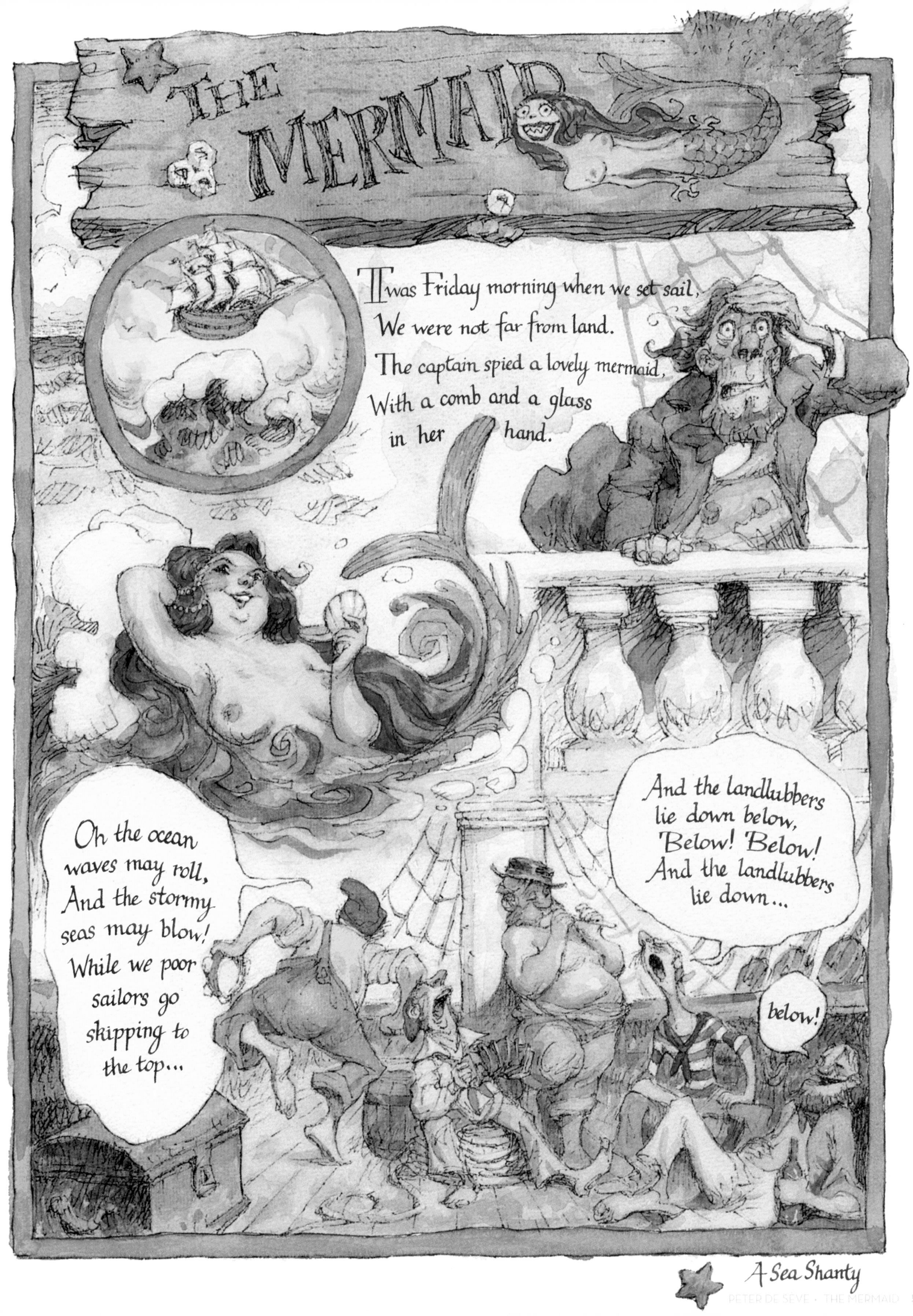
THE MERMAID
'Twas Friday morning when we set sail,
We were not far from land.
The captain spied a lovely mermaid,
With a comb and a glass in her hand.
Oh the ocean waves may roll, And the stormy seas may blow! While we poor sailors go skipping to the top...
And the landlubbers lie down below, Below! Below! And the landlubbers lie down...
below!

A Sea Shanty

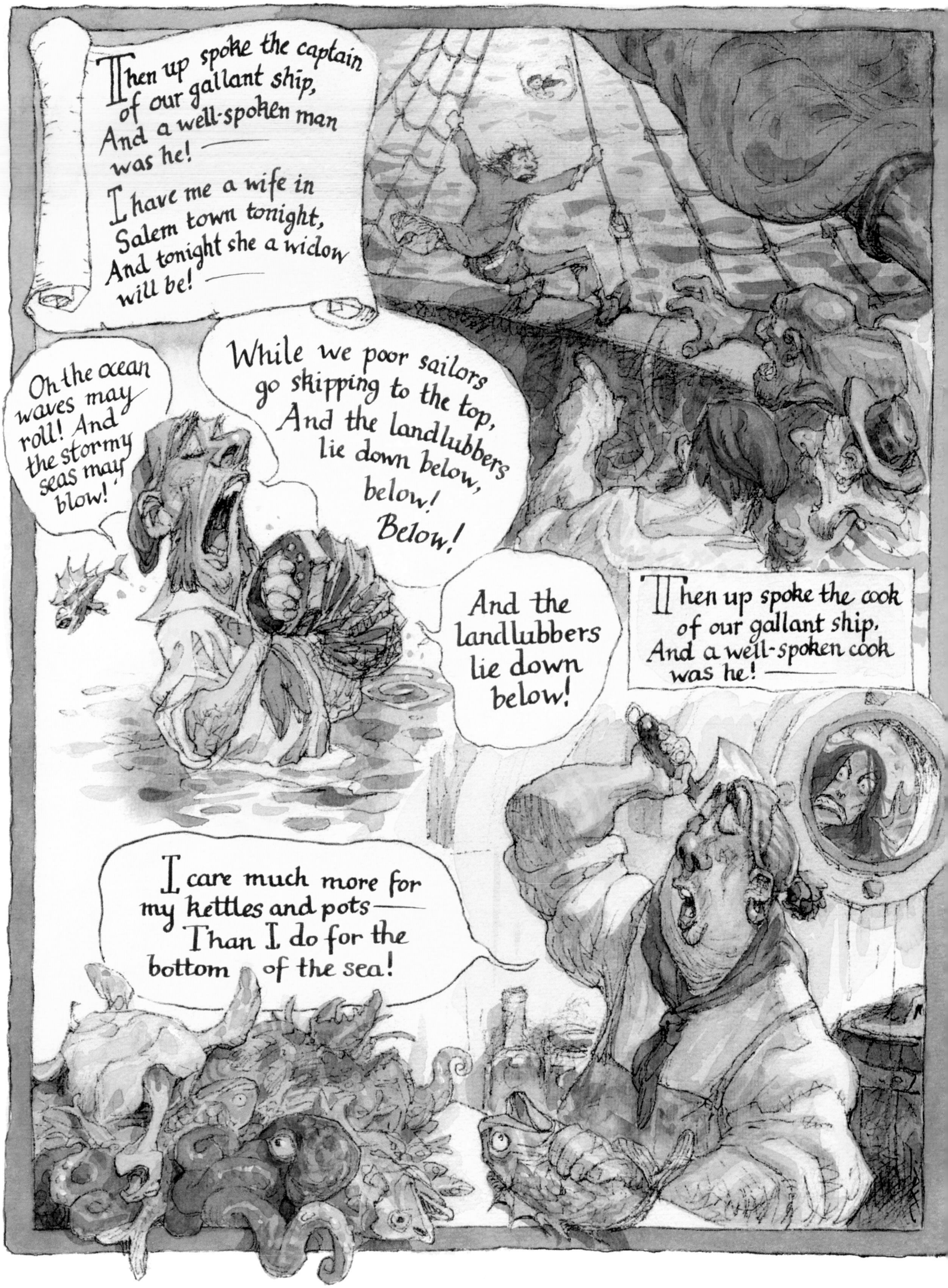
Then up spoke the captain of our gallant ship, And a well-spoken man was he! — I have me a wife in Salem town tonight, And tonight she a widow will be! —
Oh the ocean waves may roll! And the stormy seas may blow!
While we poor sailors go skipping to the top, And the landlubbers lie down below, below! Below!
And the landlubbers lie down below!
Then up spoke the cook of our gallant ship, And a well-spoken cook was he! —
I care much more for my kettles and pots — Than I do for the bottom of the sea!

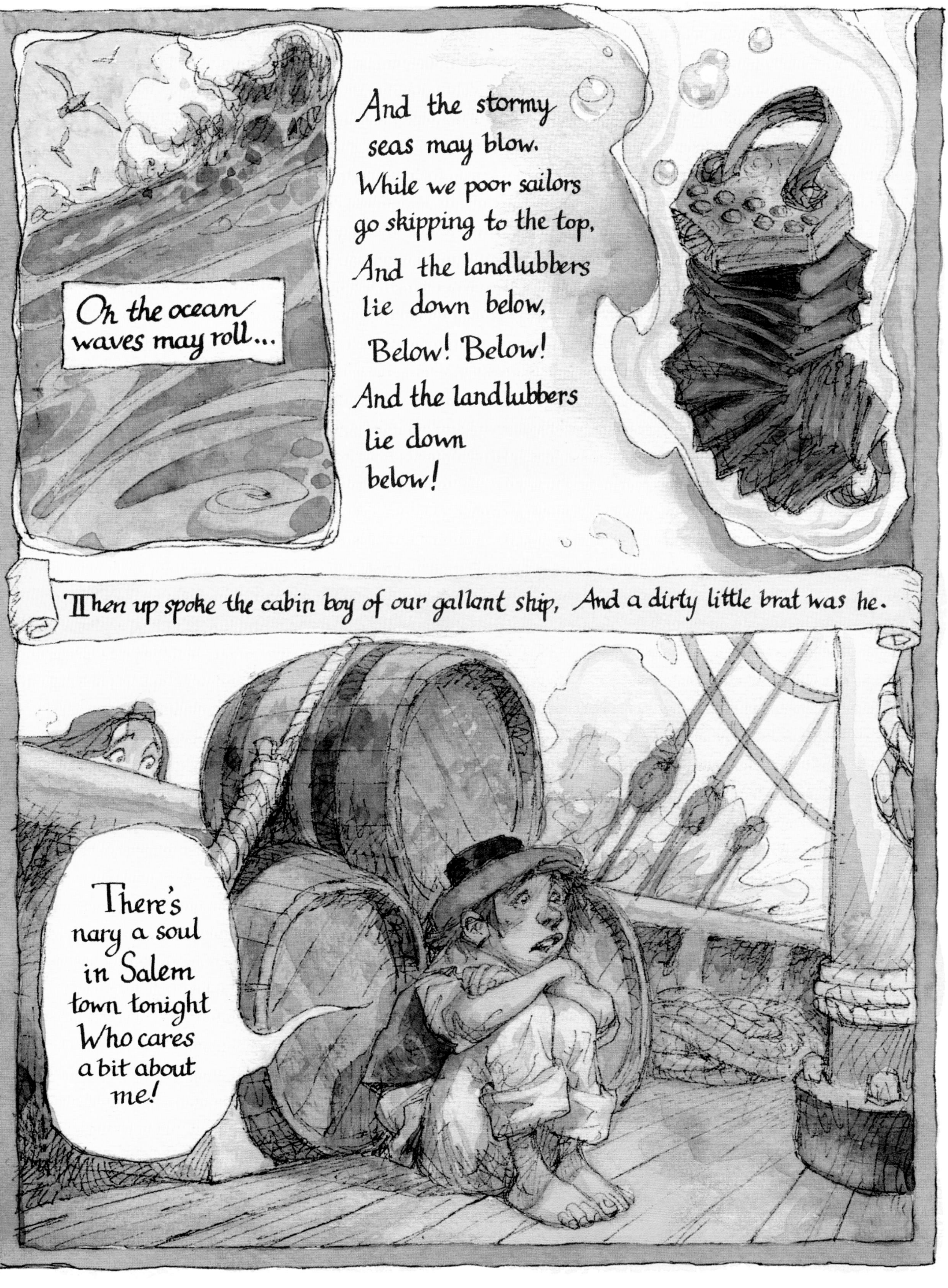
On the ocean waves may roll...
And the stormy seas may blow.
While we poor sailors go skipping to the top,
And the landlubbers lie down below,
Below! Below!
And the landlubbers lie down below!
Then up spoke the cabin boy of our gallant ship, And a dirty little brat was he.
There's nary a soul in Salem town tonight Who cares a bit about me!

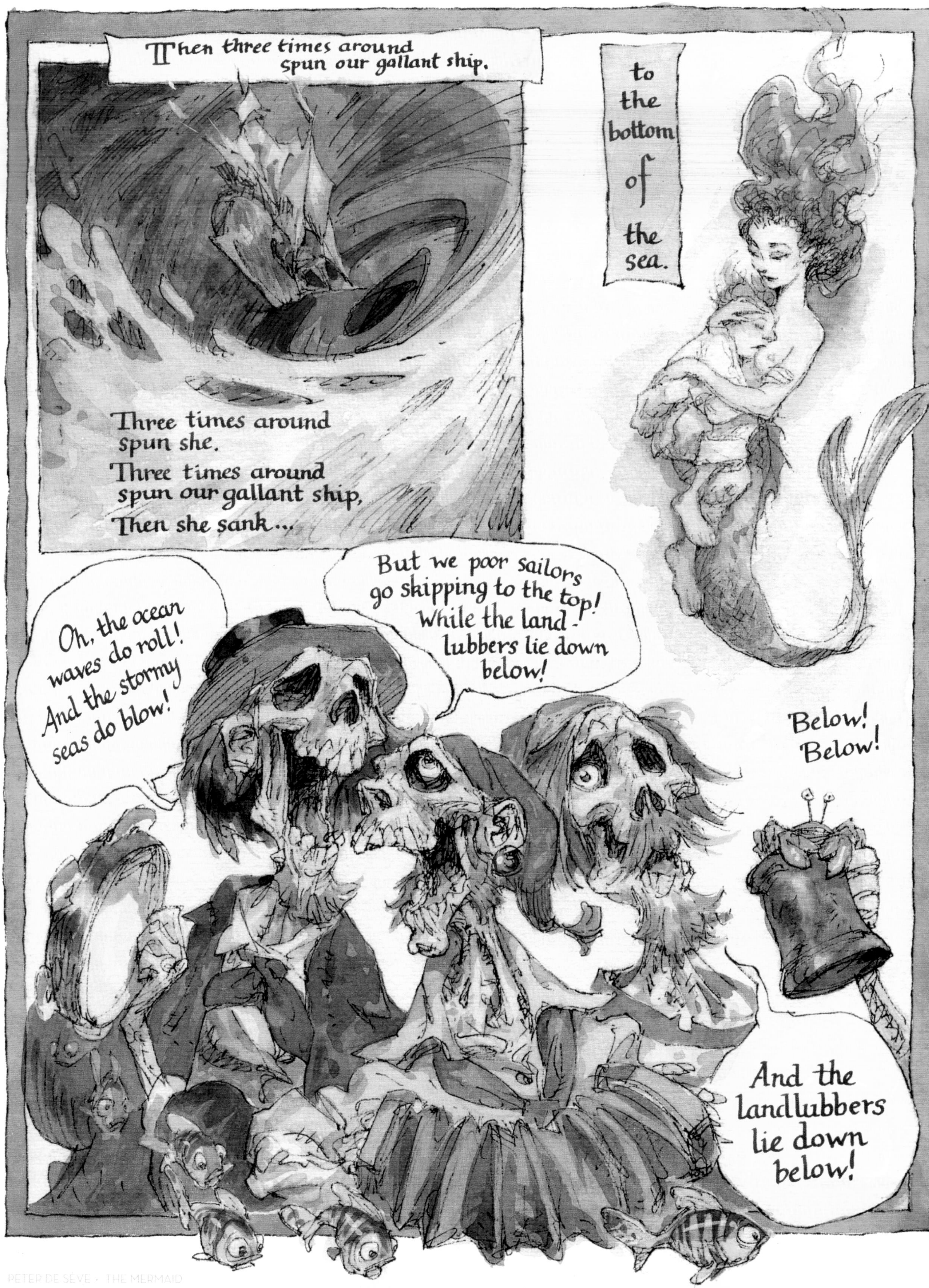
Then three times around spun our gallant ship.
Three times around spun she.
Three times around spun our gallant ship,
Then she sank...
to the bottom of the sea.
Oh, the ocean waves do roll! And the stormy seas do blow!
But we poor sailors go skipping to the top! While the land-lubbers lie down below!
Below! Below!
And the landlubbers lie down below!

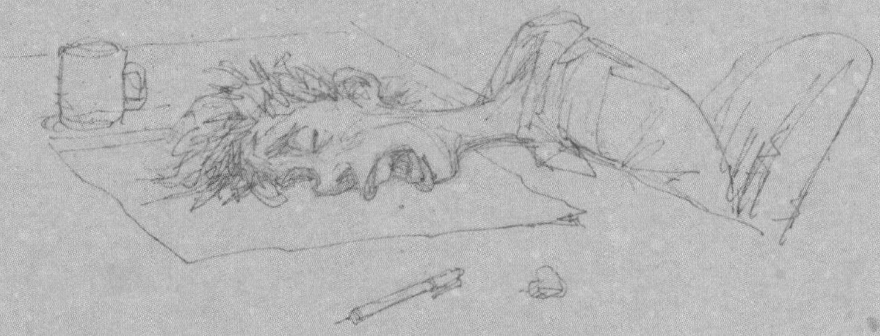

OUT OF PICTURE

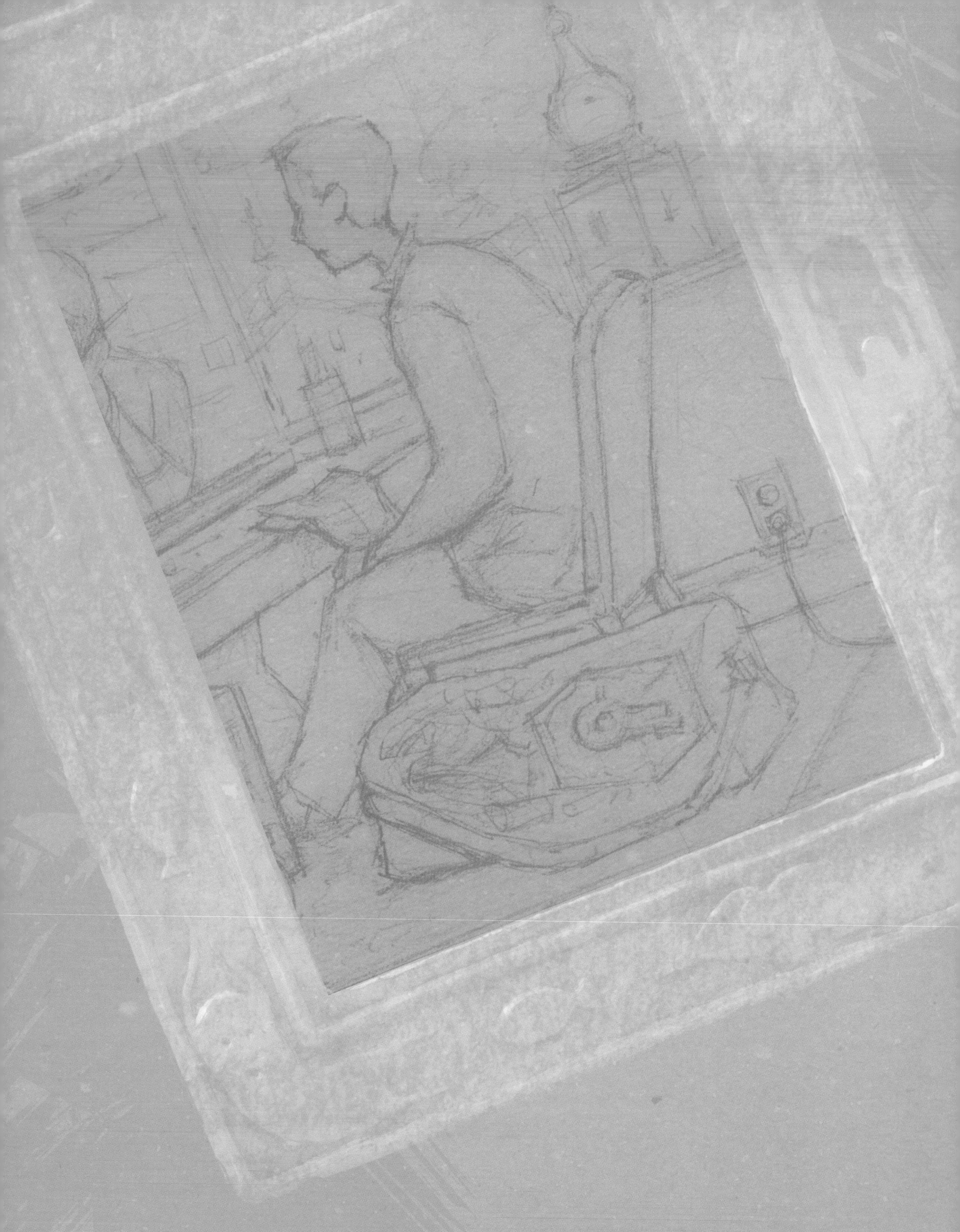

DAVID GORDON

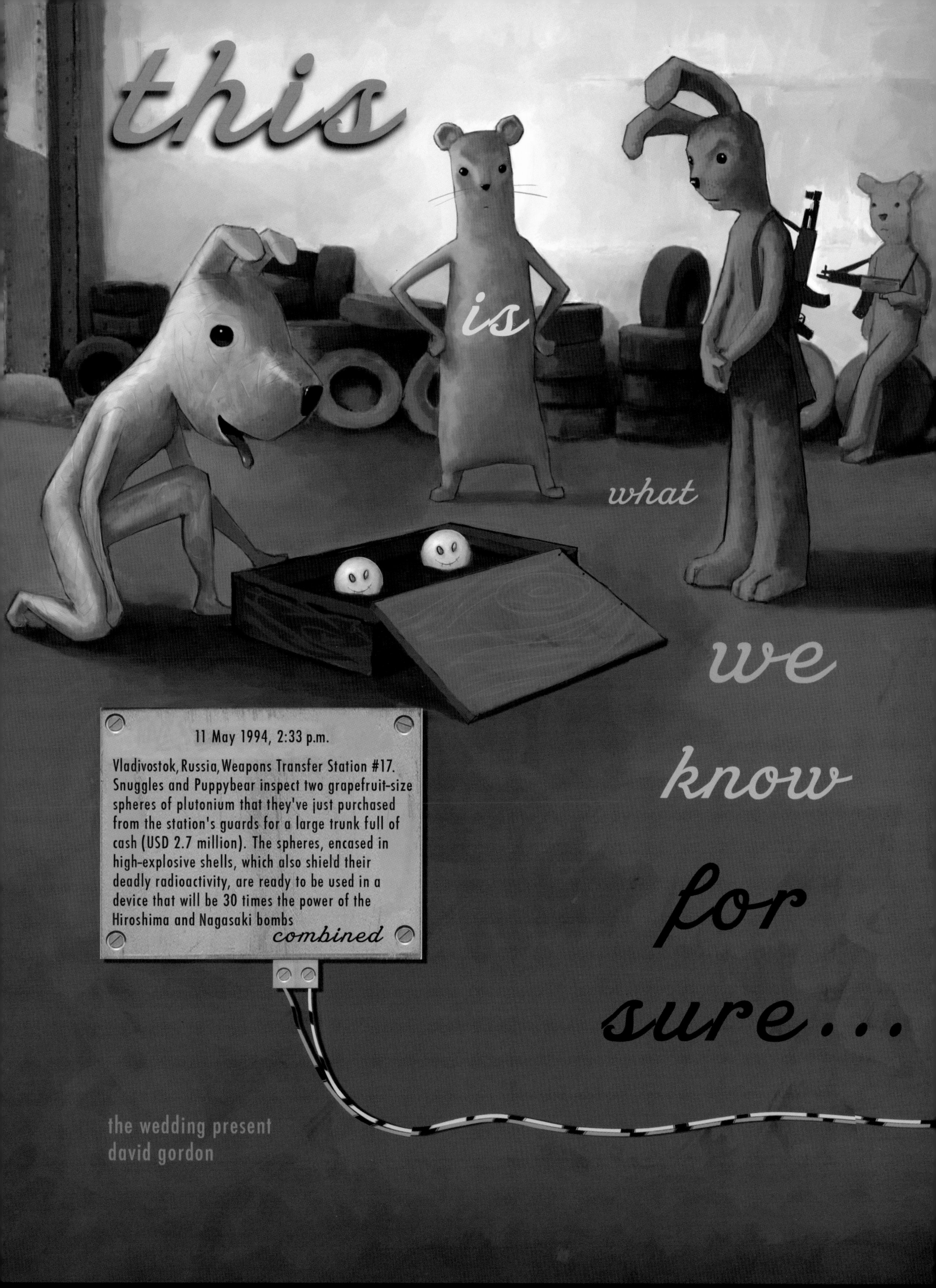
this
is
what
we
know
for
sure...
11 May 1994, 2:33 p.m.
Vladivostok, Russia, Weapons Transfer Station #17. Snuggles and Puppybear inspect two grapefruit-size spheres of plutonium that they've just purchased from the station's guards for a large trunk full of cash (USD 2.7 million). The spheres, encased in high-explosive shells, which also shield their deadly radioactivity, are ready to be used in a device that will be 30 times the power of the Hiroshima and Nagasaki bombs combined
the wedding present
david gordon

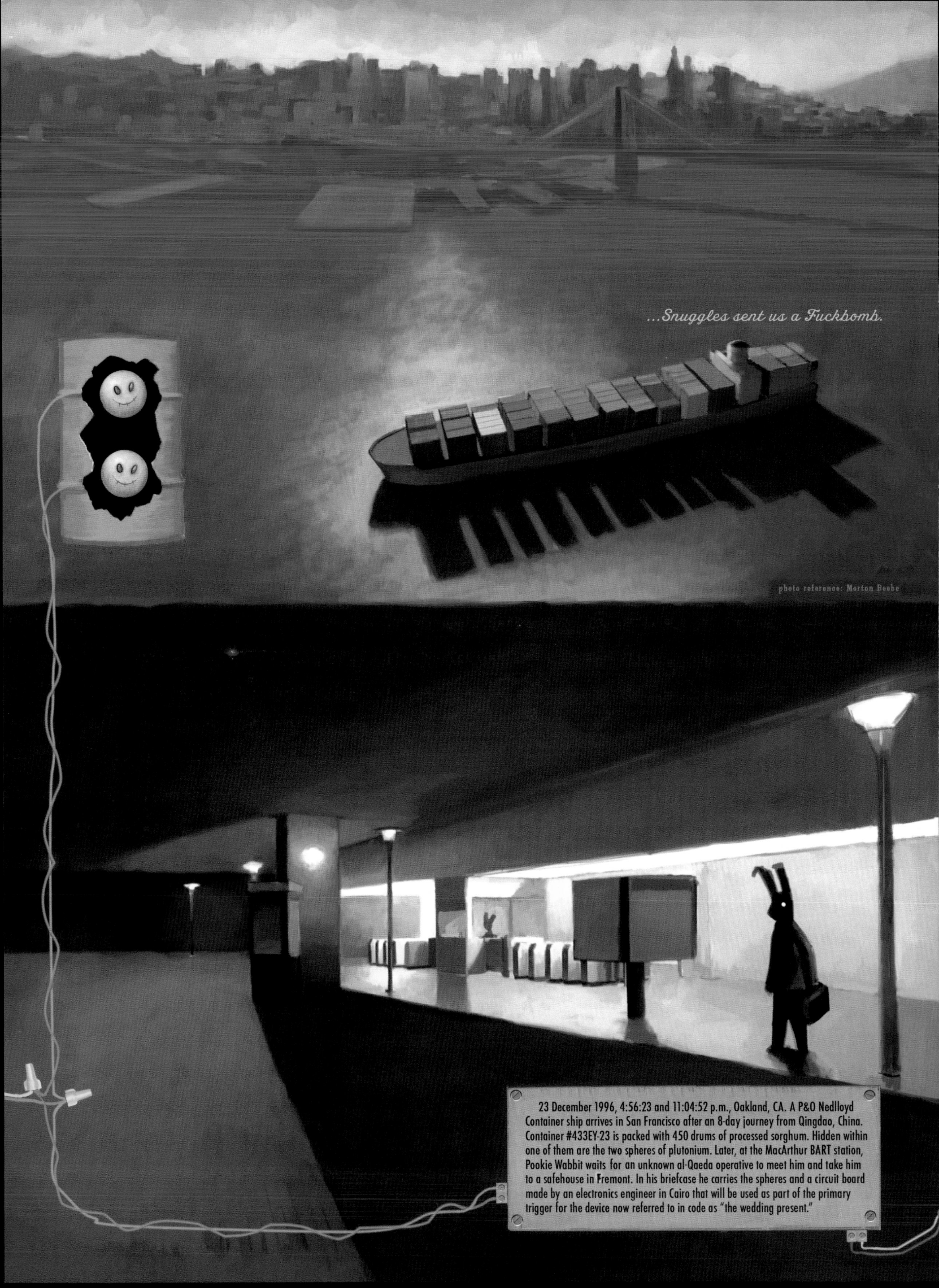

...Snuggles sent us a Fuckbomb.
photo reference: Morton Beebe
23 December 1996, 4:56:23 and 11:04:52 p.m., Oakland, CA. A P&O Nedlloyd Container ship arrives in San Francisco after an 8-day journey from Qingdao, China. Container #433EY-23 is packed with 450 drums of processed sorghum. Hidden within one of them are the two spheres of plutonium. Later, at the MacArthur BART station, Pookie Wabbit waits for an unknown al-Qaeda operative to meet him and take him to a safehouse in Fremont. In his briefcase he carries the spheres and a circuit board made by an electronics engineer in Cairo that will be used as part of the primary trigger for the device now referred to in code as "the wedding present."

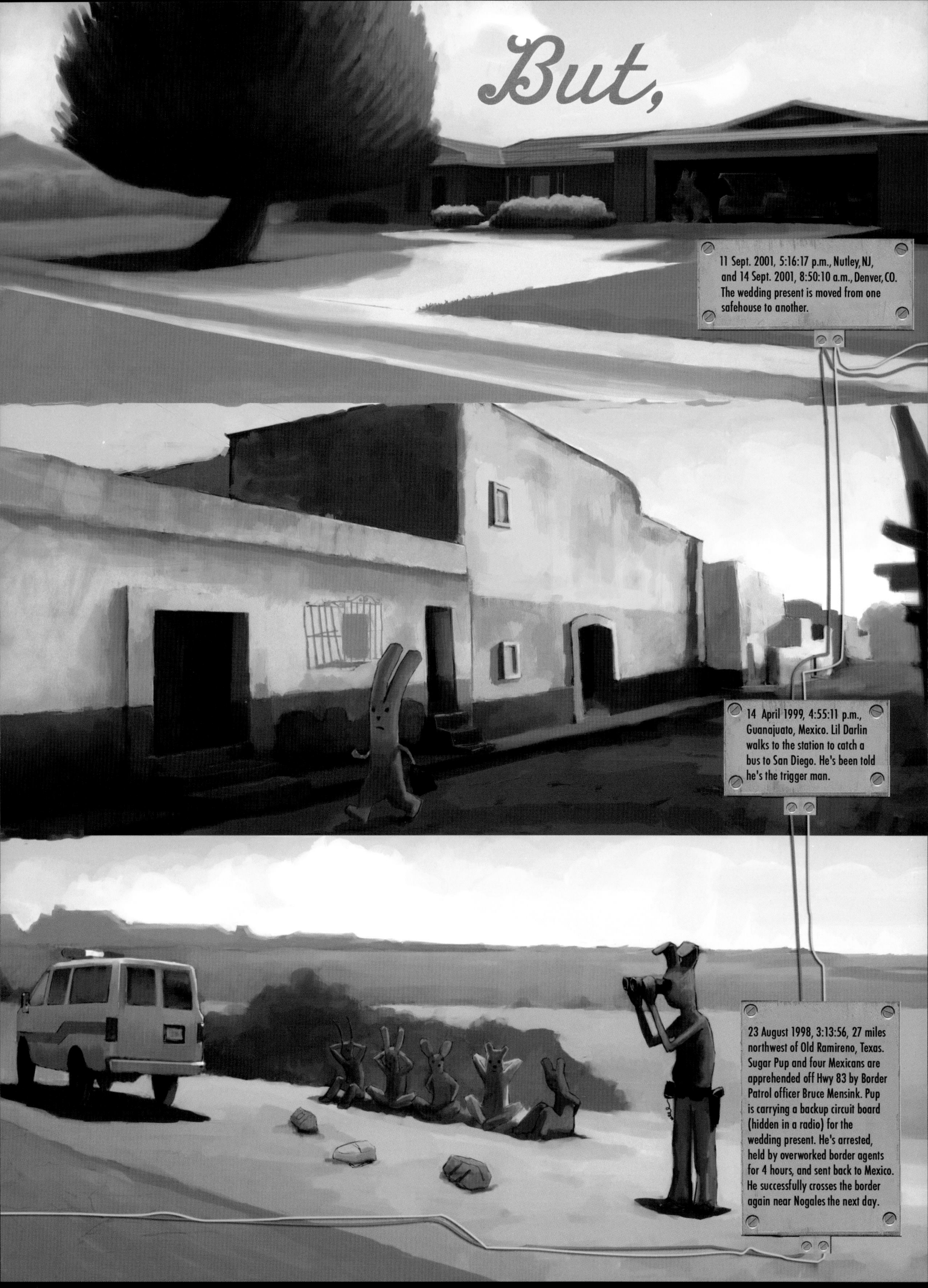
But,
11 Sept. 2001, 5:16:17 p.m., Nutley, NJ, and 14 Sept. 2001, 8:50:10 a.m., Denver, CO. The wedding present is moved from one safehouse to another.
14 April 1999, 4:55:11 p.m., Guanajuato, Mexico. Lil Darlin walks to the station to catch a bus to San Diego. He's been told he's the trigger man.
23 August 1998, 3:13:56, 27 miles northwest of Old Ramireno, Texas. Sugar Pup and four Mexicans are apprehended off Hwy 83 by Border Patrol officer Bruce Mensink. Pup is carrying a backup circuit board (hidden in a radio) for the wedding present. He's arrested, held by overworked border agents for 4 hours, and sent back to Mexico. He successfully crosses the border again near Nogales the next day.

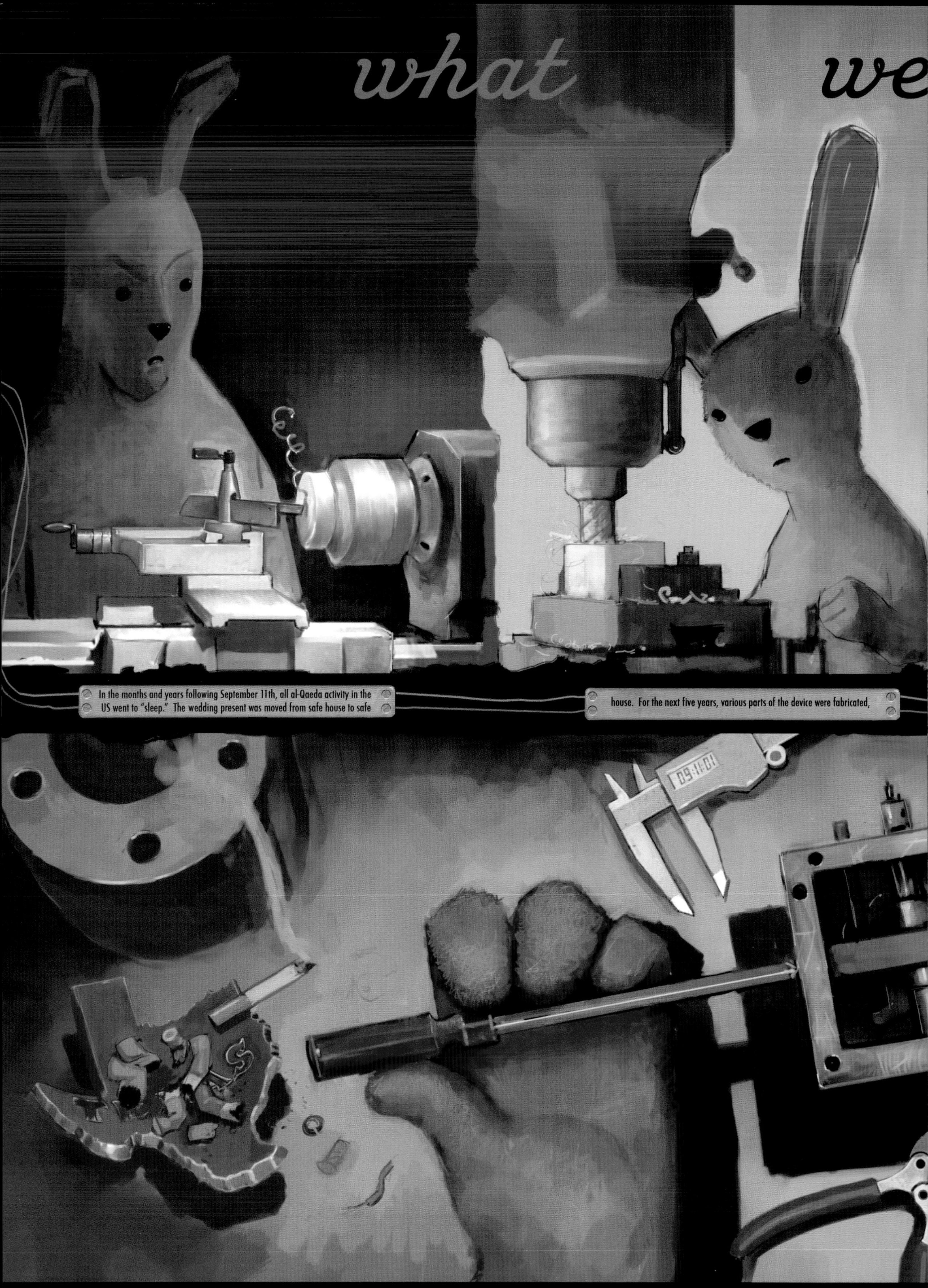
what
we
In the months and years following September 11th, all al-Qaeda activity in the US went to "sleep." The wedding present was moved from safe house to safe
house. For the next five years, various parts of the device were fabricated,
09:11:01

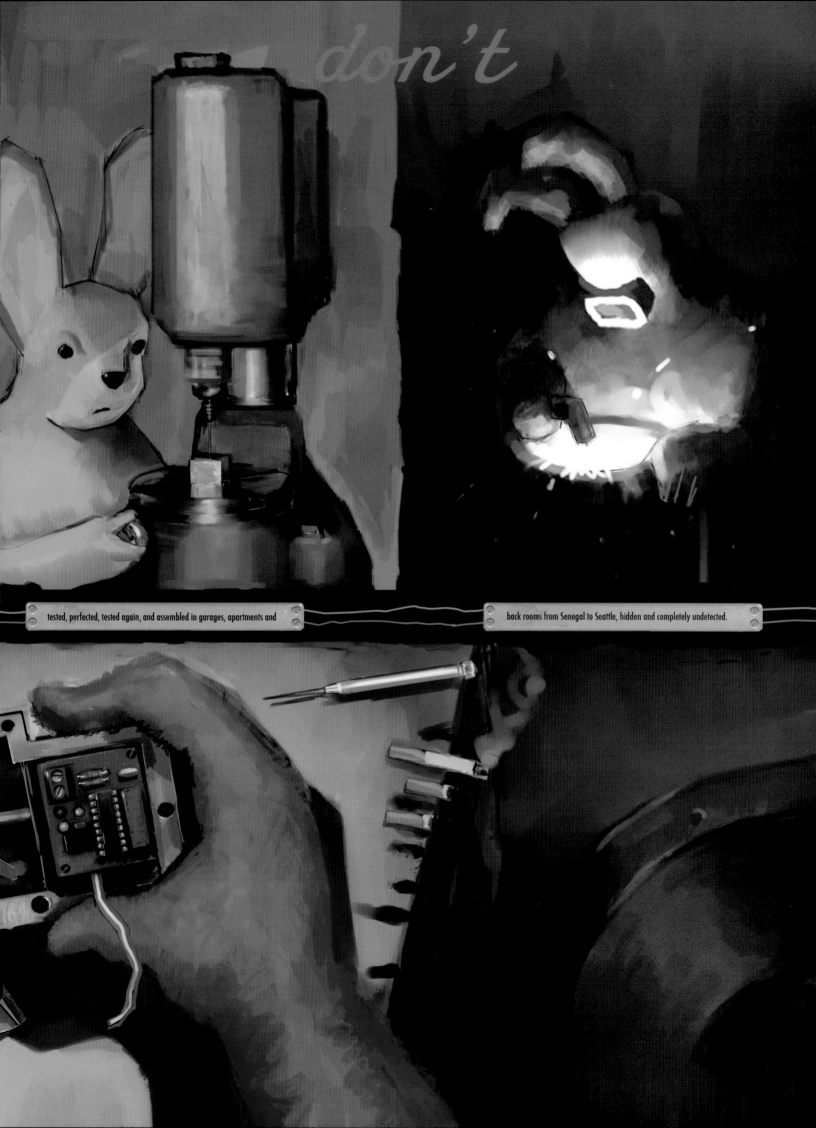

tested, perfected, tested again, and assembled in garages, apartments and back rooms from Senegal to Seattle, hidden and completely undetected.

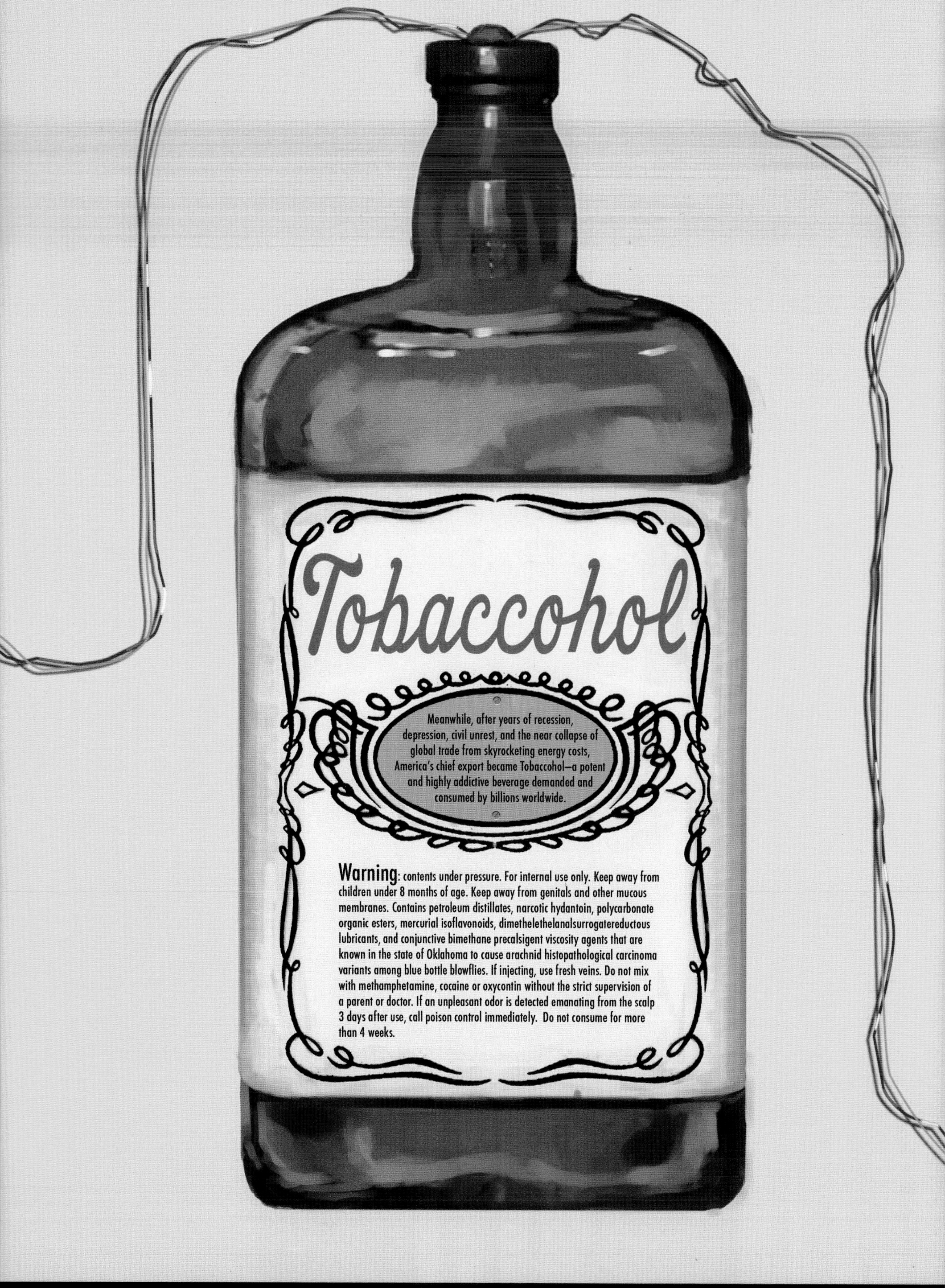
Tobaccohol
Meanwhile, after years of recession, depression, civil unrest, and the near collapse of global trade from skyrocketing energy costs, America's chief export became Tobaccohol—a potent and highly addictive beverage demanded and consumed by billions worldwide.
Warning: contents under pressure. For internal use only. Keep away from children under 8 months of age. Keep away from genitals and other mucous membranes. Contains petroleum distillates, narcotic hydantoin, polycarbonate organic esters, mercurial isoflavonoids, dimethelethelanalsurrogatereductous lubricants, and conjunctive bimethane precalsigent viscosity agents that are known in the state of Oklahoma to cause arachnid histopathological carcinoma variants among blue bottle blowflies. If injecting, use fresh veins. Do not mix with methamphetamine, cocaine or oxycontin without the strict supervision of a parent or doctor. If an unpleasant odor is detected emanating from the scalp 3 days after use, call poison control immediately. Do not consume for more than 4 weeks.

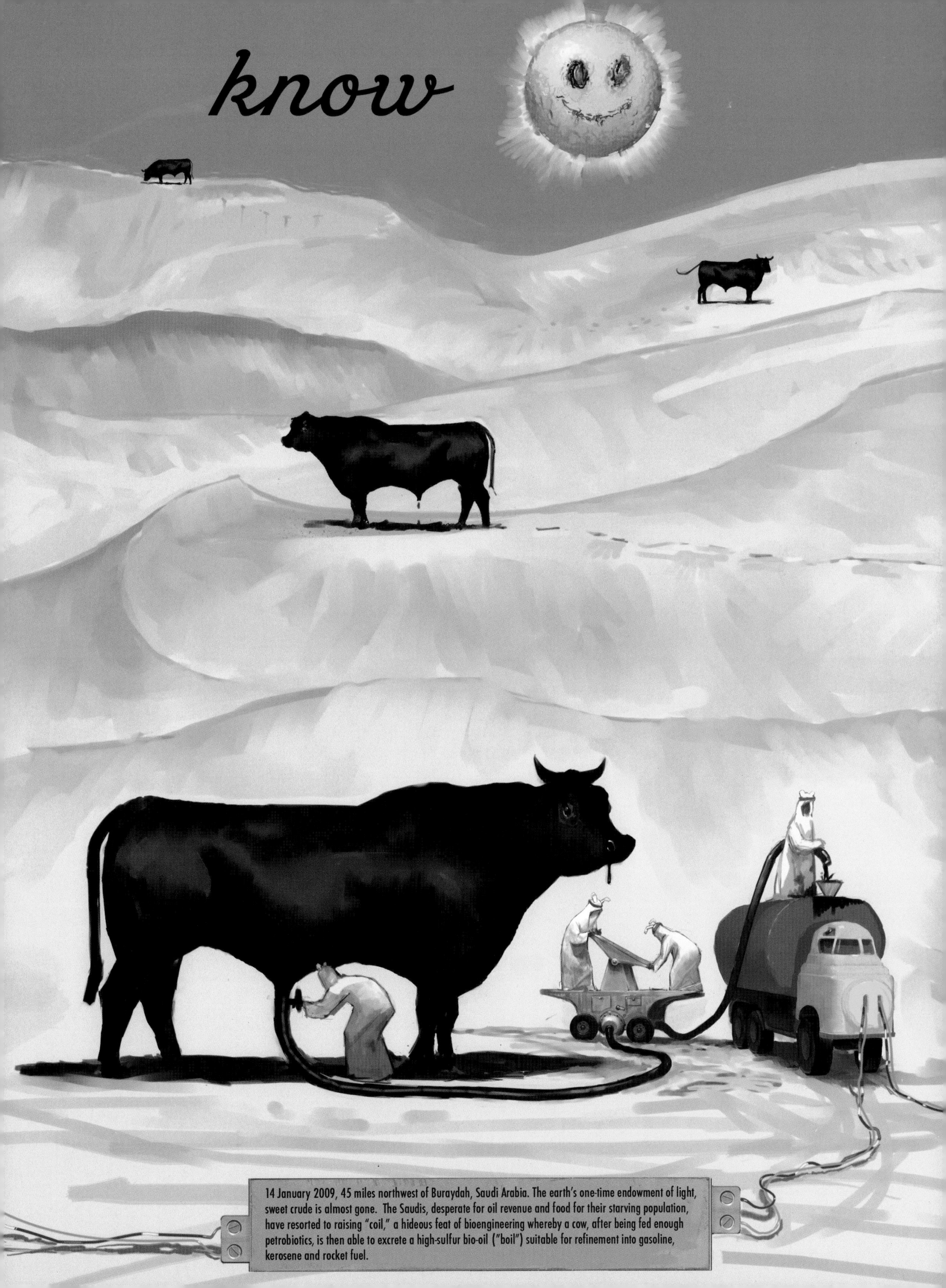
know

14 January 2009, 45 miles northwest of Buraydah, Saudi Arabia. The earth's one-time endowment of light, sweet crude is almost gone. The Saudis, desperate for oil revenue and food for their starving population, have resorted to raising "coil," a hideous feat of bioengineering whereby a cow, after being fed enough petrobiotics, is then able to excrete a high-sulfur bio-oil ("boil") suitable for refinement into gasoline, kerosene and rocket fuel.

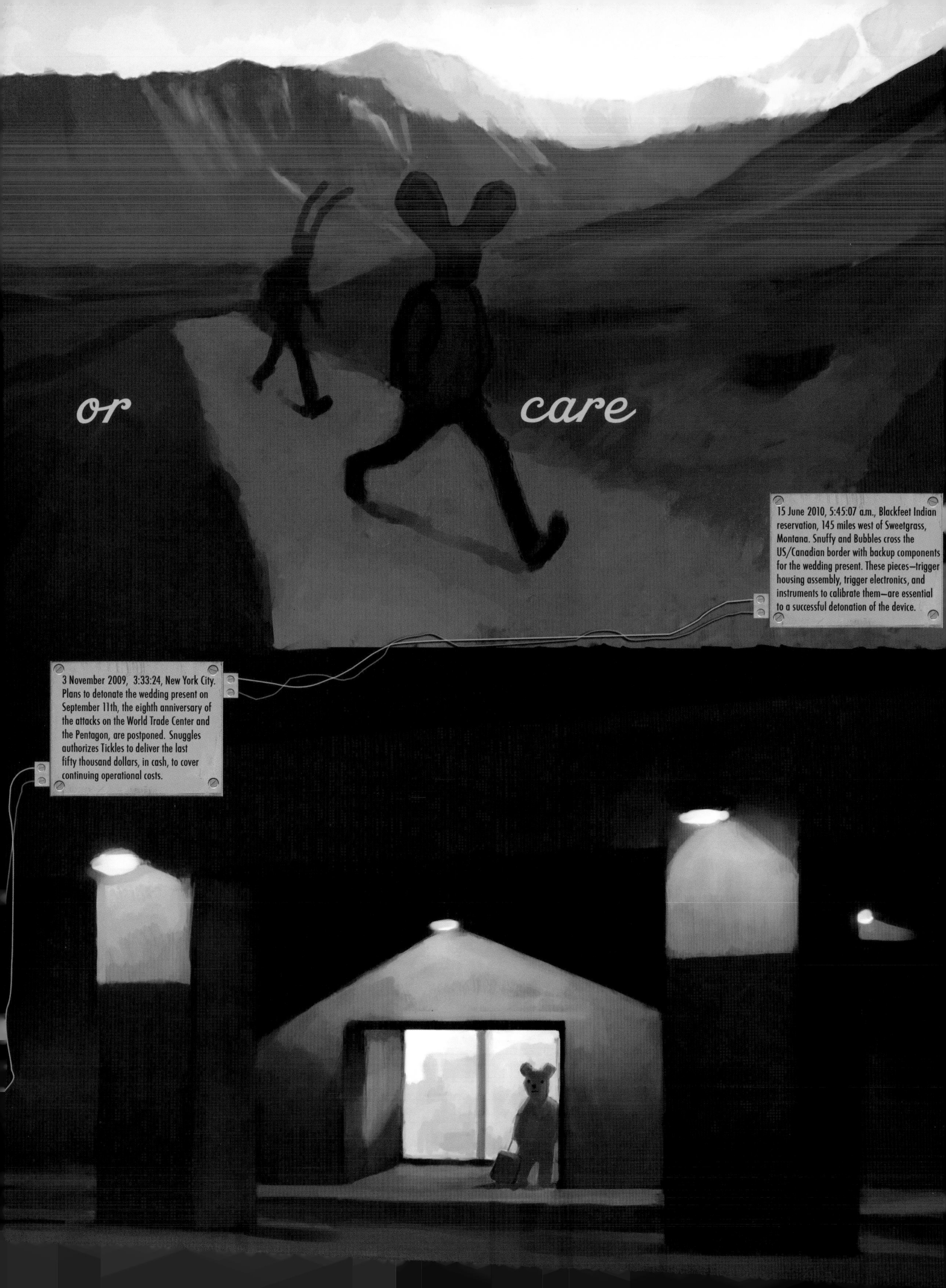
or
care
15 June 2010, 5:45:07 a.m., Blackfeet Indian reservation, 145 miles west of Sweetgrass, Montana. Snuffy and Bubbles cross the US/Canadian border with backup components for the wedding present. These pieces—trigger housing assembly, trigger electronics, and instruments to calibrate them—are essential to a successful detonation of the device.
3 November 2009, 3:33:24, New York City. Plans to detonate the wedding present on September 11th, the eighth anniversary of the attacks on the World Trade Center and the Pentagon, are postponed. Snuggles authorizes Tickles to deliver the last fifty thousand dollars, in cash, to cover continuing operational costs.

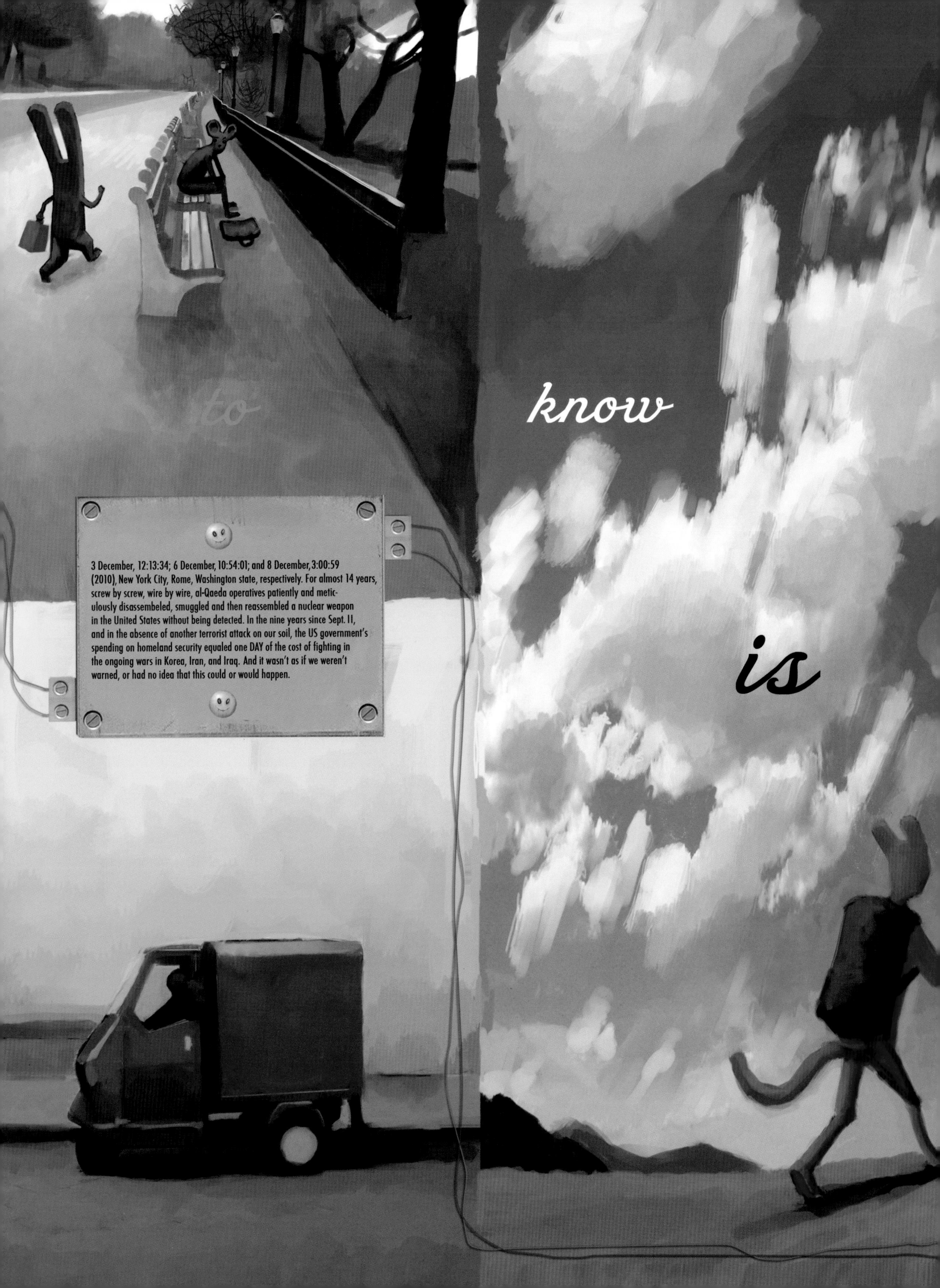
to
know
3 December, 12:13:34; 6 December, 10:54:01; and 8 December, 3:00:59 (2010), New York City, Rome, Washington state, respectively. For almost 14 years, screw by screw, wire by wire, al-Qaeda operatives patiently and meticulously disassembeled, smuggled and then reassembled a nuclear weapon in the United States without being detected. In the nine years since Sept. 11, and in the absence of another terrorist attack on our soil, the US government's spending on homeland security equaled one DAY of the cost of fighting in the ongoing wars in Korea, Iran, and Iraq. And it wasn't as if we weren't warned, or had no idea that this could or would happen.
is

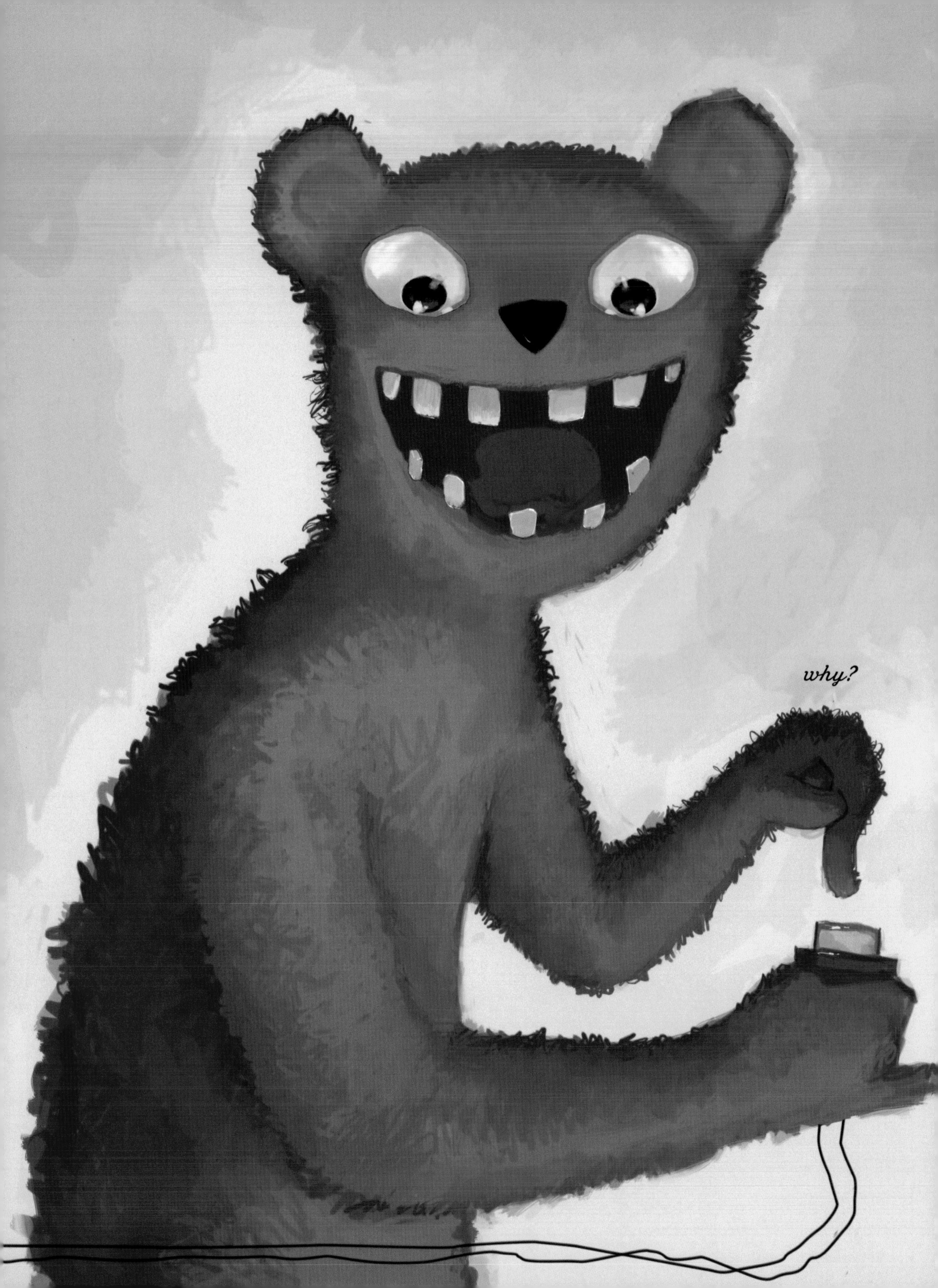

why?

OUT OF PICTURE

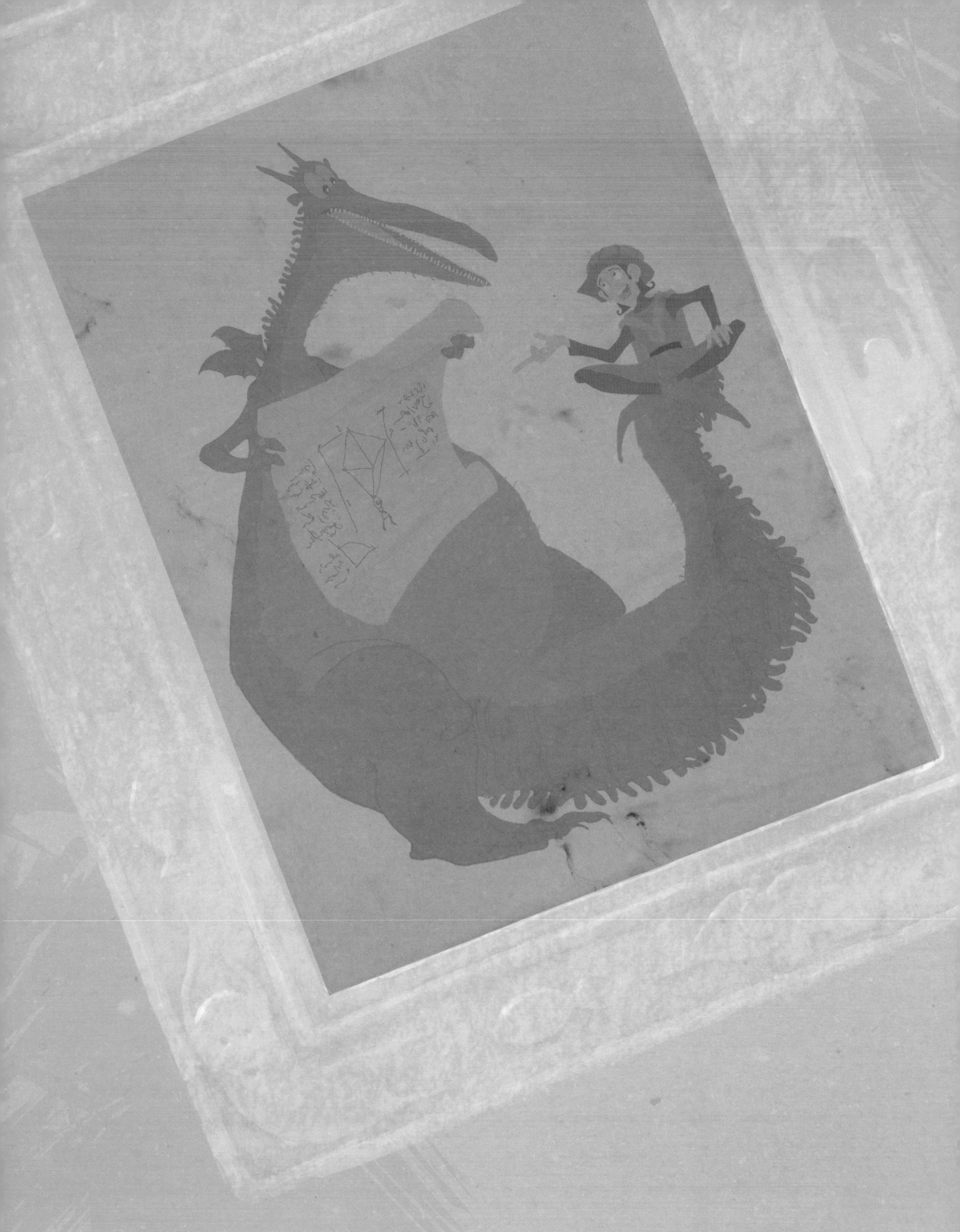

ANDREA BLASICH

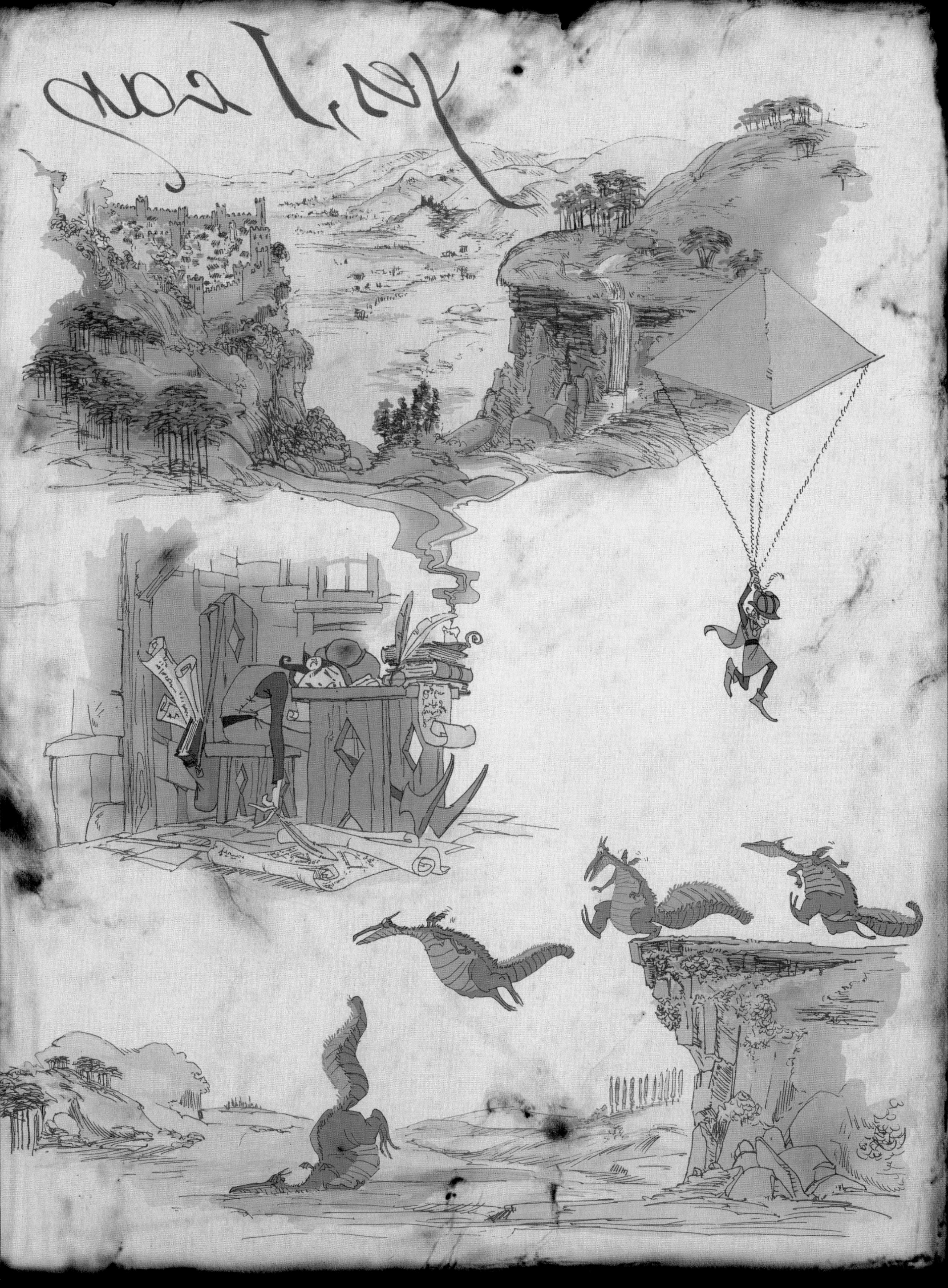

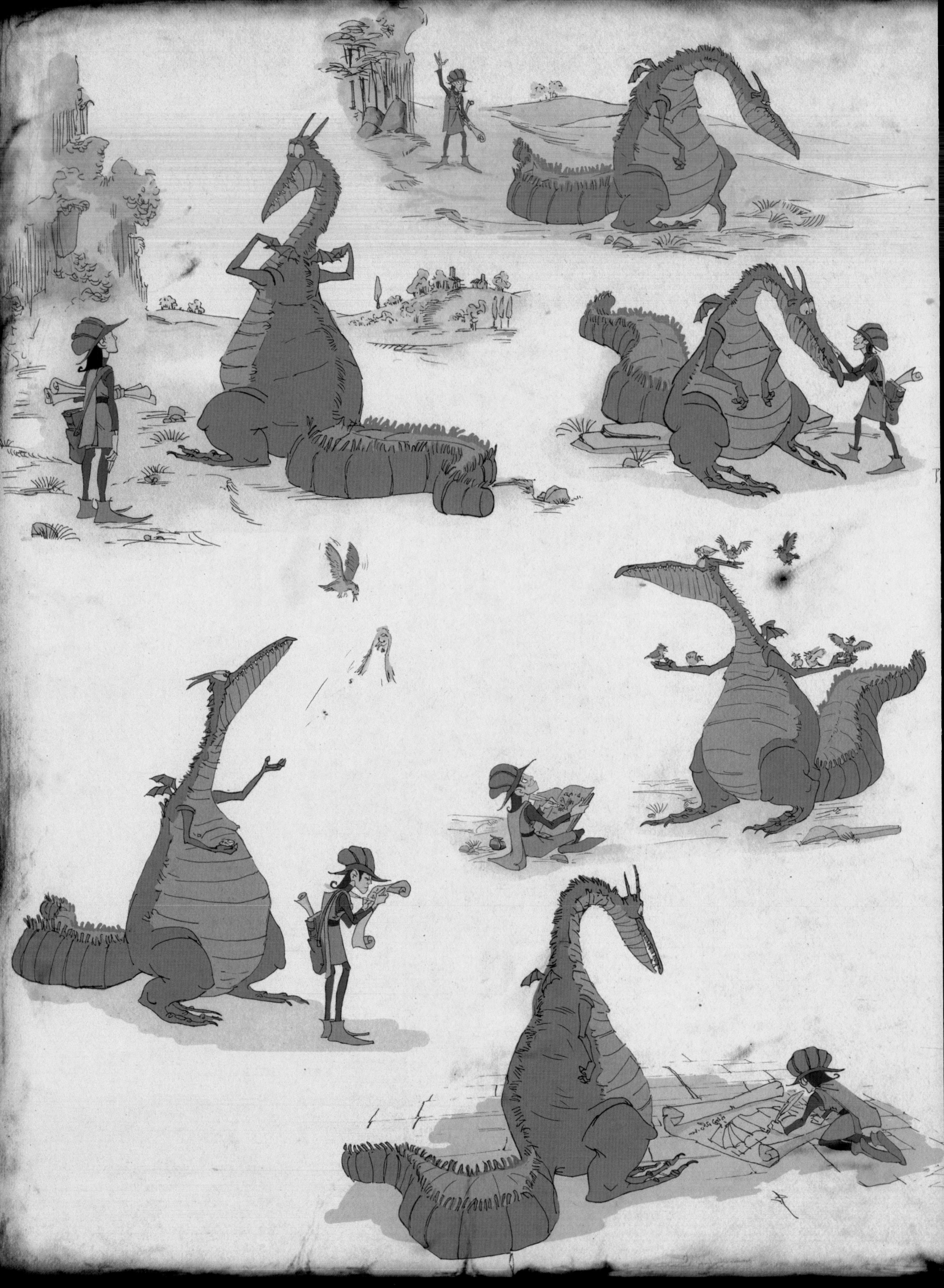

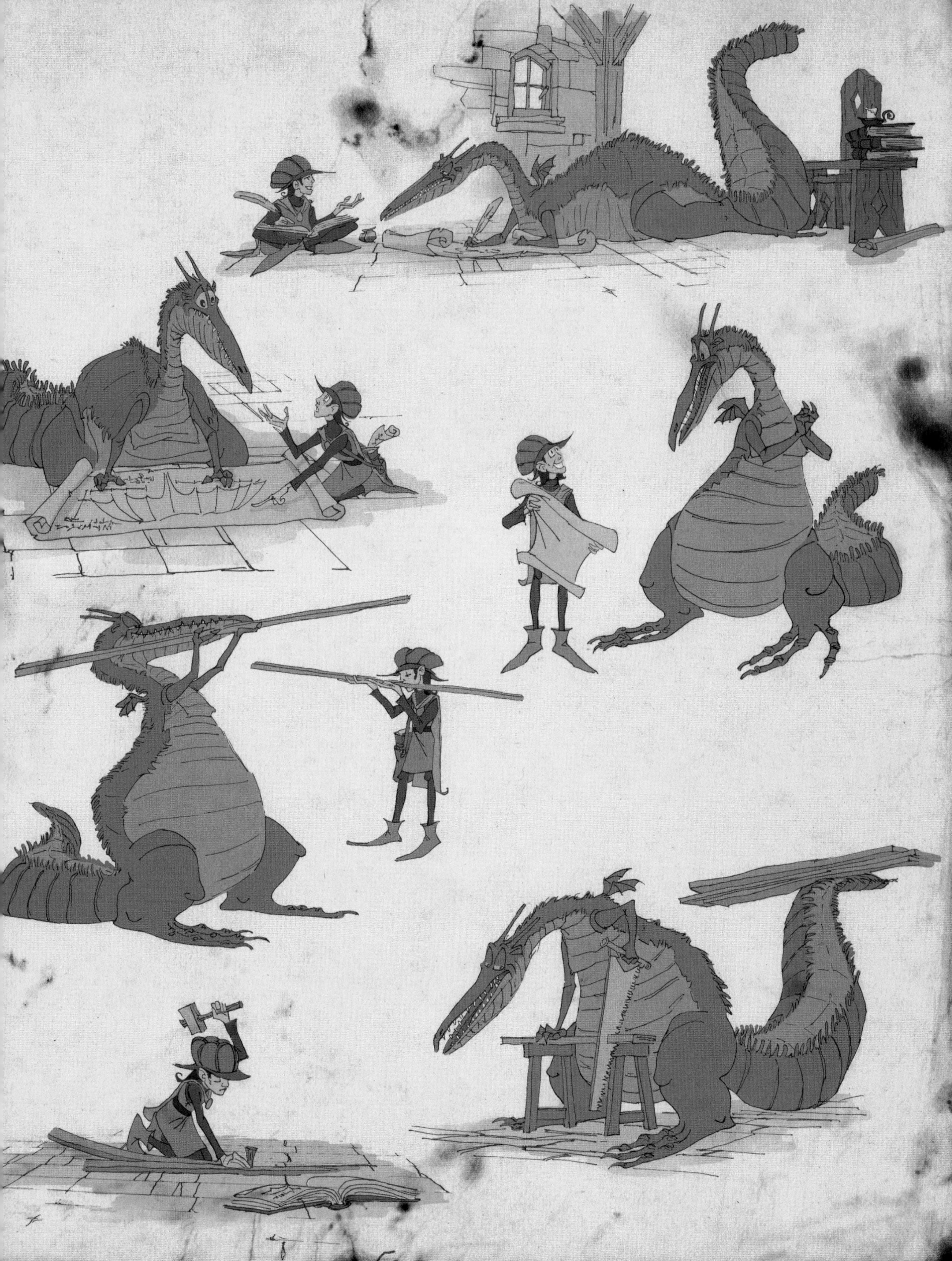

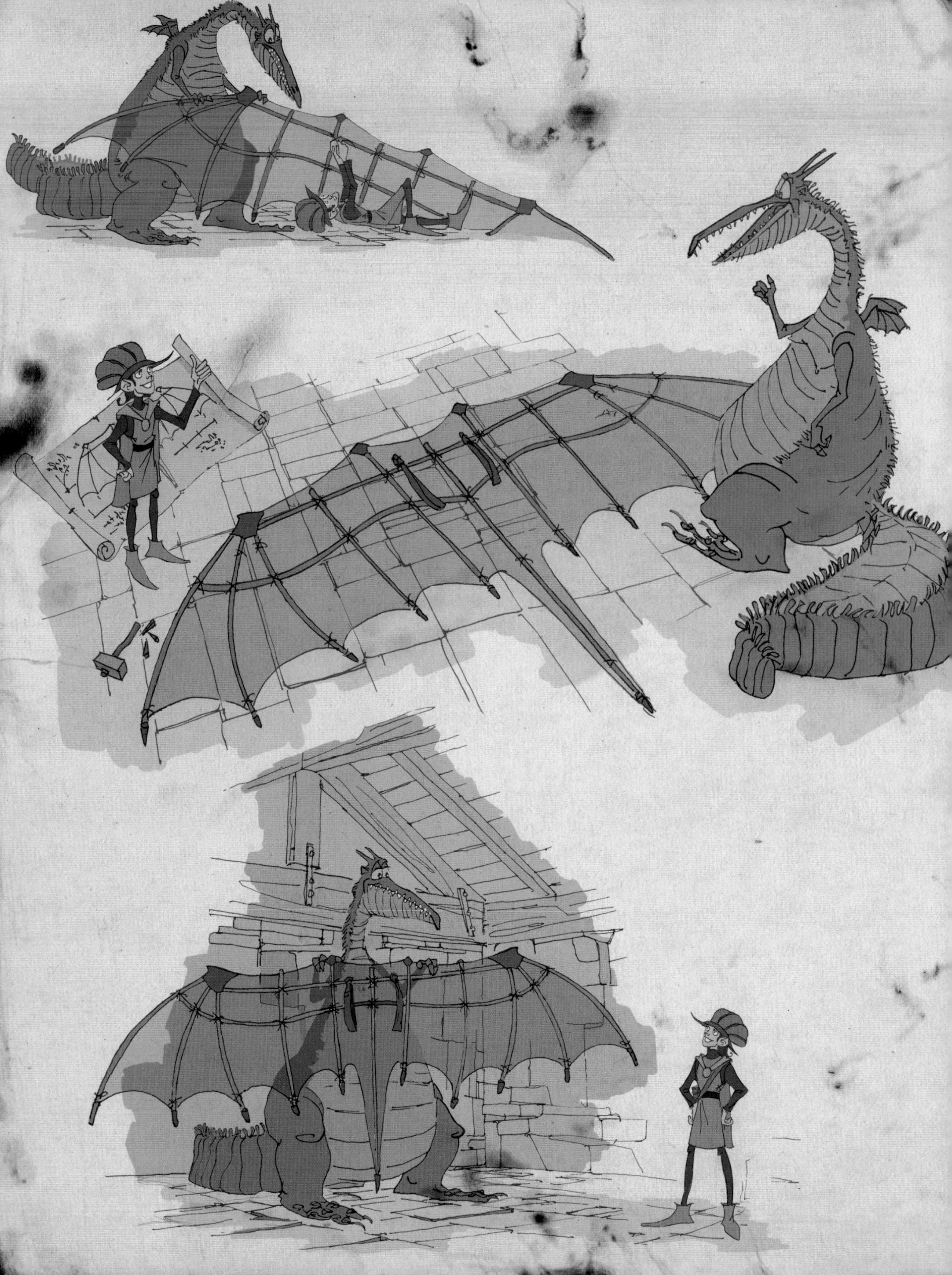

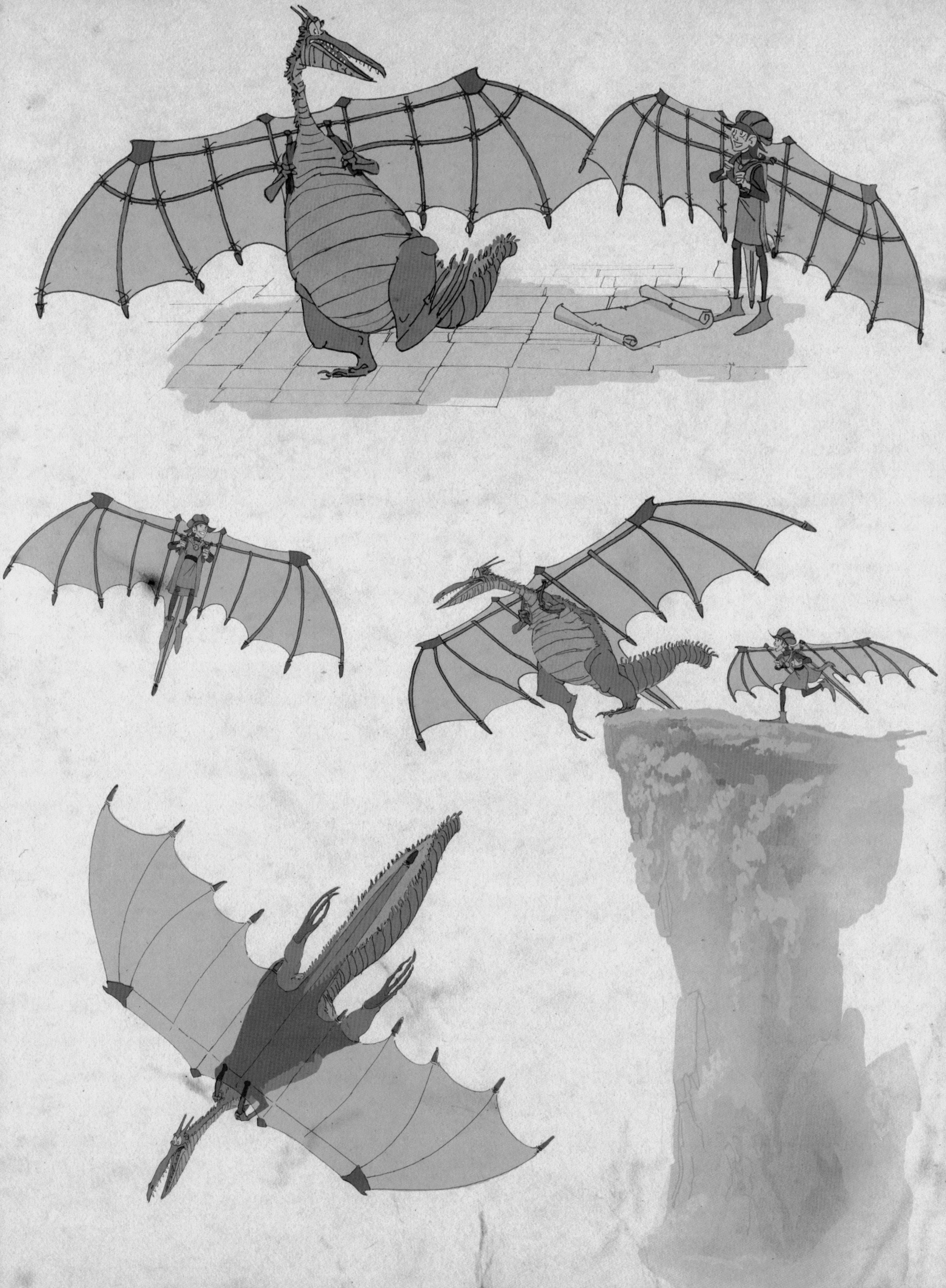

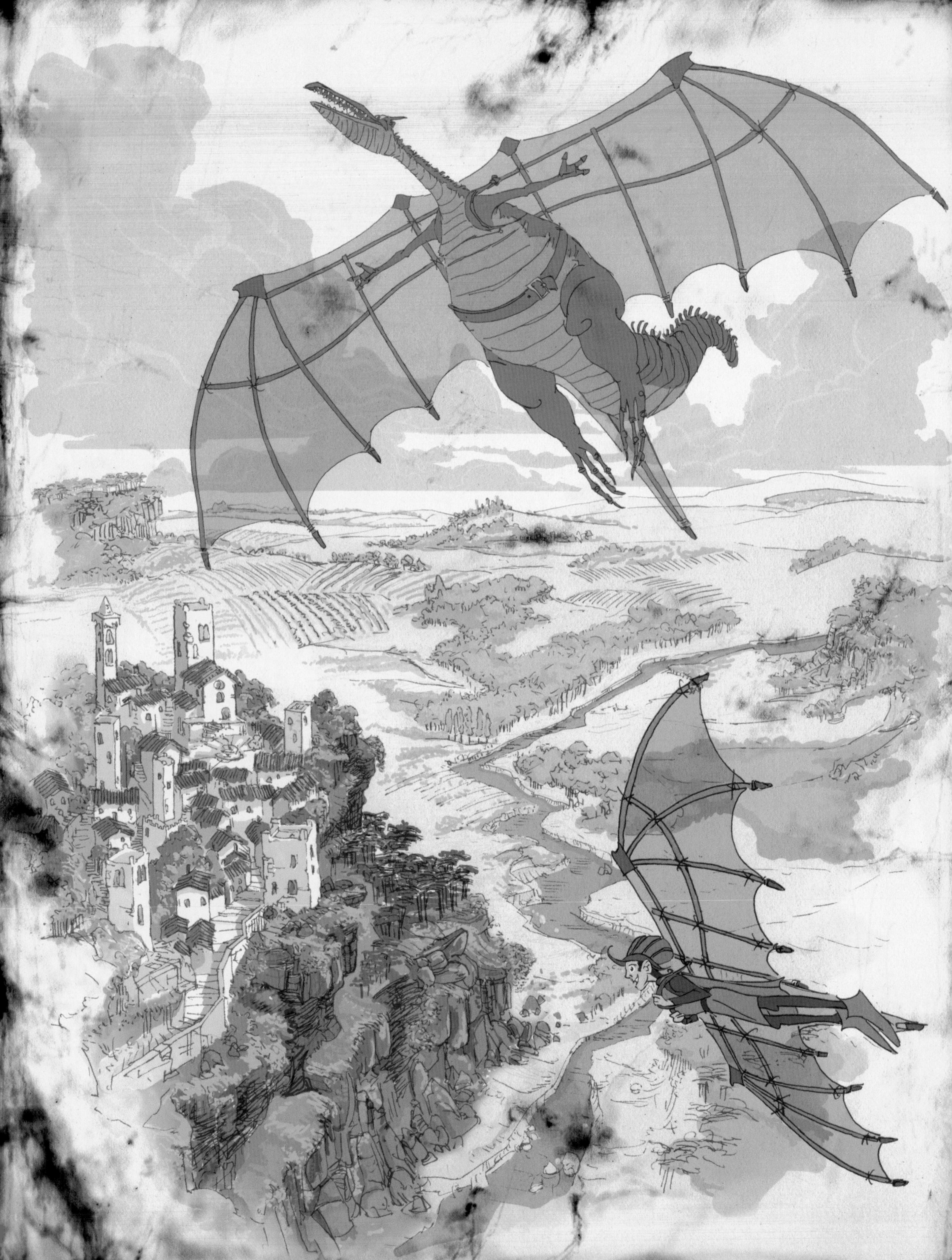

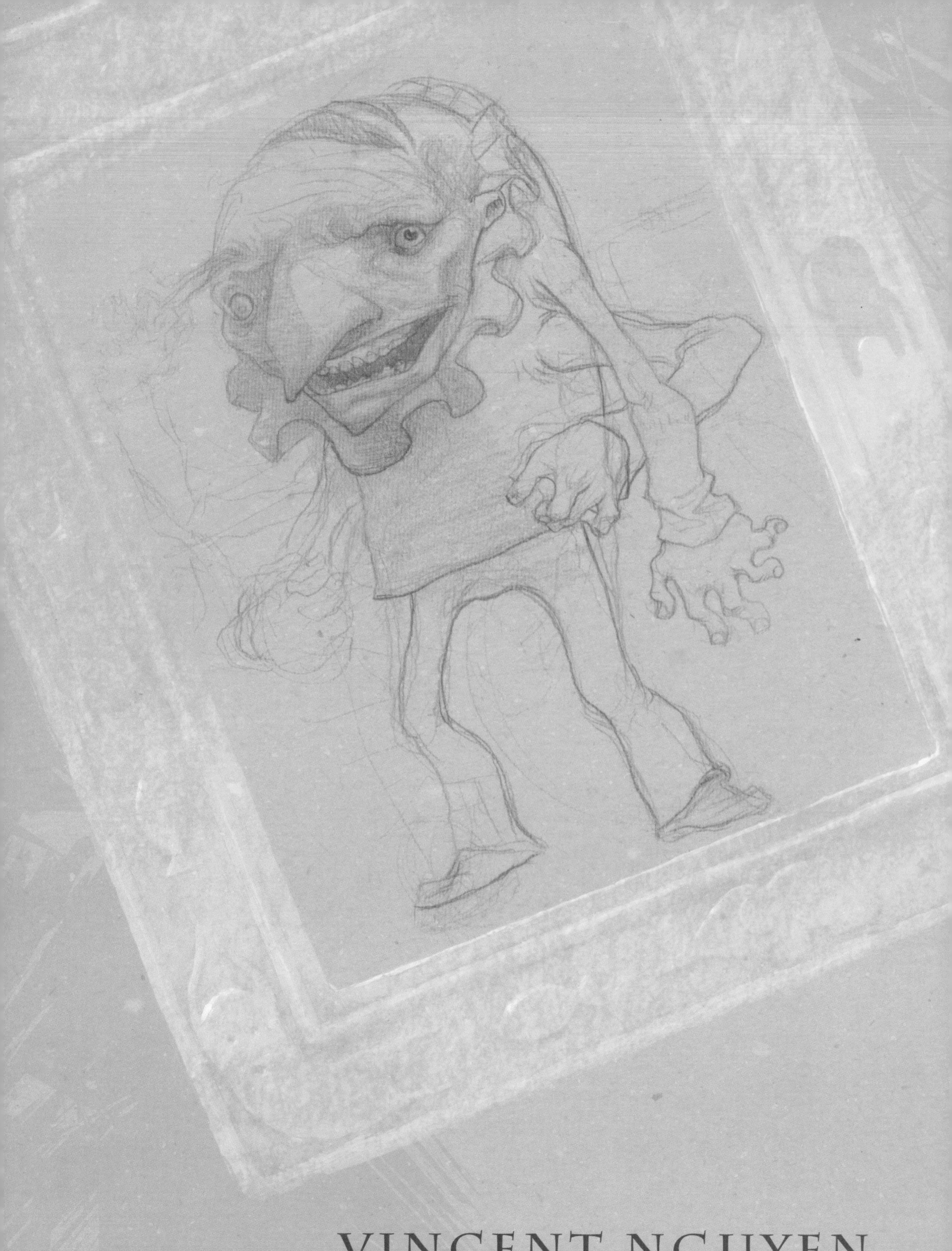

VINCENT NGUYEN

DOMESTICITY

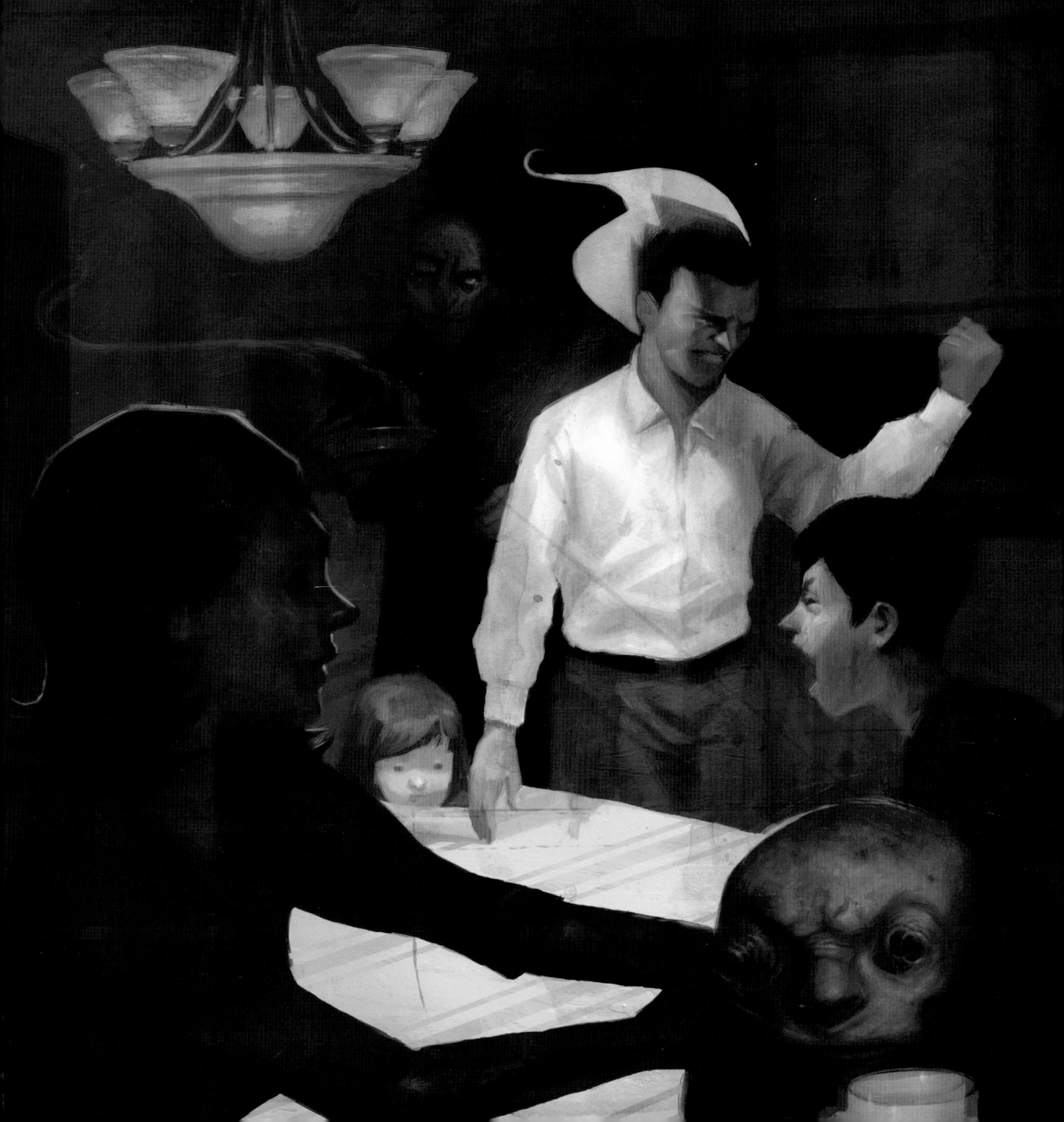

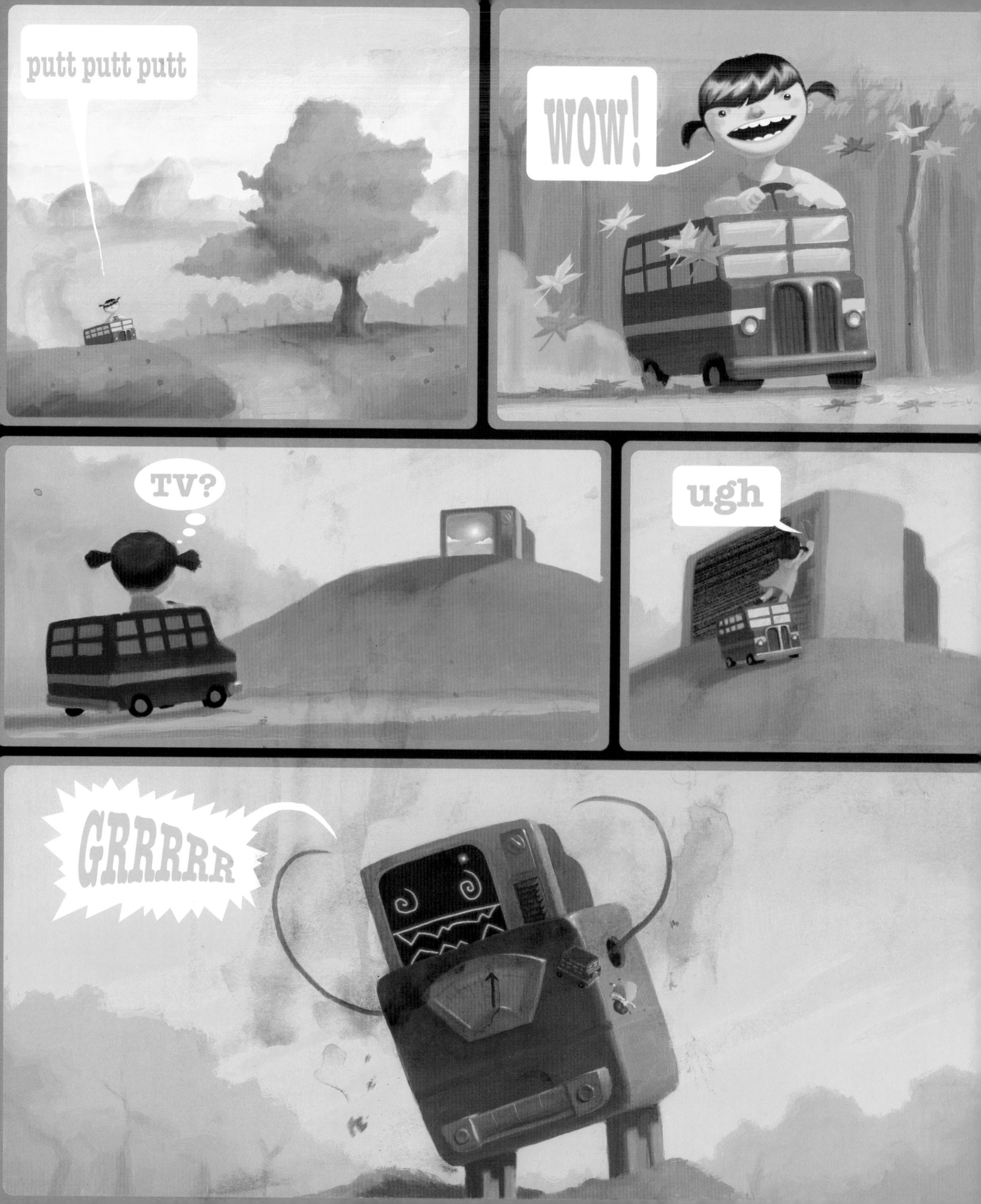
putt putt putt
WOW!
TV?
ugh
GRRRRR

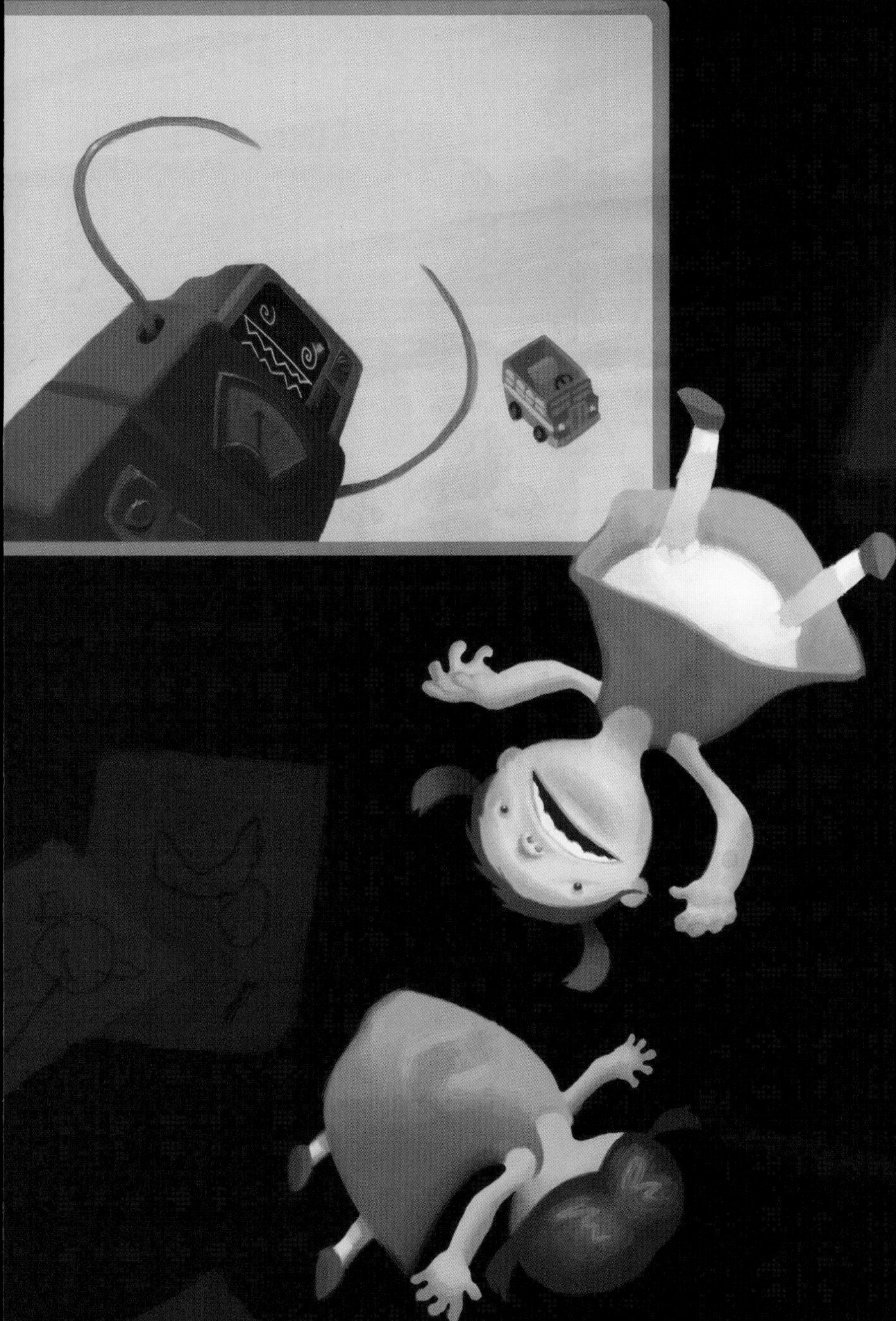

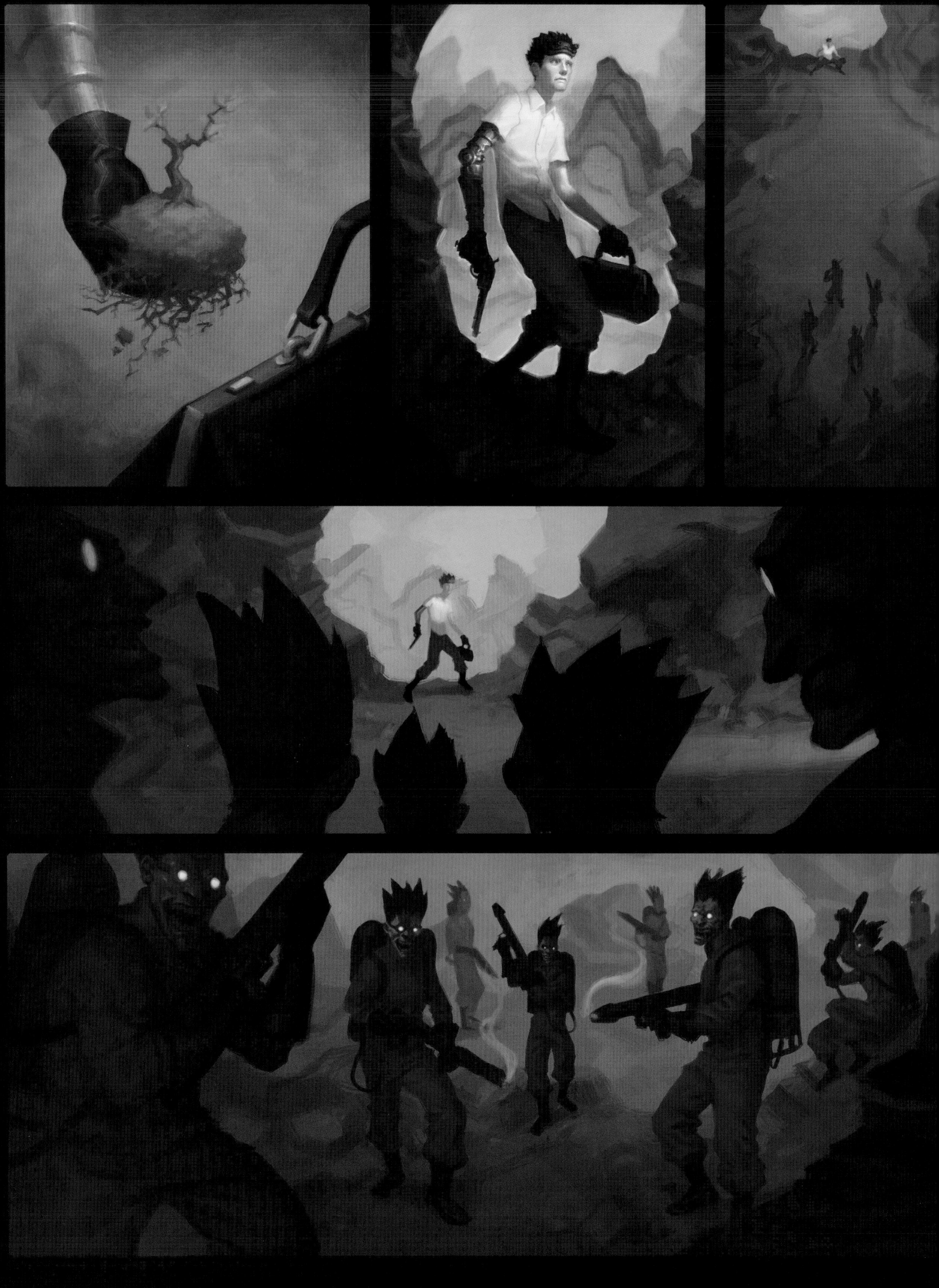

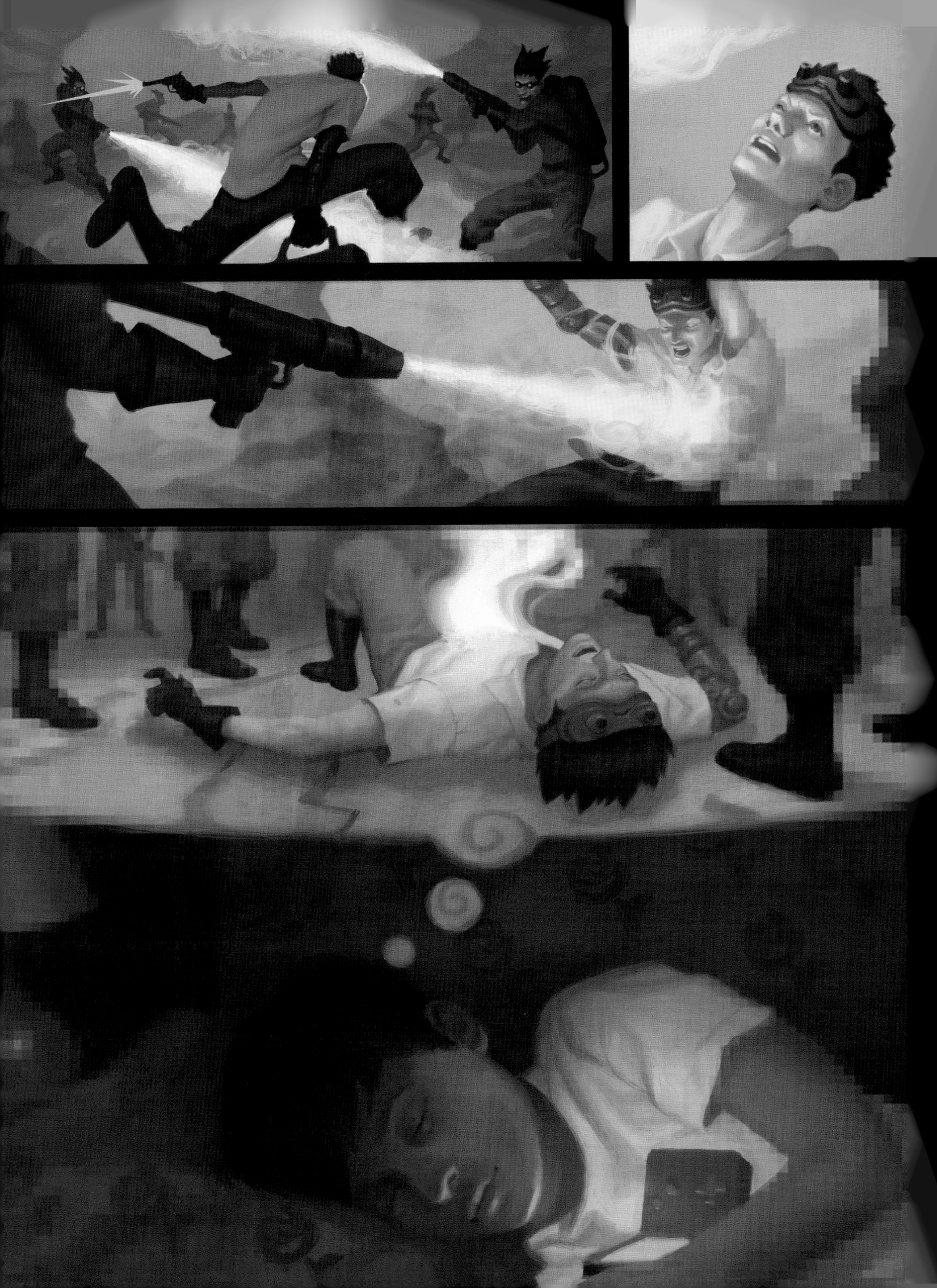

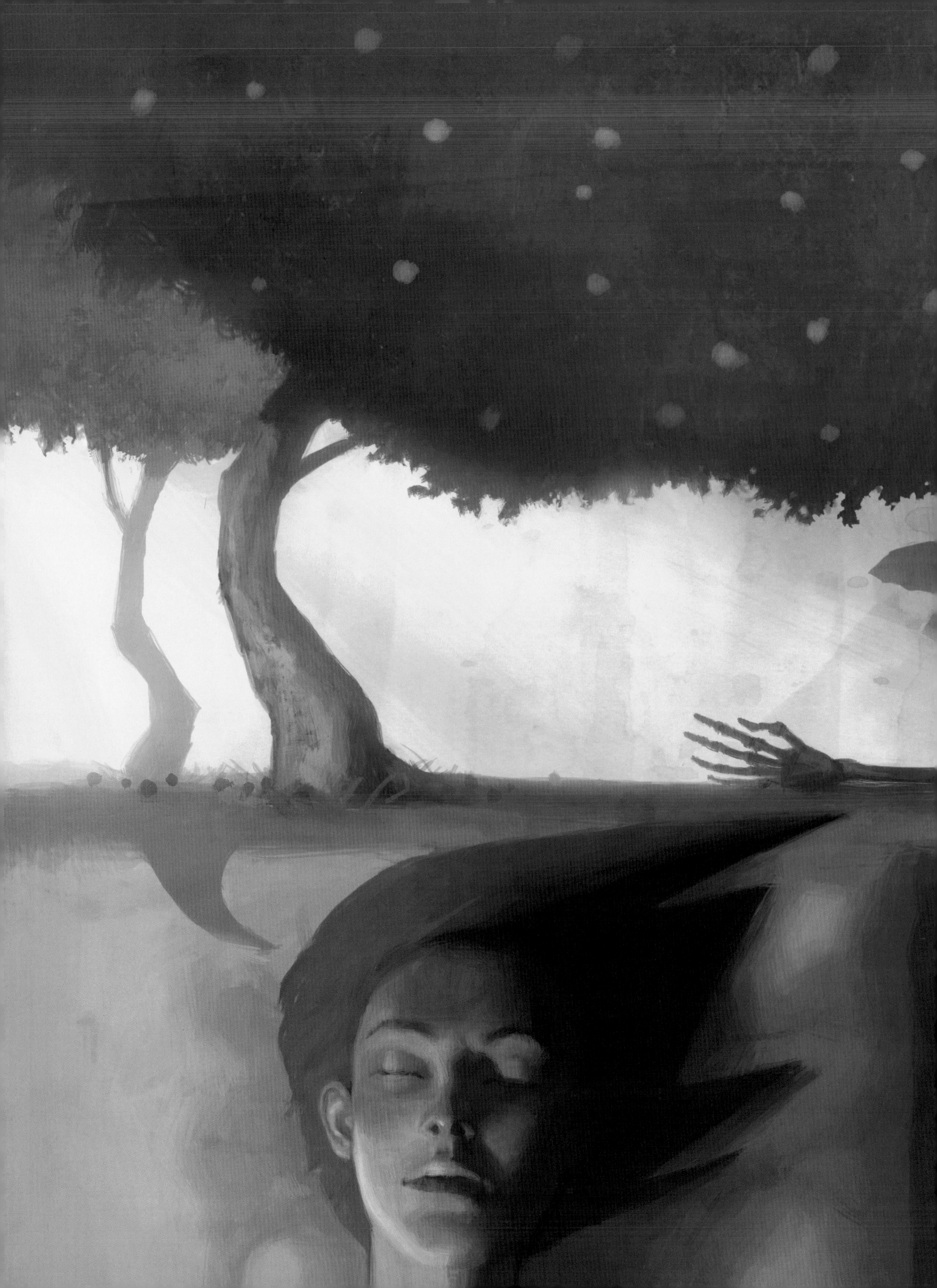

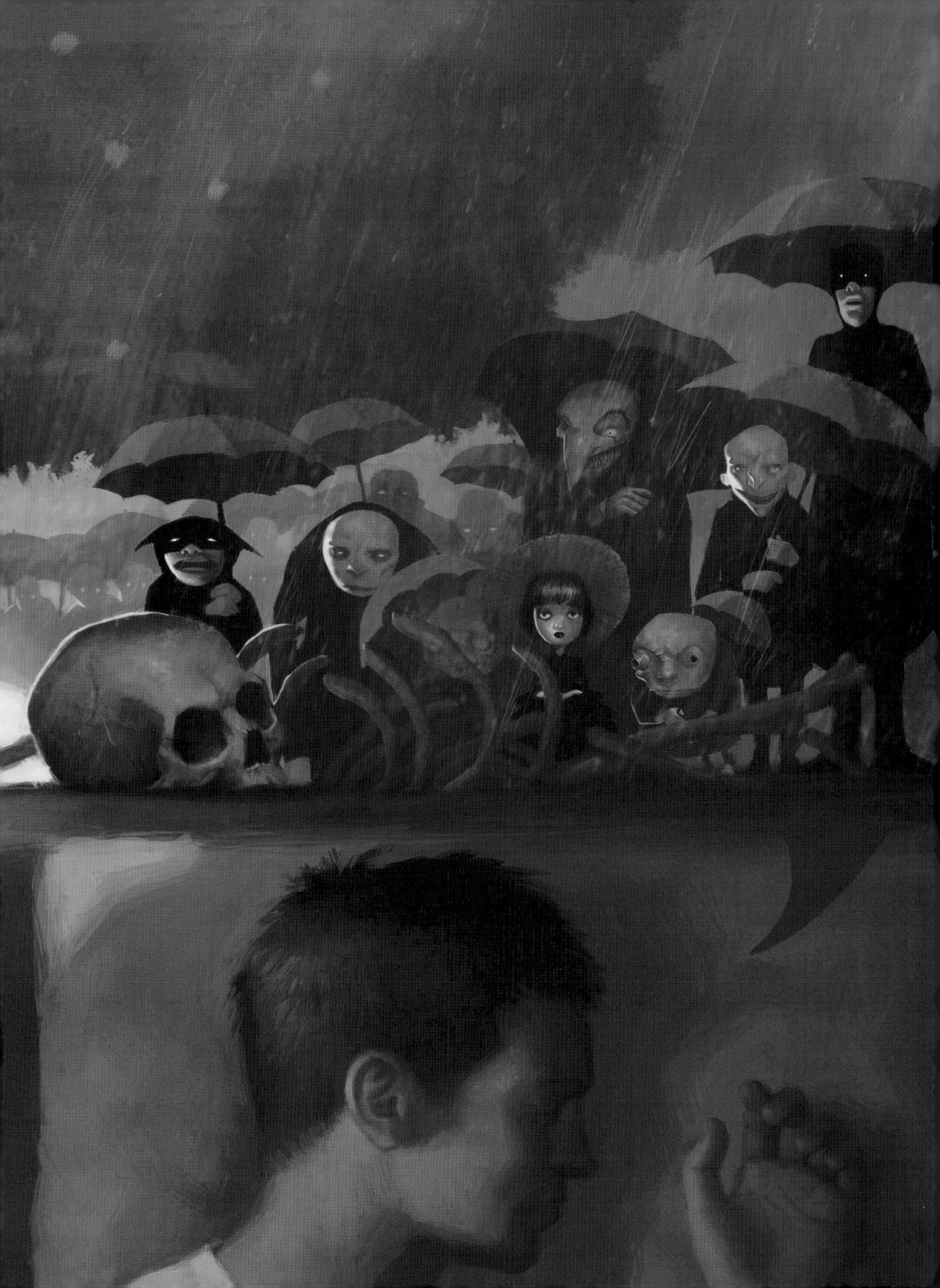

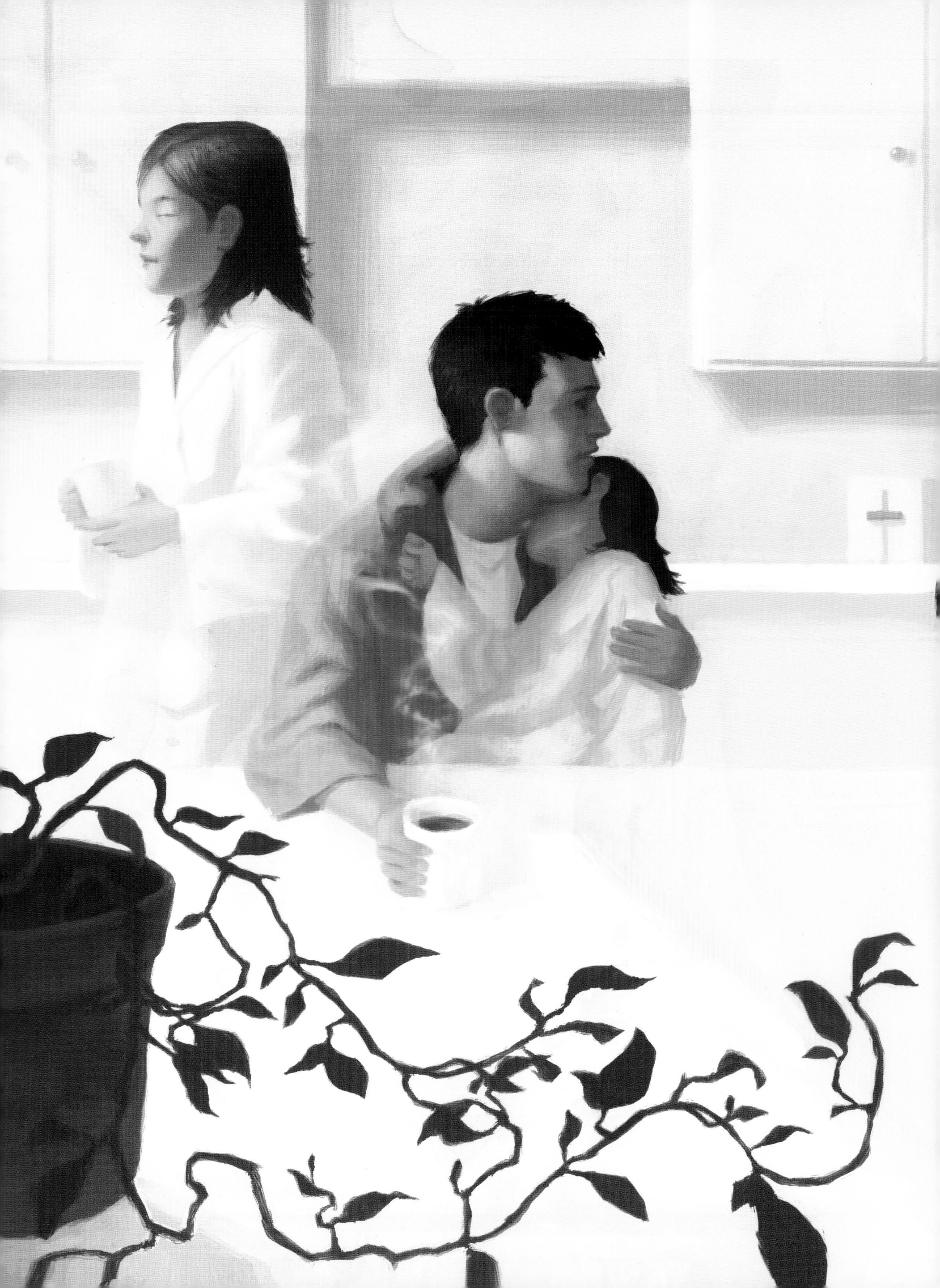

OUT OF PICTURE

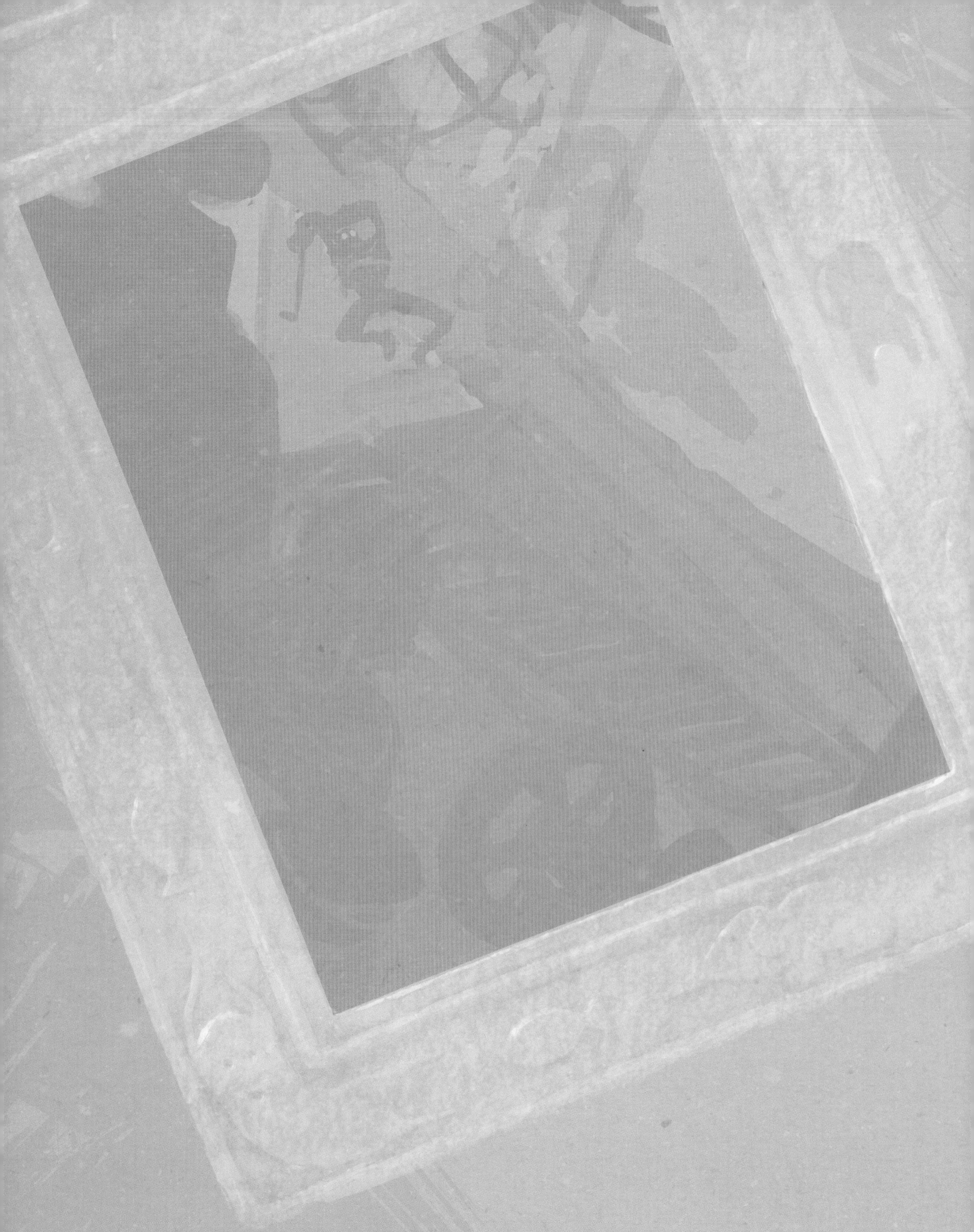

NASH DUNNIGAN

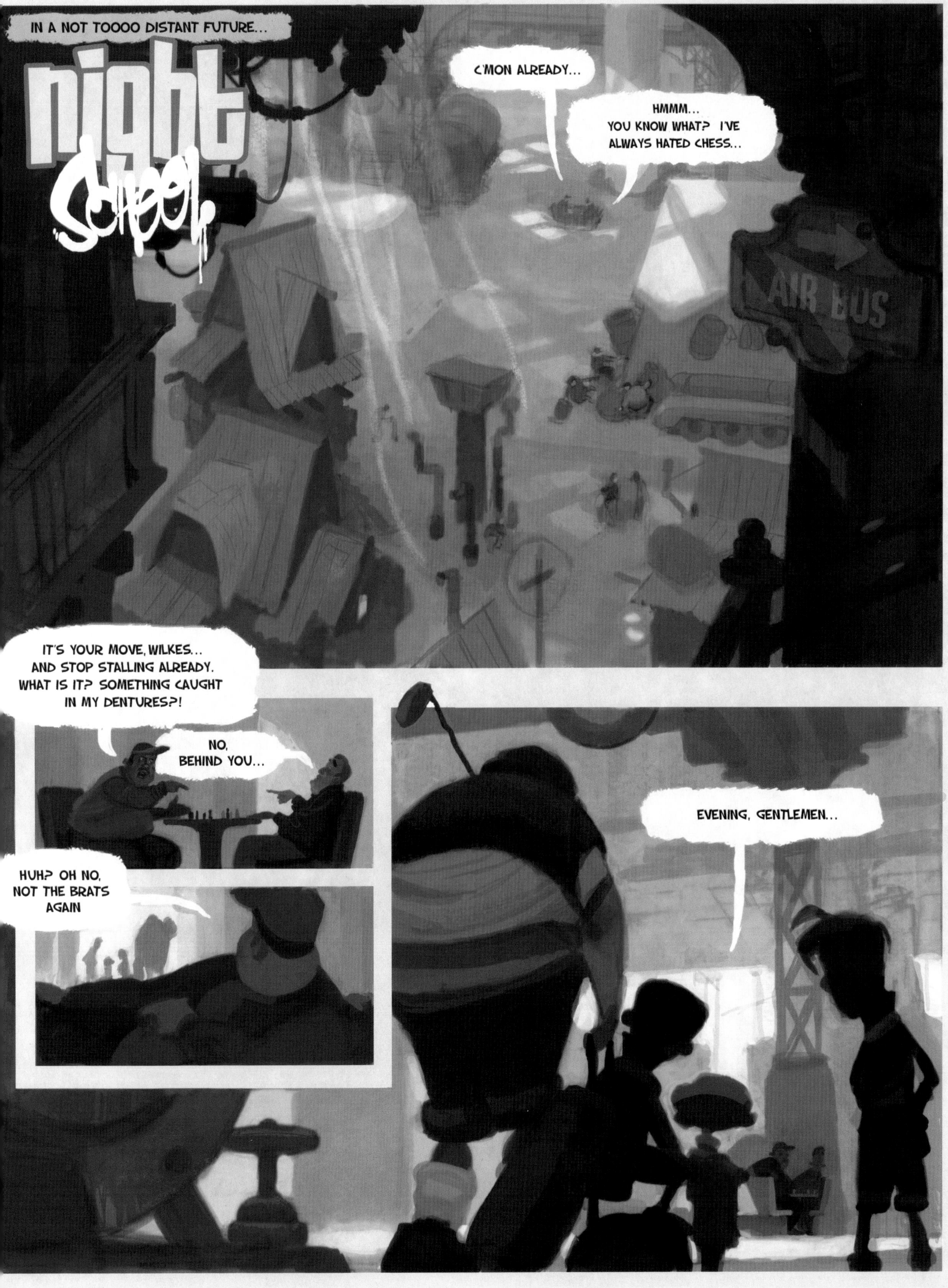
IN A NOT TOOOO DISTANT FUTURE...
night school
C'MON ALREADY...
HMMM... YOU KNOW WHAT? I'VE ALWAYS HATED CHESS...
AIR BUS
IT'S YOUR MOVE, WILKES... AND STOP STALLING ALREADY. WHAT IS IT? SOMETHING CAUGHT IN MY DENTURES?!
NO, BEHIND YOU...
HUH? OH NO, NOT THE BRATS AGAIN
EVENING, GENTLEMEN...

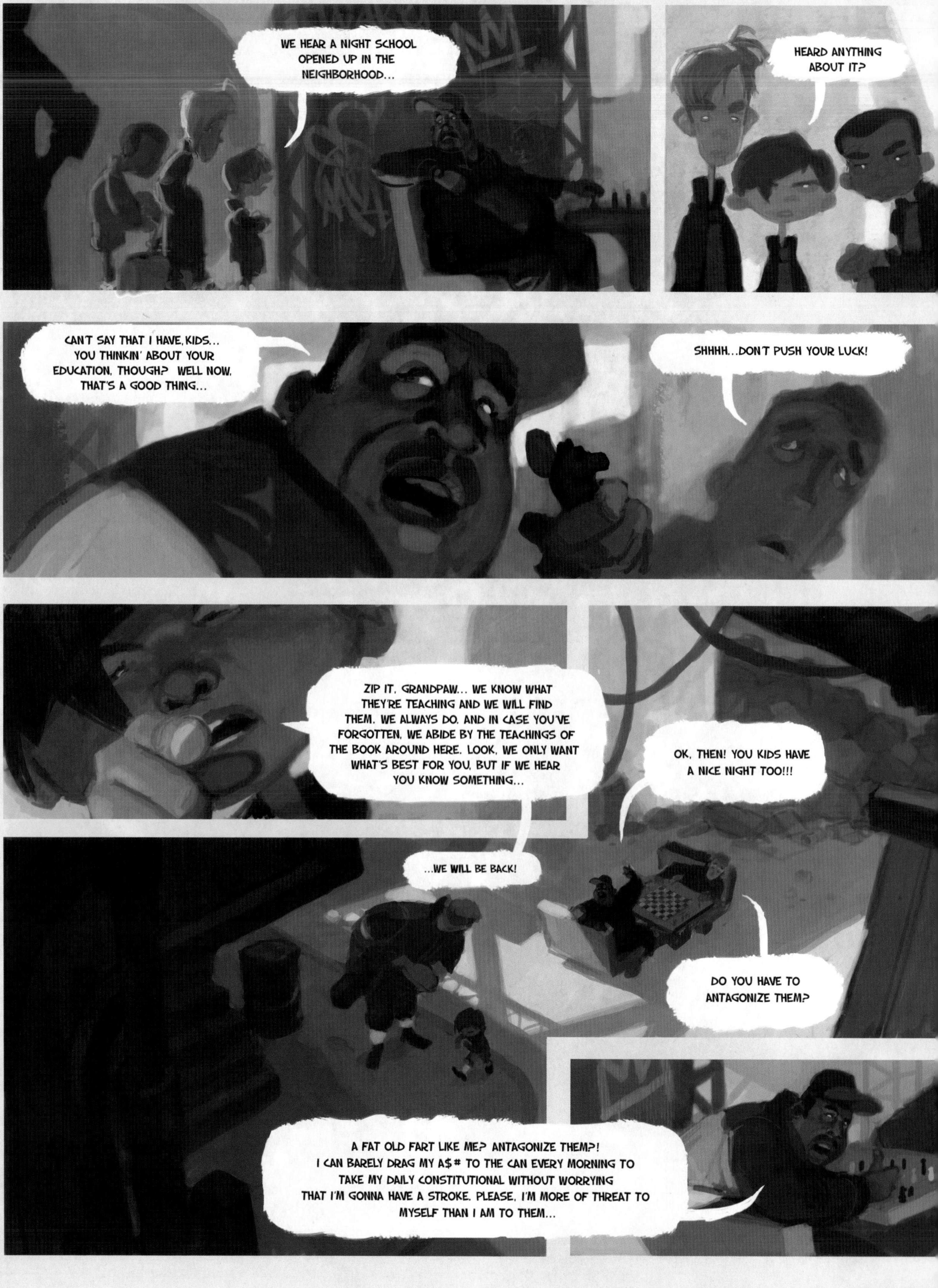
WE HEAR A NIGHT SCHOOL OPENED UP IN THE NEIGHBORHOOD...
HEARD ANYTHING ABOUT IT?
CAN'T SAY THAT I HAVE, KIDS... YOU THINKIN' ABOUT YOUR EDUCATION, THOUGH? WELL NOW, THAT'S A GOOD THING...
SHHHH...DON'T PUSH YOUR LUCK!
ZIP IT, GRANDPAW... WE KNOW WHAT THEY'RE TEACHING AND WE WILL FIND THEM. WE ALWAYS DO. AND IN CASE YOU'VE FORGOTTEN, WE ABIDE BY THE TEACHINGS OF THE BOOK AROUND HERE. LOOK, WE ONLY WANT WHAT'S BEST FOR YOU, BUT IF WE HEAR YOU KNOW SOMETHING...
OK, THEN! YOU KIDS HAVE A NICE NIGHT TOO!!!
...WE WILL BE BACK!
DO YOU HAVE TO ANTAGONIZE THEM?
A FAT OLD FART LIKE ME? ANTAGONIZE THEM?! I CAN BARELY DRAG MY A$# TO THE CAN EVERY MORNING TO TAKE MY DAILY CONSTITUTIONAL WITHOUT WORRYING THAT I'M GONNA HAVE A STROKE. PLEASE, I'M MORE OF THREAT TO MYSELF THAN I AM TO THEM...

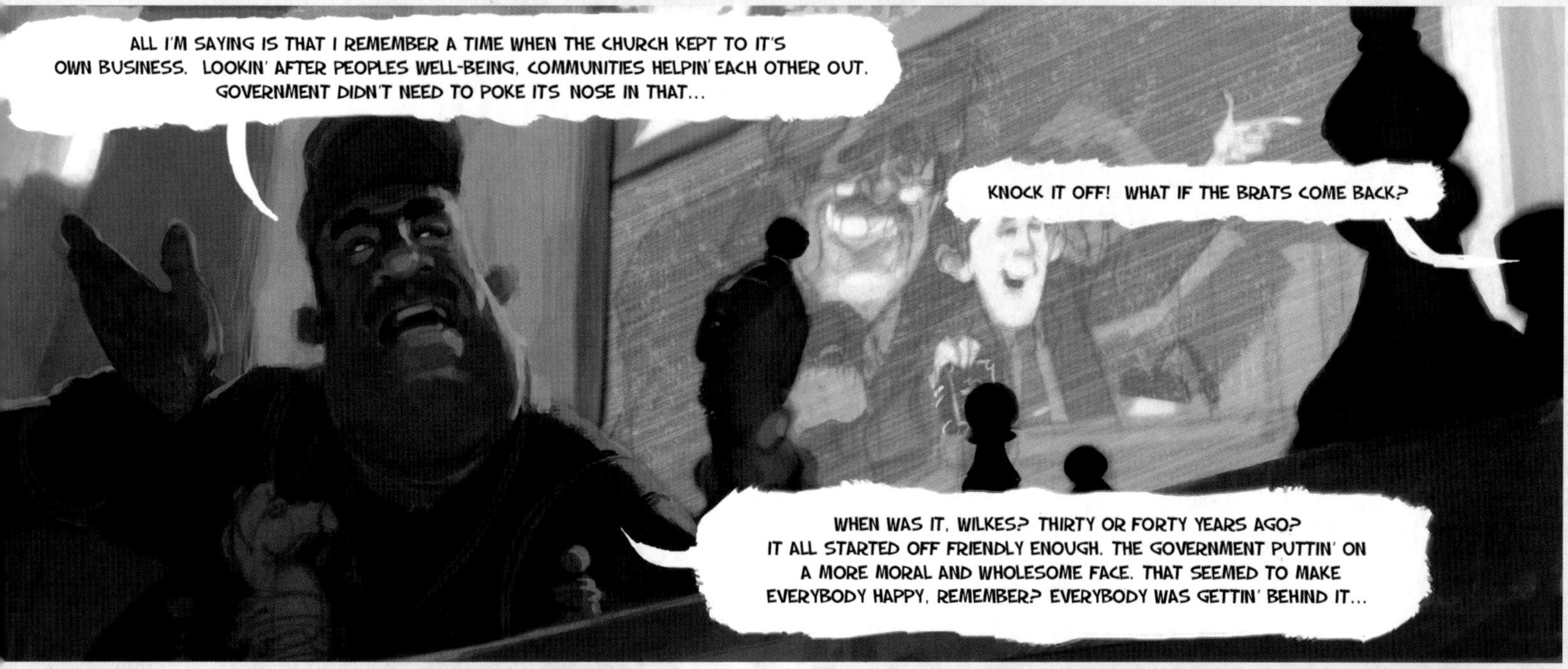
ALL I'M SAYING IS THAT I REMEMBER A TIME WHEN THE CHURCH KEPT TO IT'S OWN BUSINESS. LOOKIN' AFTER PEOPLES WELL-BEING, COMMUNITIES HELPIN' EACH OTHER OUT. GOVERNMENT DIDN'T NEED TO POKE ITS NOSE IN THAT...
KNOCK IT OFF! WHAT IF THE BRATS COME BACK?
WHEN WAS IT, WILKES? THIRTY OR FORTY YEARS AGO? IT ALL STARTED OFF FRIENDLY ENOUGH. THE GOVERNMENT PUTTIN' ON A MORE MORAL AND WHOLESOME FACE. THAT SEEMED TO MAKE EVERYBODY HAPPY, REMEMBER? EVERYBODY WAS GETTIN' BEHIND IT...

BUT REMEMBER THAT ANTI-EVOLUTION SHOWDOWN IN 2112?
IT WAS "SCIENTISTS VERSUS 'GENE' THE CREATIONIST DINO" AT THE SUPREME COURT.

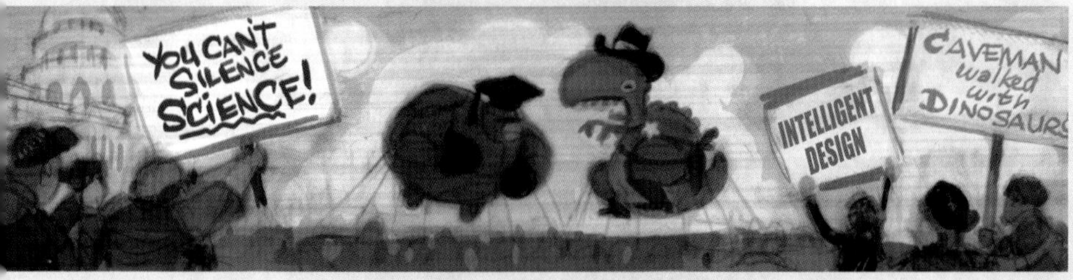
YOU CAN'T SILENCE SCIENCE!
CAVEMAN walked with DINOSAURS
INTELLIGENT DESIGN

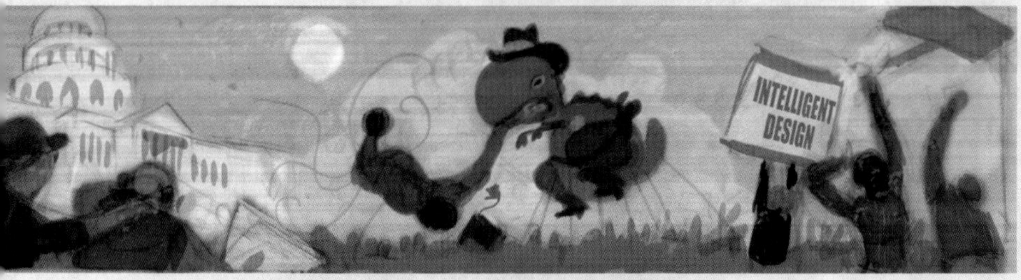
INTELLIGENT DESIGN

THAT 50-FOOT INFLATABLE CHIMP WASN'T THE ONLY THING
TO GET THE WIND KNOCKED OUT OF IT THAT DAY...

THINGS CHANGED....IT WAS QUIET, ALMOST NOBODY NOTICED. THE GOVERNMENT STARTED PICKIN' UP THE TAB FOR THOSE 'FAITH BASED INITIATIVES.' THEY GOT TO CHOOSE WHICH ONES, TOO. BUT WHO WAS WATCHING THEM? YOU REMEMBER THAT PRESIDENT? USED TO SAY THINGS LIKE, "OUR RIGHTS ARE DERIVED FROM THE BIBLE," AND THAT IT WAS THEIR "GUIDEBOOK FOR GOOD GOVERNMENT..." THAT WAS BEFORE THE BIG WAR STARTED, WHEN PATRIOTISM GOT ALL MIXED UP WITH RIGHTEOUSNESS AND THEIR HOLY MISSION. WE'VE BEEN LIVIN' WITH THAT MESS FOR GOIN' ON FOURTY YEARS...

UNCLE SAM HAD BEEN RUNNIN' LOW ON CASH. WARS WERE EXPENSIVE, AFTER ALL. SO BACK HERE THEY START ENLISTING THOSE LOCAL THEOCRATS AND THEIR KIDS TO KEEP THE PEACE ON THE HOME FRONT. SEEMED LIKE A GOOD IDEA. BUT THOSE LITTLE BUGGERS GOT A SENSE OF ENTITLEMENT, LIKE THEY WERE BETTER THAN EVERYBODY ELSE. STARTED CALLIN' THEMSELVES "THEOBRATS." THEY DIDN'T EVEN NEED TO PAY THEM, JUST RETURN SOME FAVORS...

NOW LOOK AT US! MY GRANDSON HAS TO SNEAK OFF TO GOD KNOWS WHERE IN THE MIDDLE OF THE NIGHT, JUST TO LEARN THE STUFF HE WON'T GET IN SCHOOL ANYMORE...

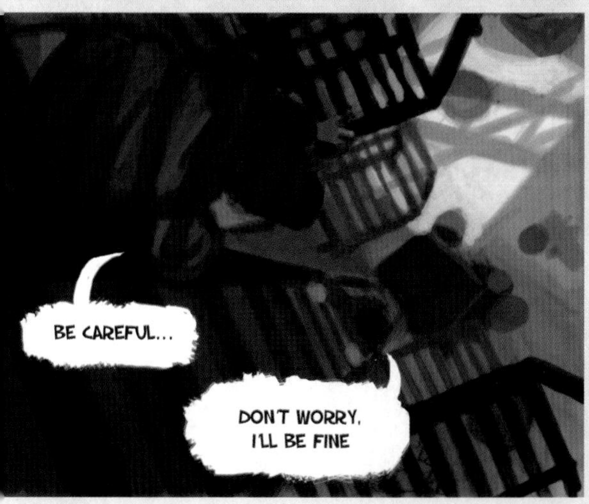
BE CAREFUL...
DON'T WORRY, I'LL BE FINE

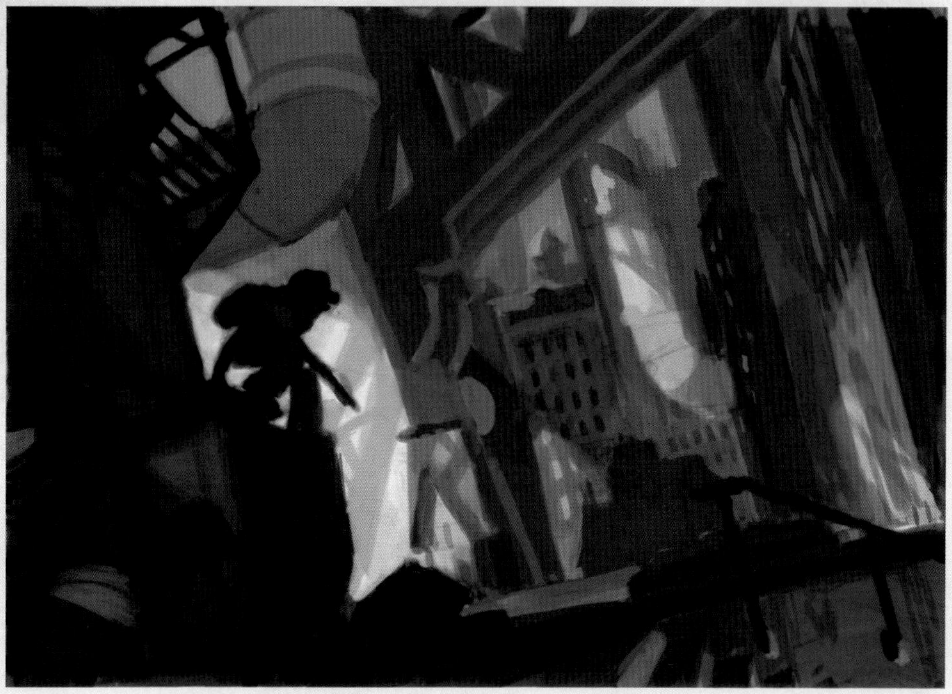

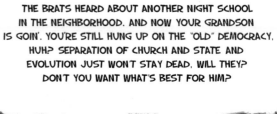

THE BRATS HEARD ABOUT ANOTHER NIGHT SCHOOL IN THE NEIGHBORHOOD. AND NOW YOUR GRANDSON IS GOIN'. YOU'RE STILL HUNG UP ON THE "OLD" DEMOCRACY, HUH? SEPARATION OF CHURCH AND STATE AND EVOLUTION JUST WON'T STAY DEAD, WILL THEY? DON'T YOU WANT WHAT'S BEST FOR HIM?

WHAT?!! GIVE ME A BREAK...

MINUTES LATER...

SHHHK

HEY!

AREN'T YOU GOING TO BE LATE FOR SCHOOL?

TINK
TINK
TINK

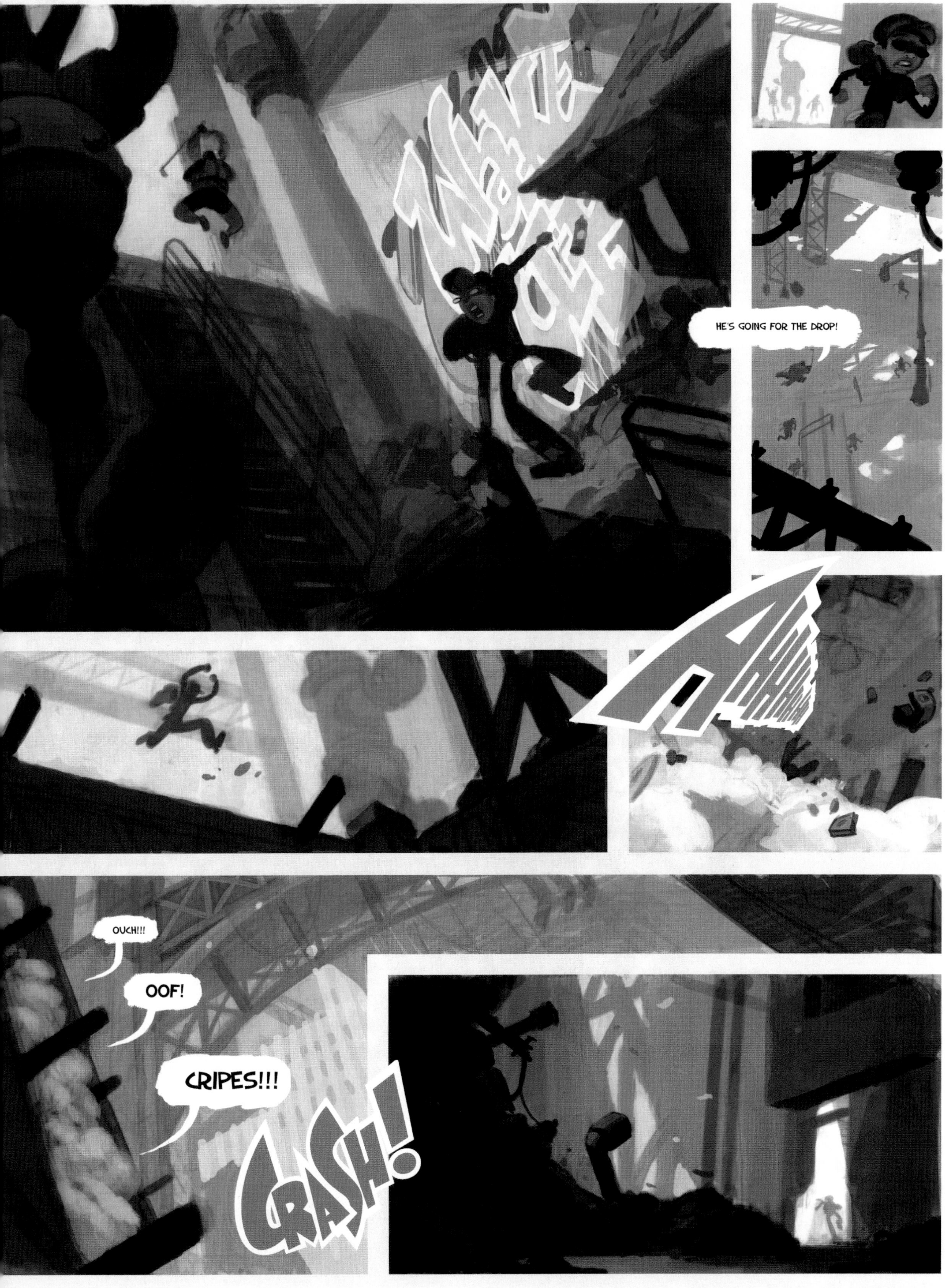
HE'S GOING FOR THE DROP!
OUCH!!!
OOF!
CRIPES!!!
CRASH!

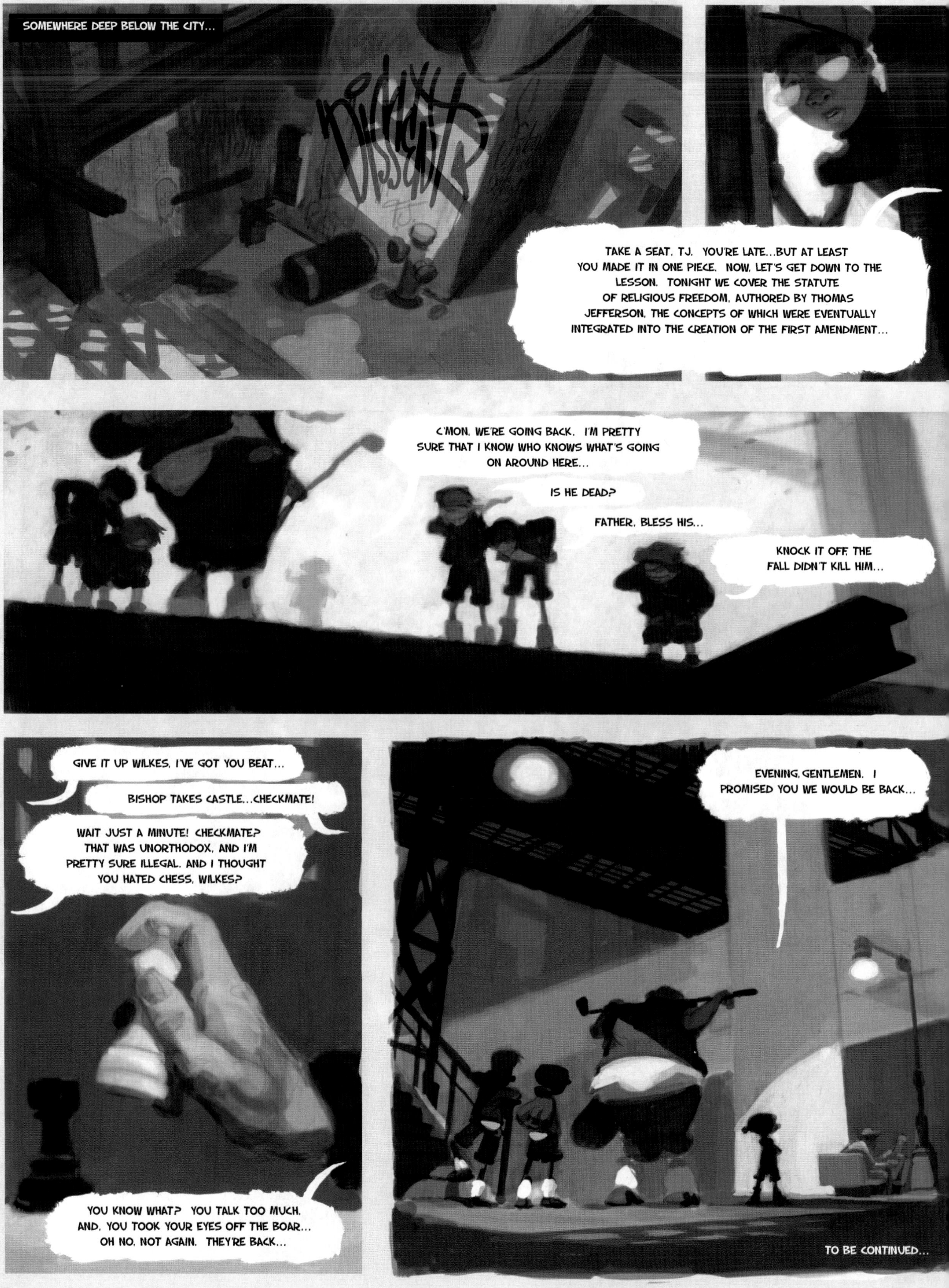
SOMEWHERE DEEP BELOW THE CITY...
TAKE A SEAT, TJ. YOU'RE LATE...BUT AT LEAST YOU MADE IT IN ONE PIECE. NOW, LET'S GET DOWN TO THE LESSON. TONIGHT WE COVER THE STATUTE OF RELIGIOUS FREEDOM, AUTHORED BY THOMAS JEFFERSON, THE CONCEPTS OF WHICH WERE EVENTUALLY INTEGRATED INTO THE CREATION OF THE FIRST AMENDMENT...
C'MON, WE'RE GOING BACK. I'M PRETTY SURE THAT I KNOW WHO KNOWS WHAT'S GOING ON AROUND HERE...
IS HE DEAD?
FATHER, BLESS HIS...
KNOCK IT OFF. THE FALL DIDN'T KILL HIM...
GIVE IT UP WILKES, I'VE GOT YOU BEAT...
BISHOP TAKES CASTLE...CHECKMATE!
WAIT JUST A MINUTE! CHECKMATE? THAT WAS UNORTHODOX, AND I'M PRETTY SURE ILLEGAL. AND I THOUGHT YOU HATED CHESS, WILKES?
YOU KNOW WHAT? YOU TALK TOO MUCH. AND, YOU TOOK YOUR EYES OFF THE BOAR... OH NO, NOT AGAIN. THEY'RE BACK...
EVENING, GENTLEMEN. I PROMISED YOU WE WOULD BE BACK...
TO BE CONTINUED...

OUT OF PICTURE

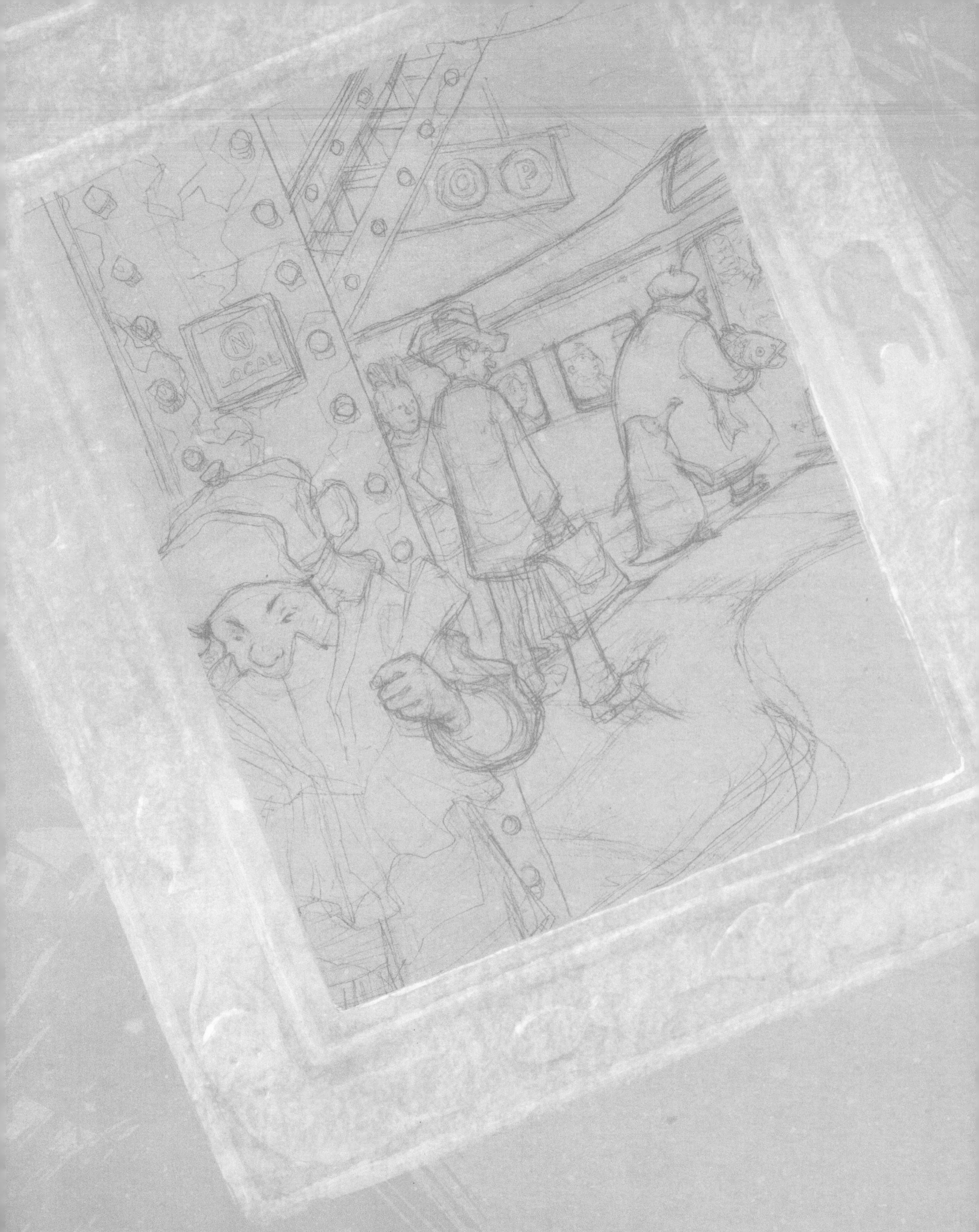
N
LOCAL

ROBERT MACKENZIE

AROUND THE CORNER

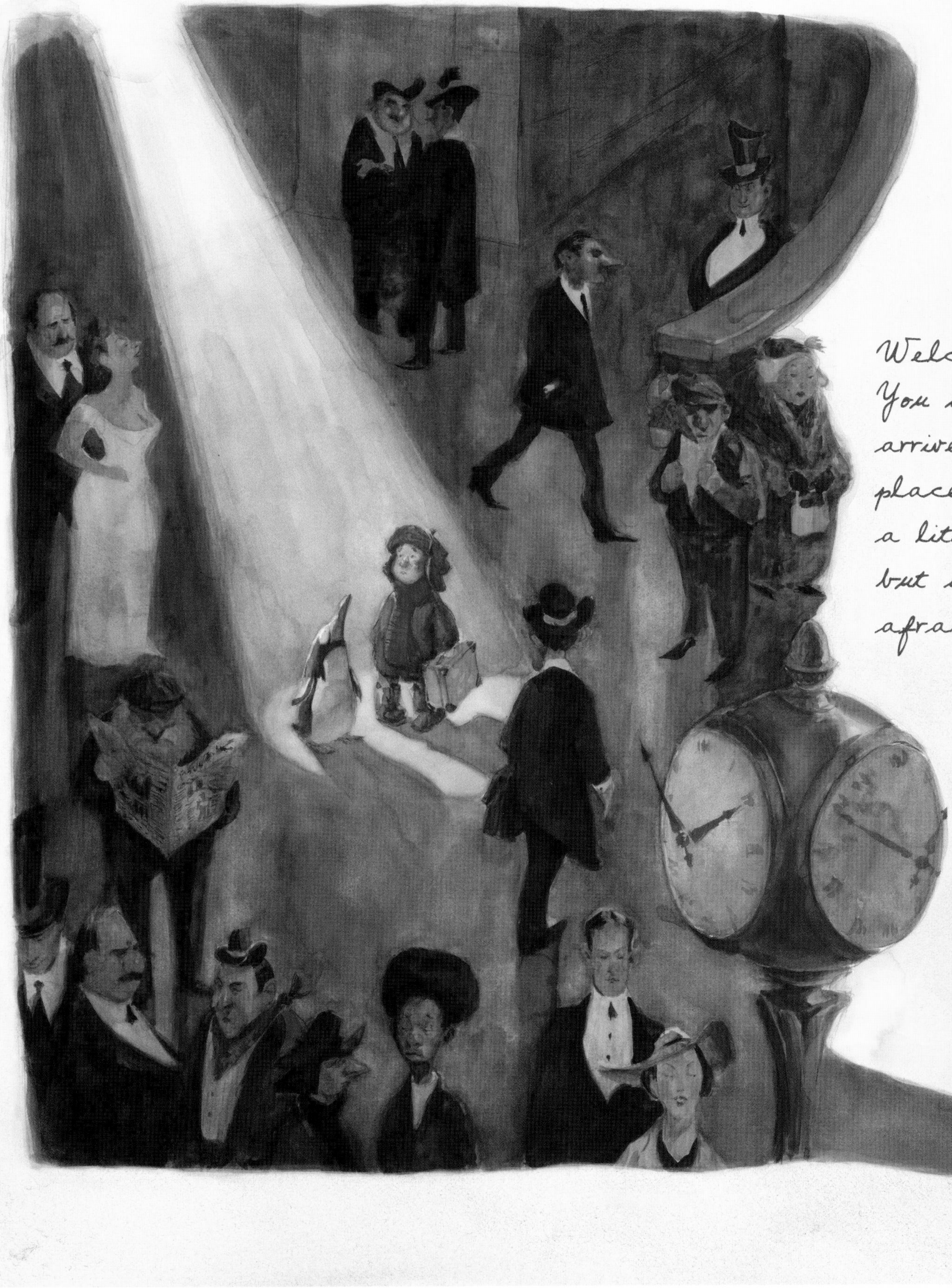

Welcome!
You have finally
arrived. This
place might seem
a little scary,
but don't be
afraid.

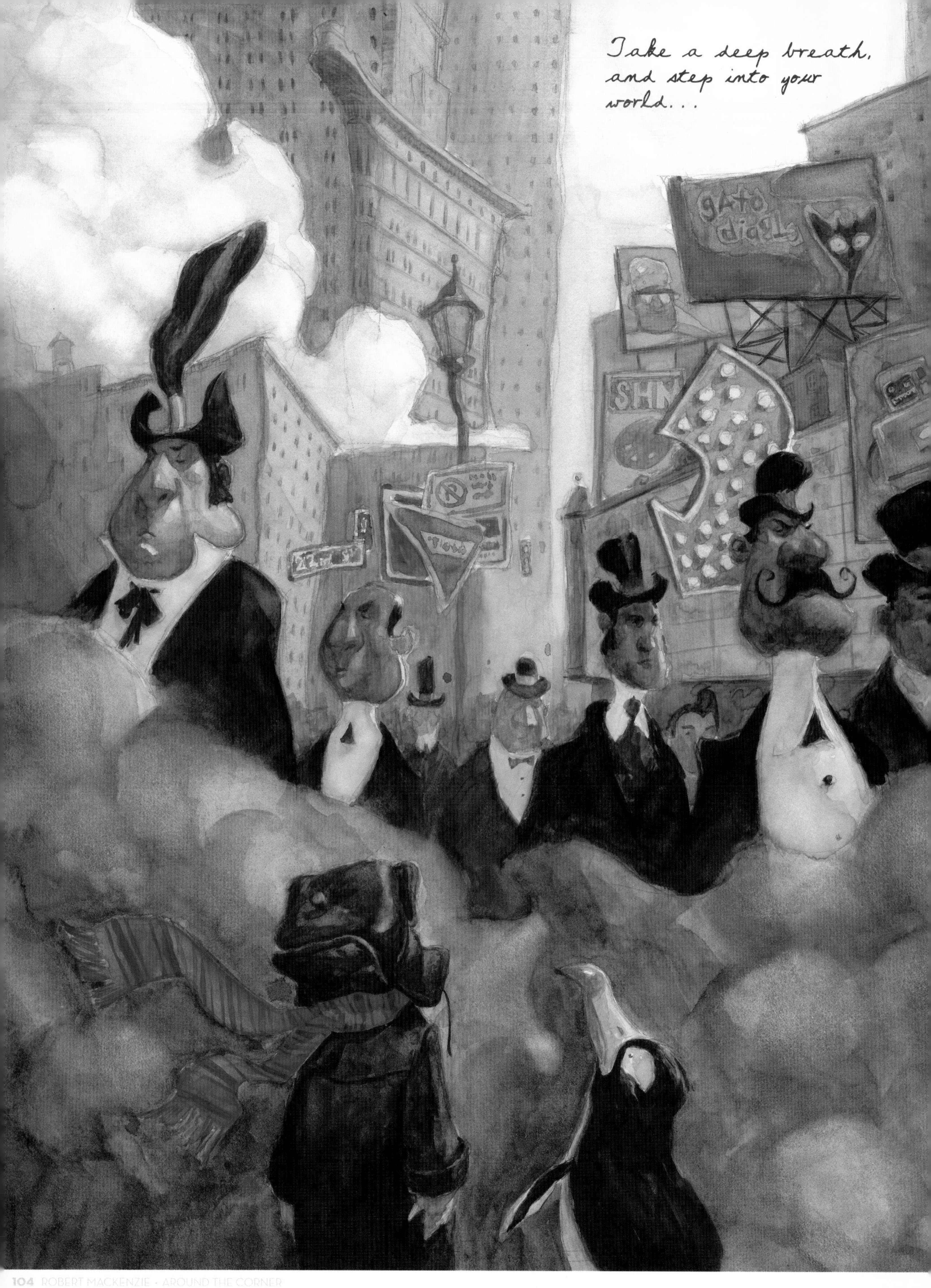
Take a deep breath,
and step into your
world...

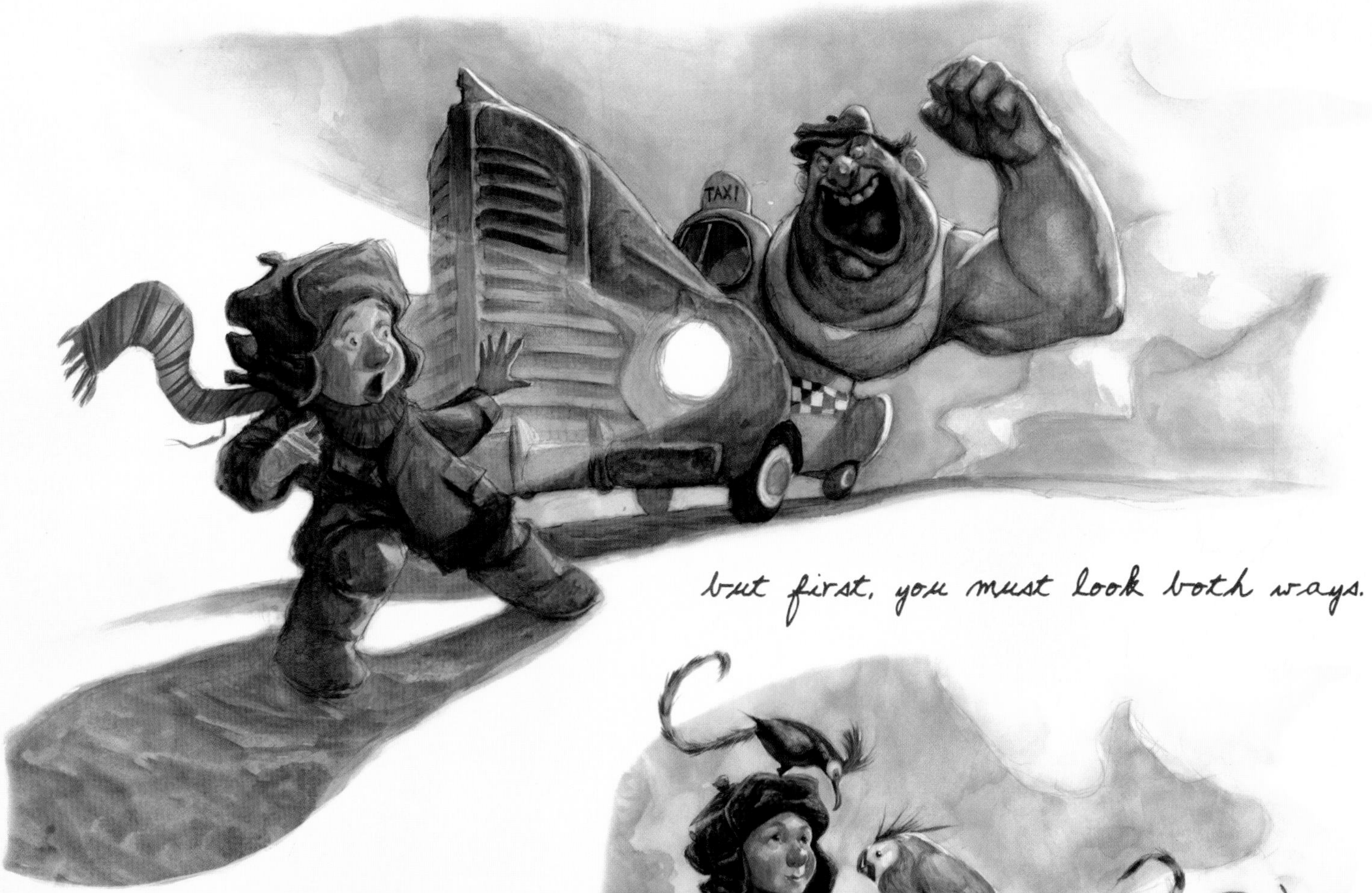
TAXI

but first, you must look both ways.

Things move a little quicker
out here, but if you take
time to reach out to others...

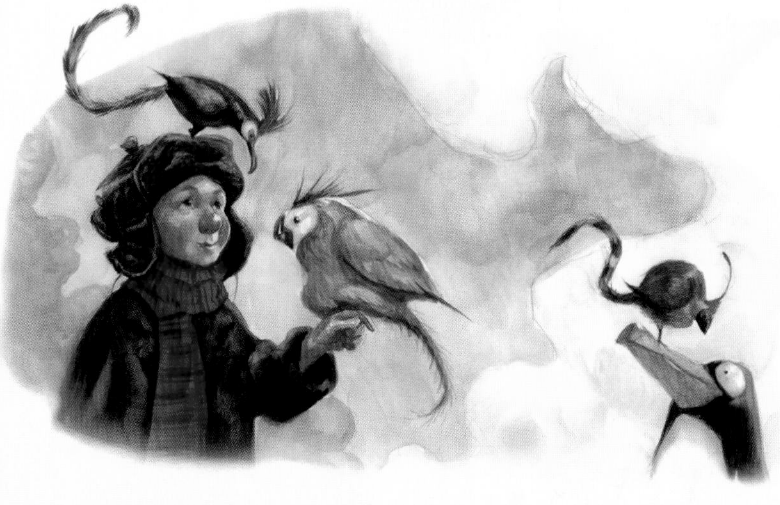

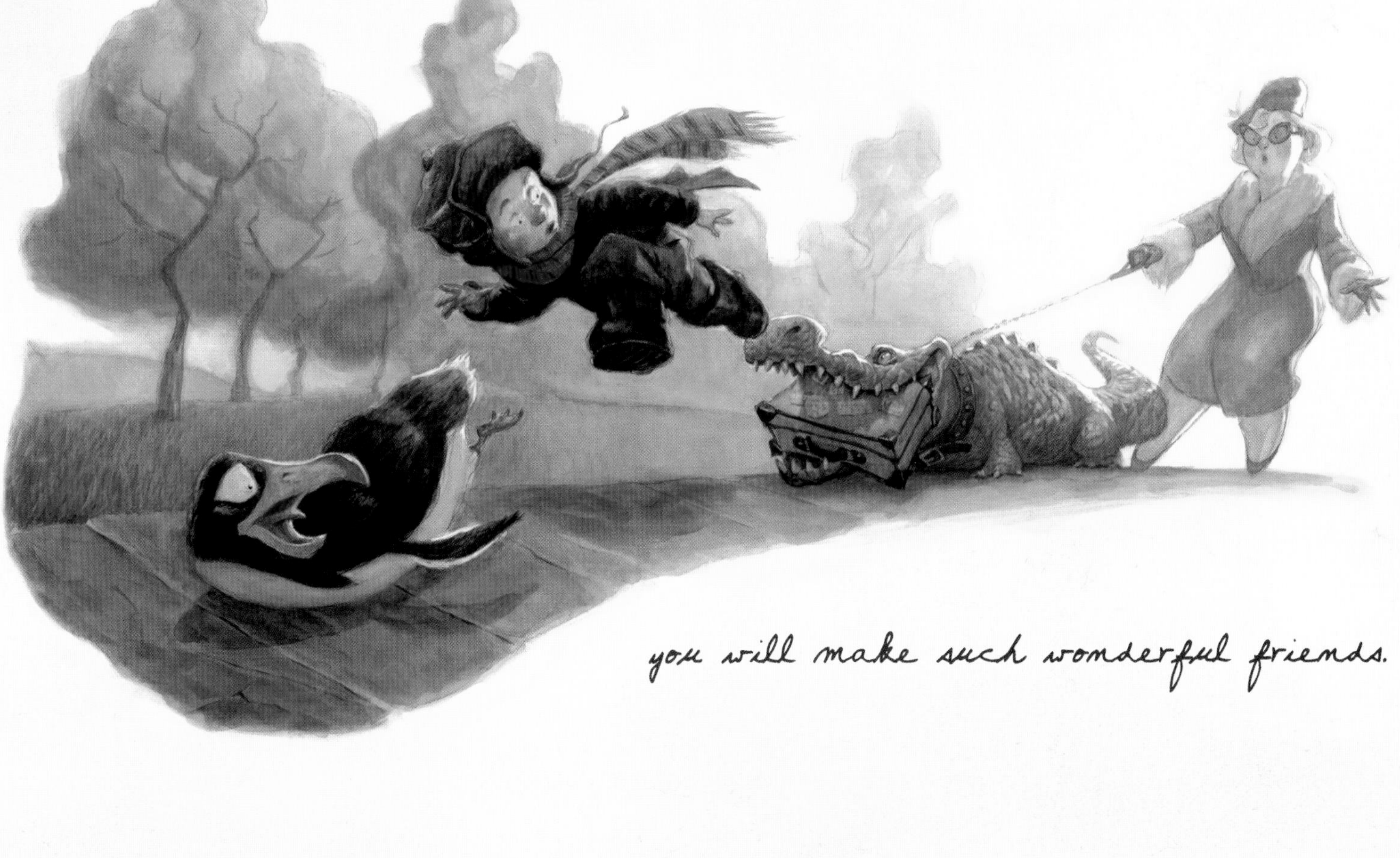

you will make such wonderful friends.

The city is filled with so many characters. . .

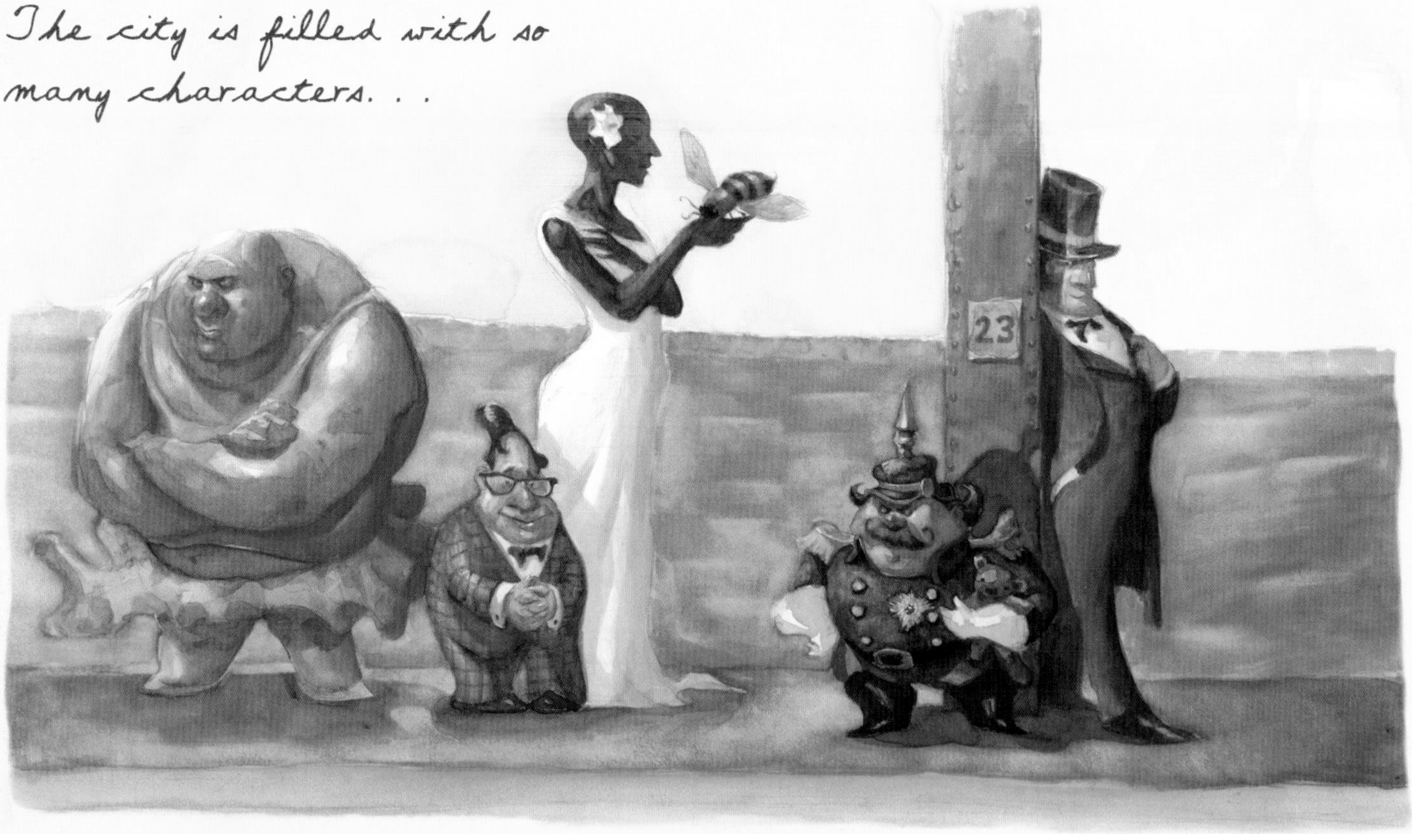
23

but be careful.

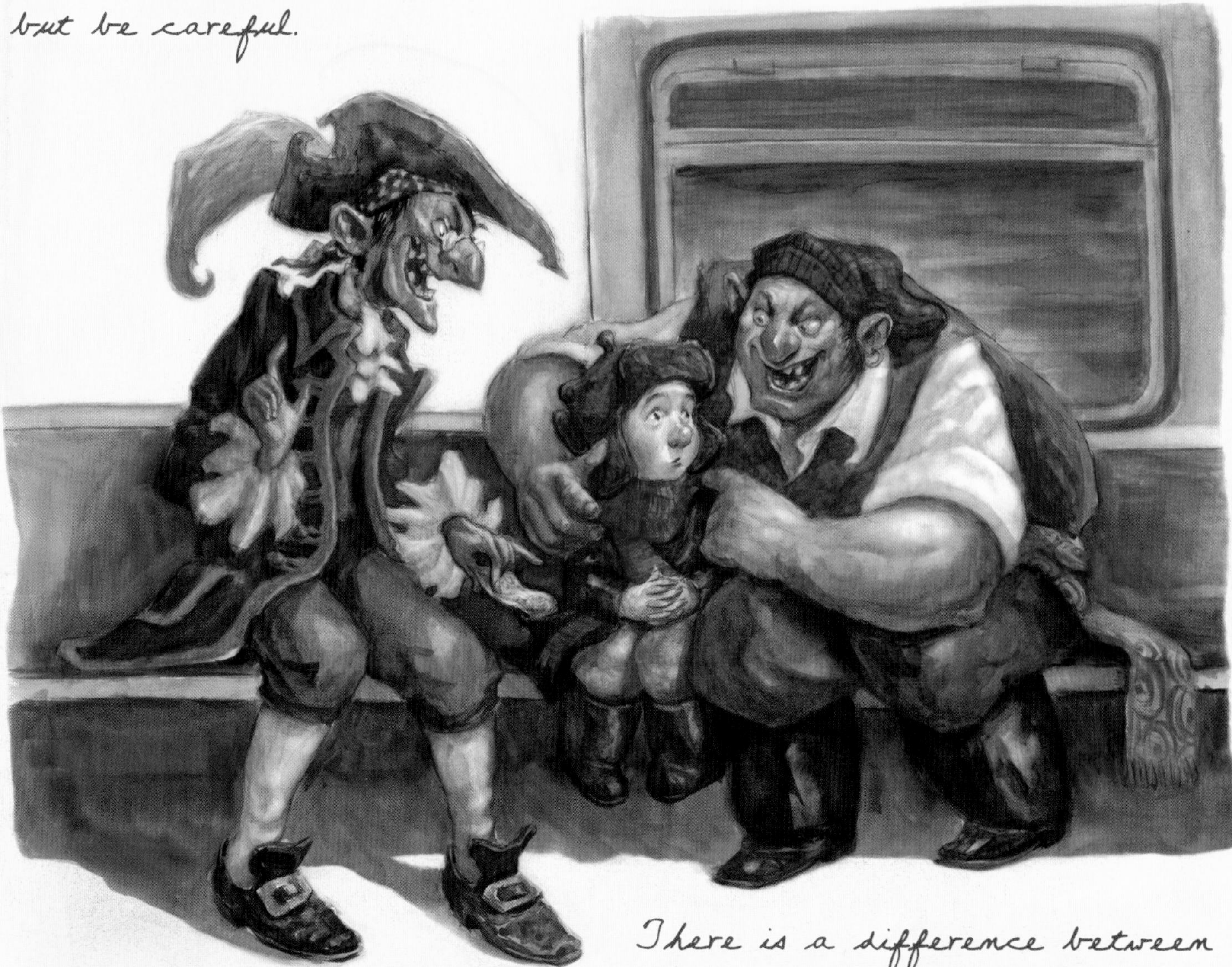

There is a difference between having character and being a character.

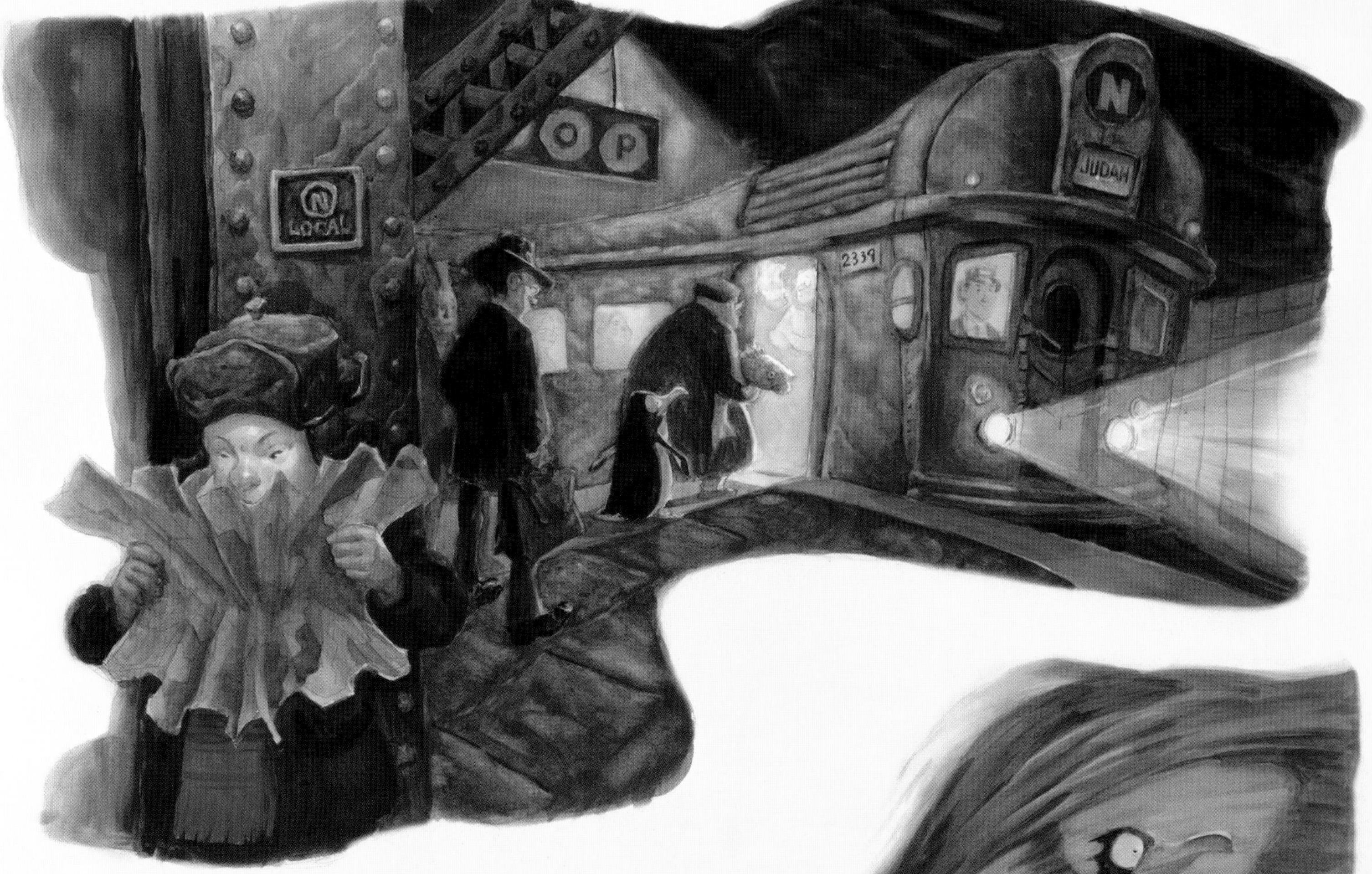
O P
N LOCAL
N
JUDAH
2339

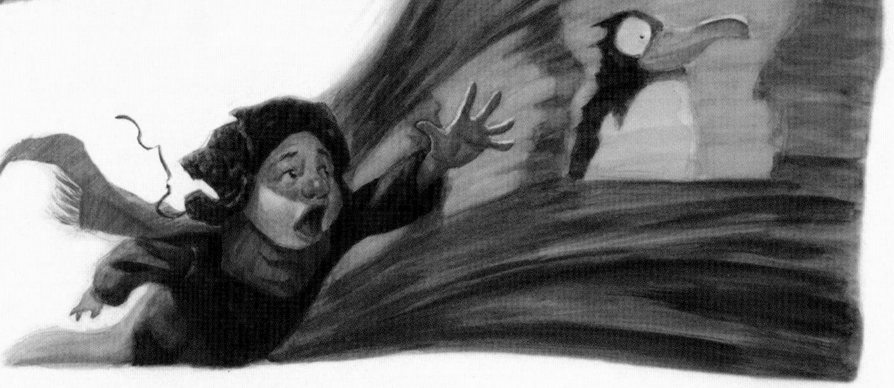

Just keep all of your valuables close to you and everything will be fine.

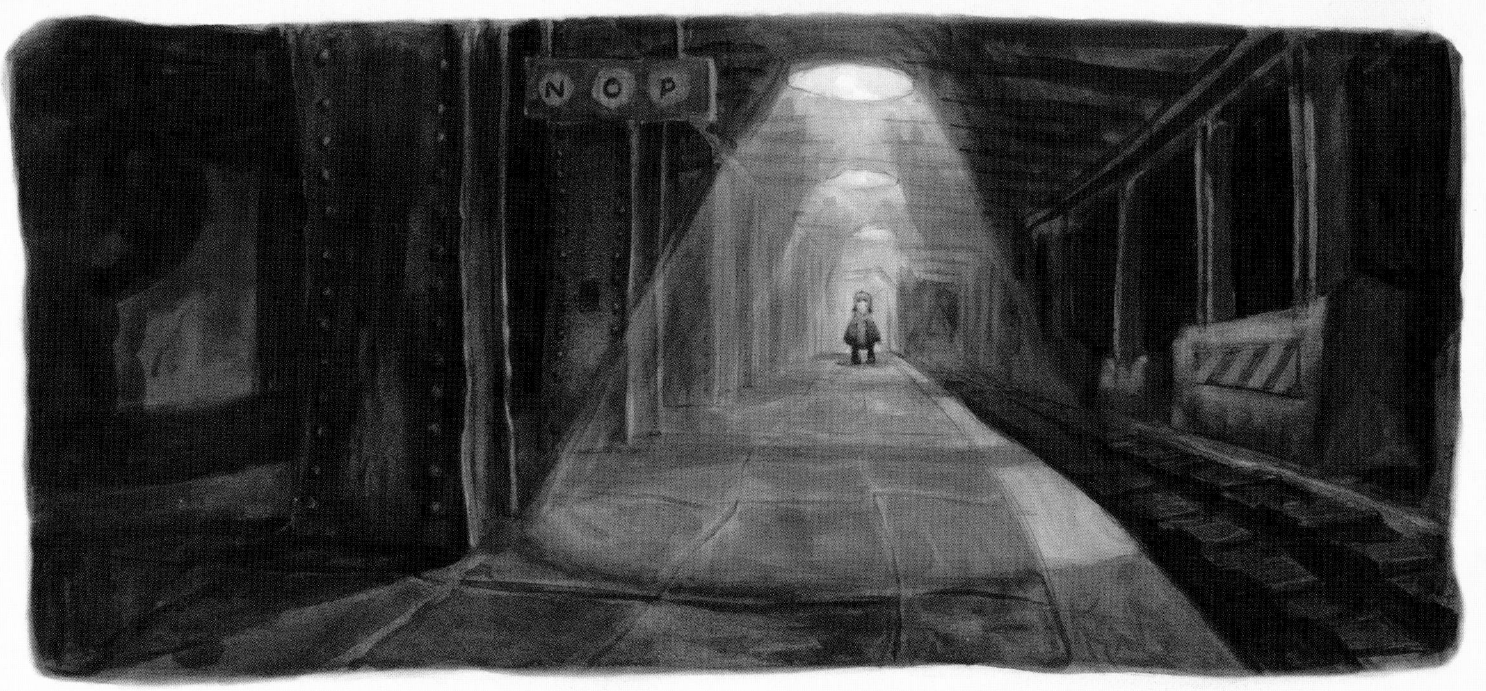
N O P

On those days when the clouds have bottled up the light—

Don't look so down.

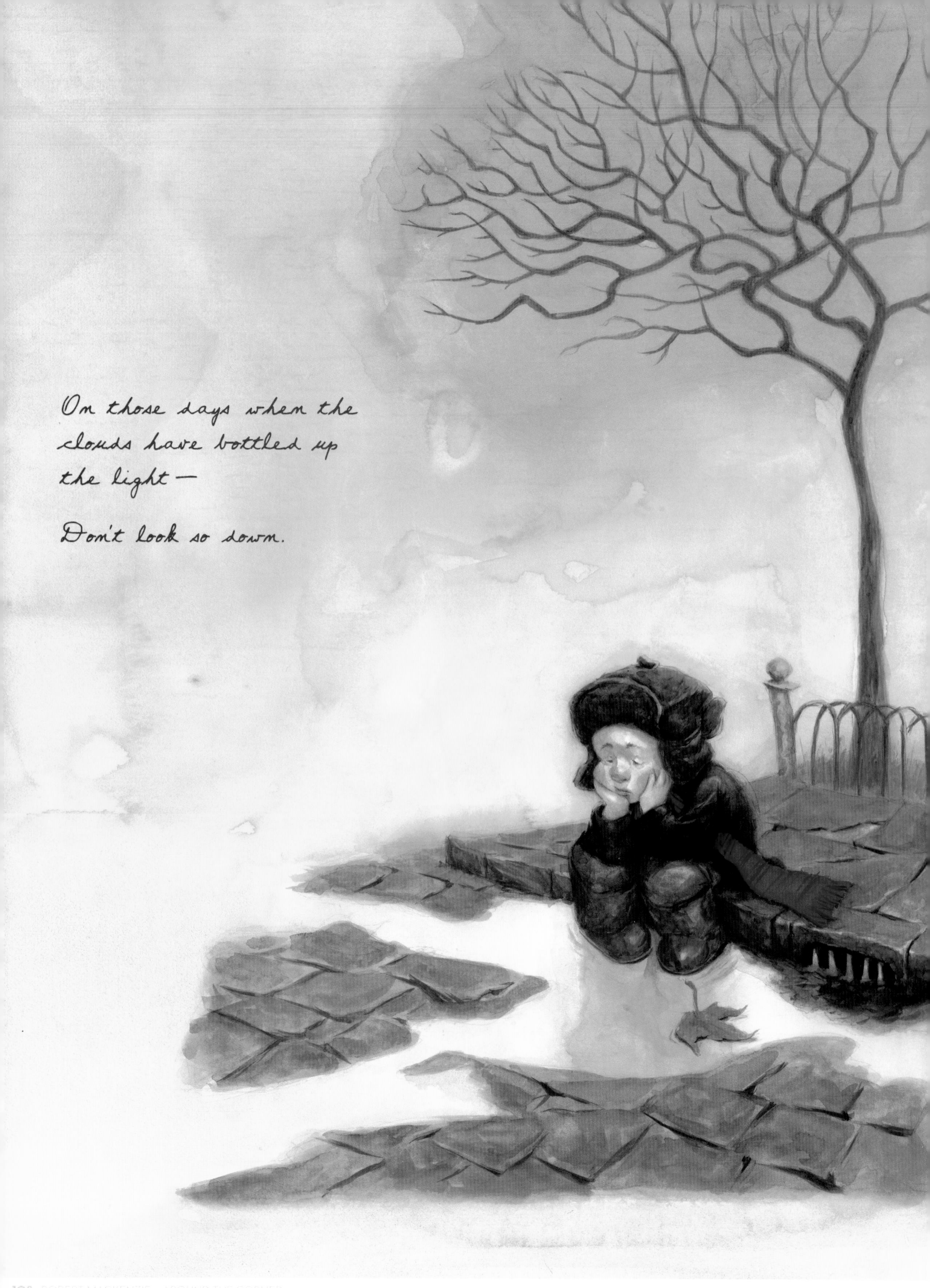

Look Within.

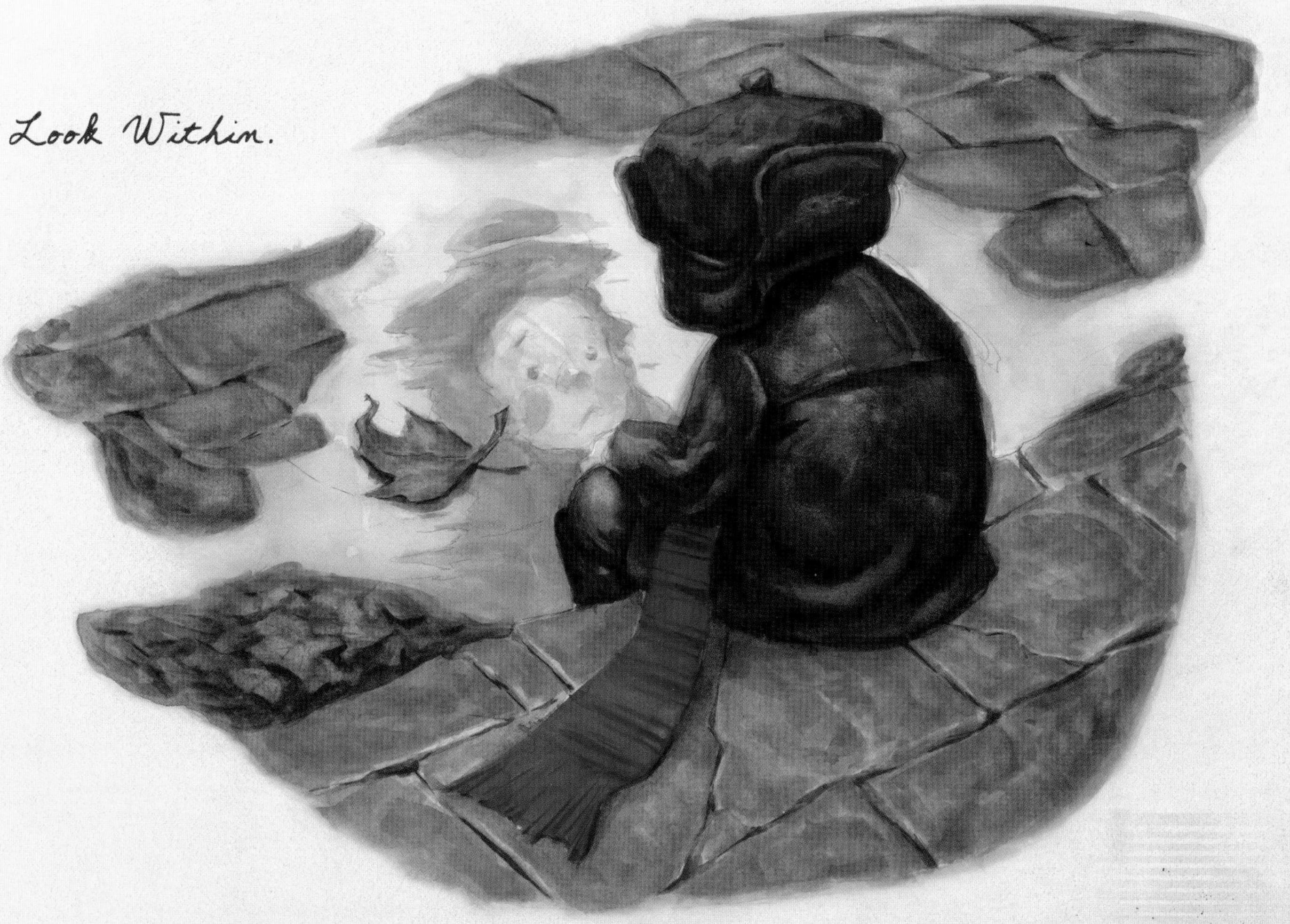

Look ahead.

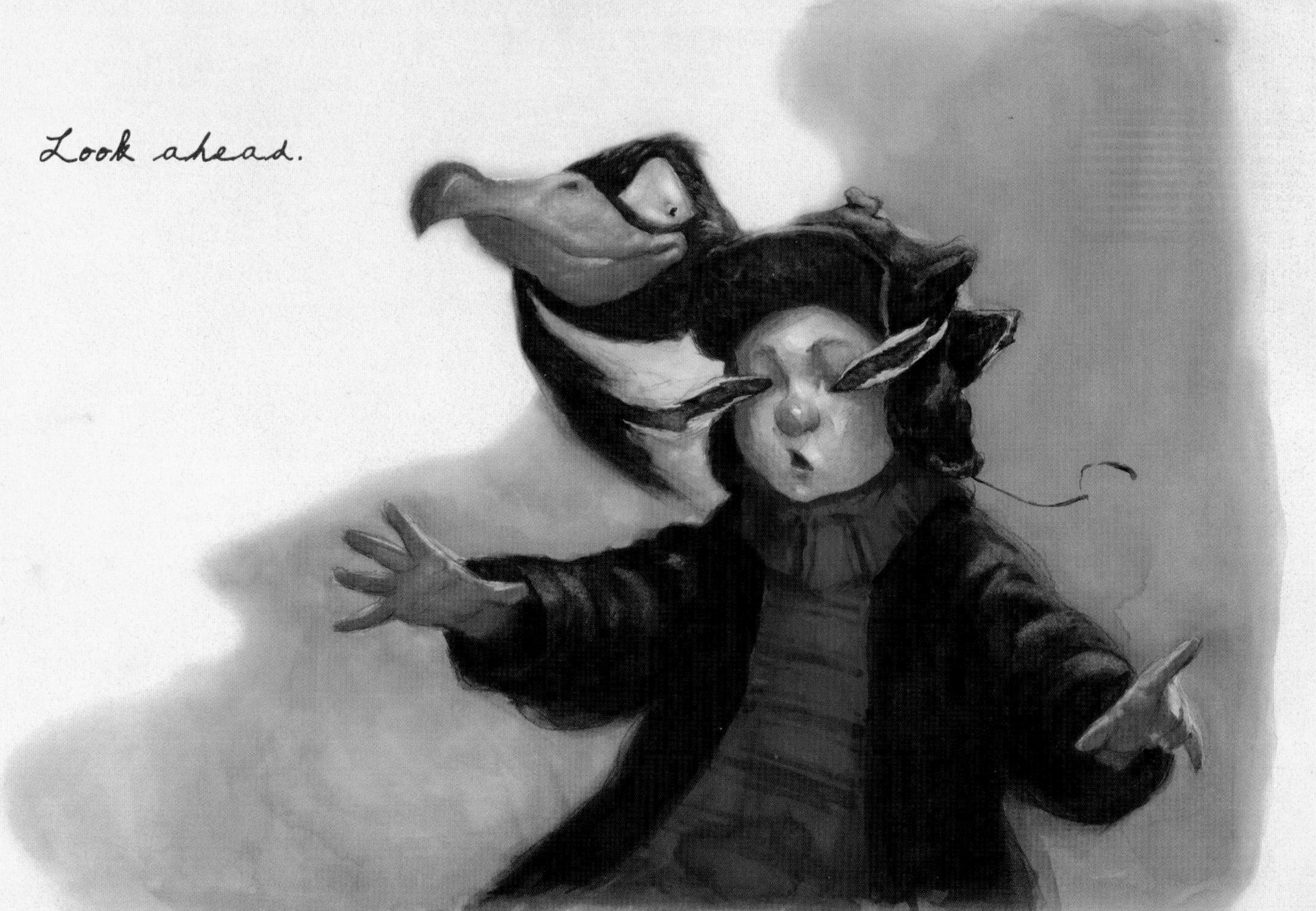

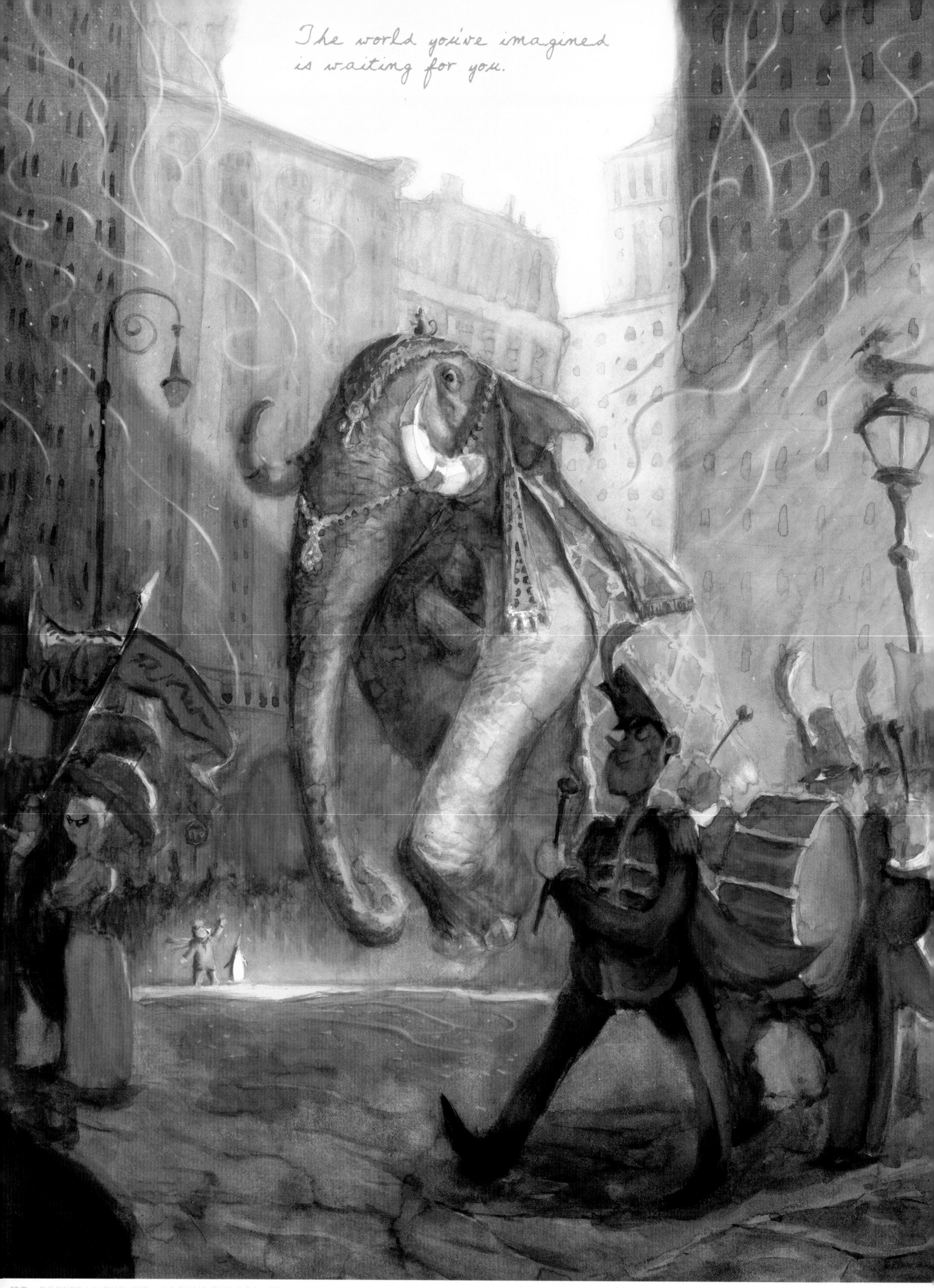
The world you've imagined
is waiting for you.

Since we were given the opportunity to do a second edition of Out of Picture 1, we wanted to make it special. The following section is comprised of some of the thinking that went into our stories: doodles, rough layouts, color studies, character sketches.... These give a small glimpse into the unique processes of each artist.

We hope you enjoy them.

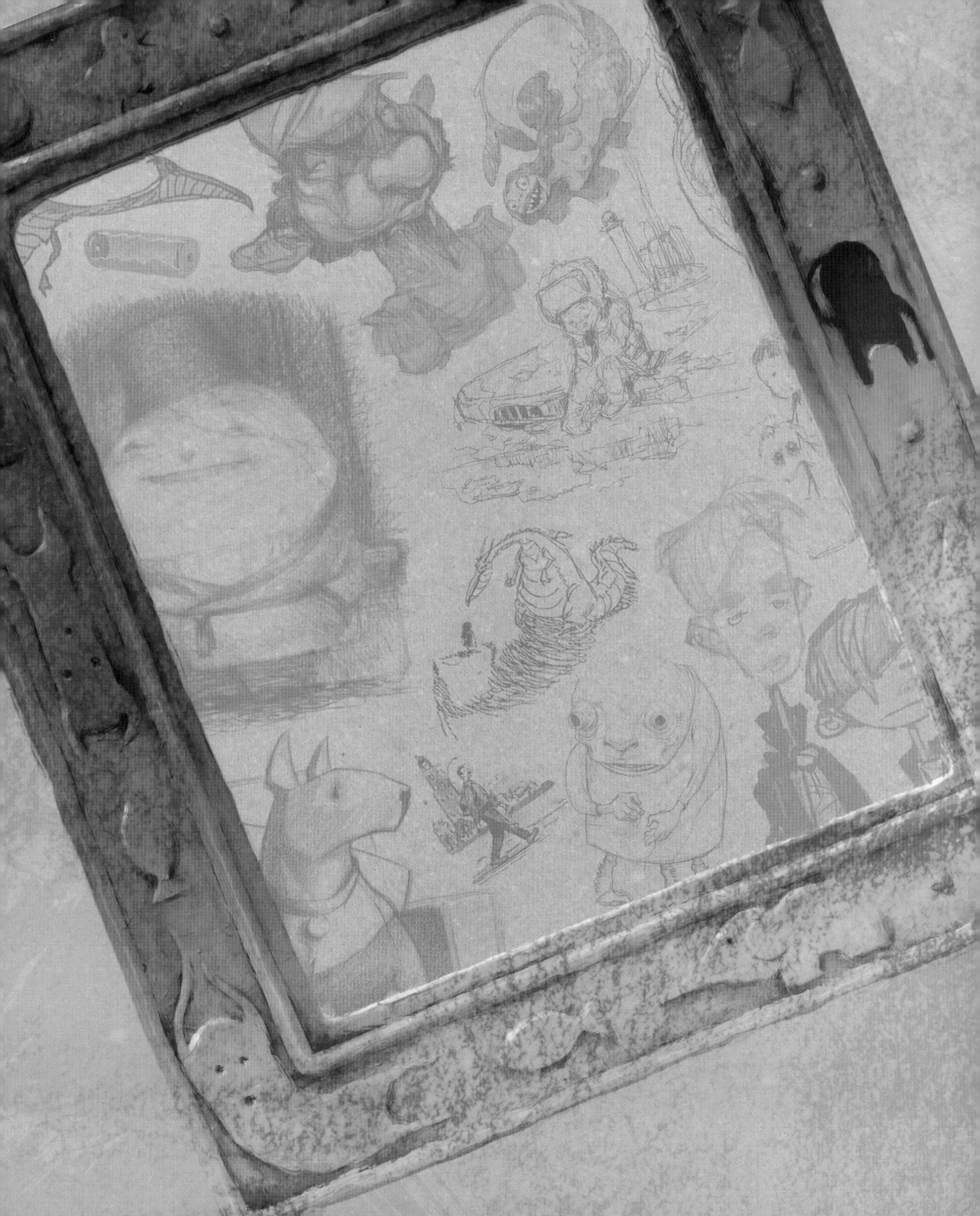

DEVELOPMENT GALLERY

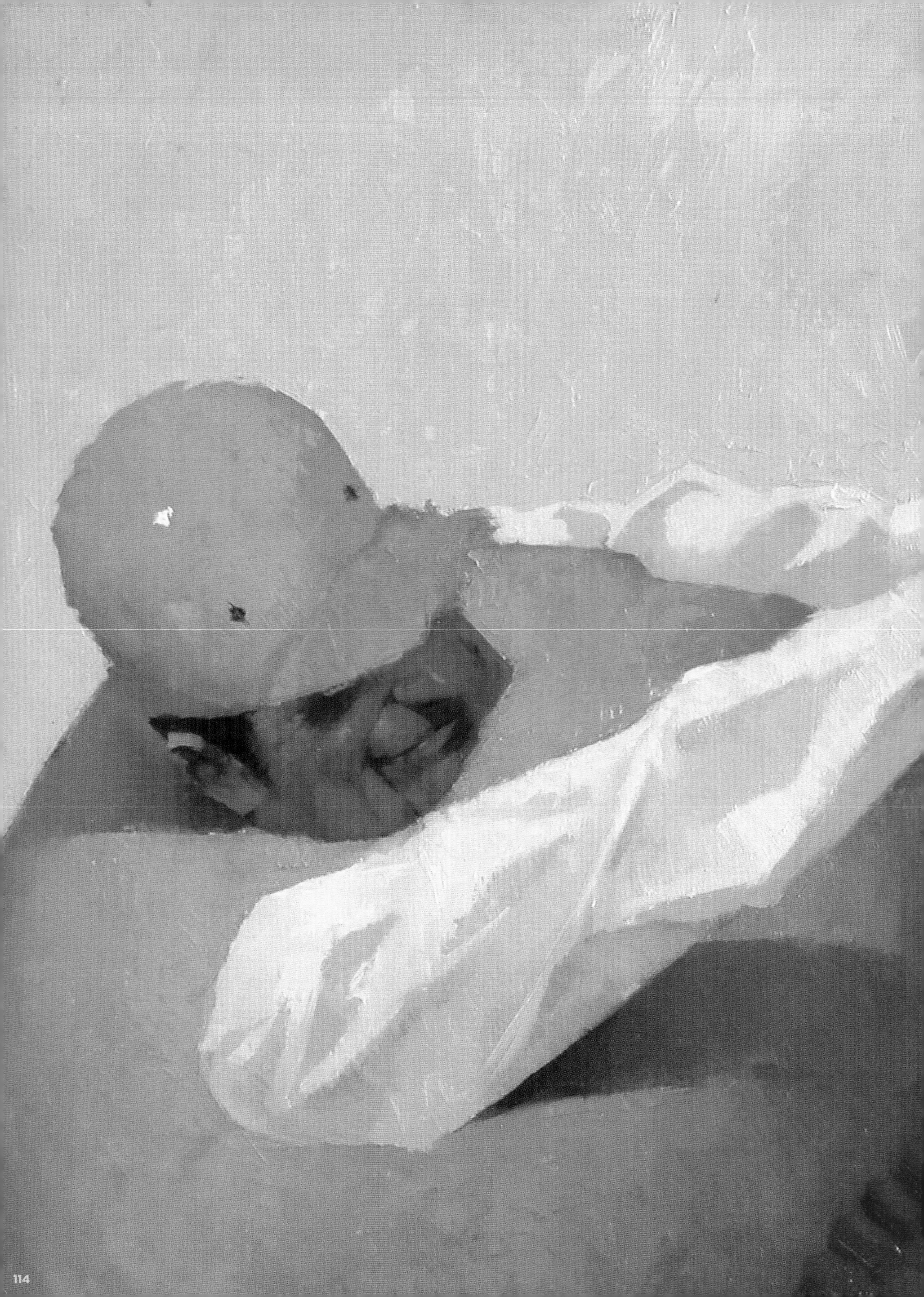

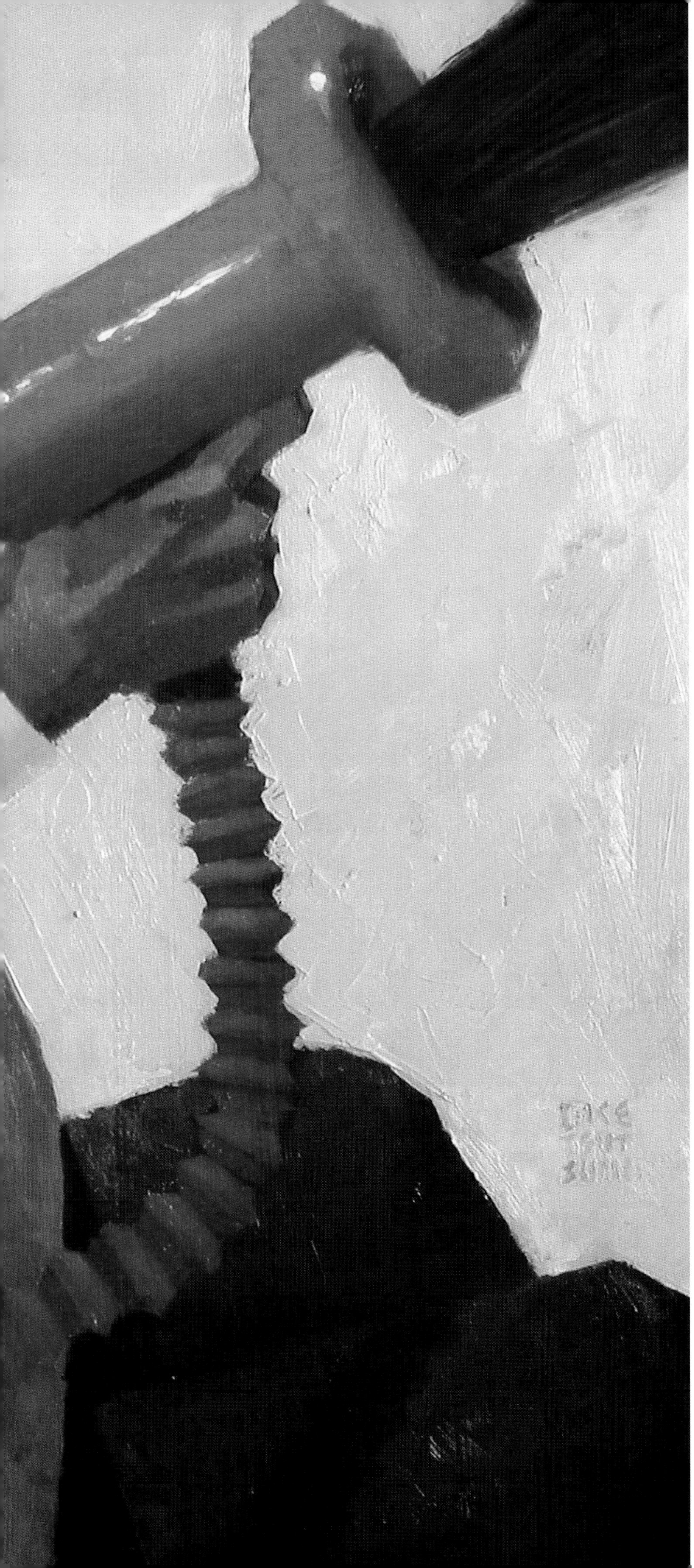

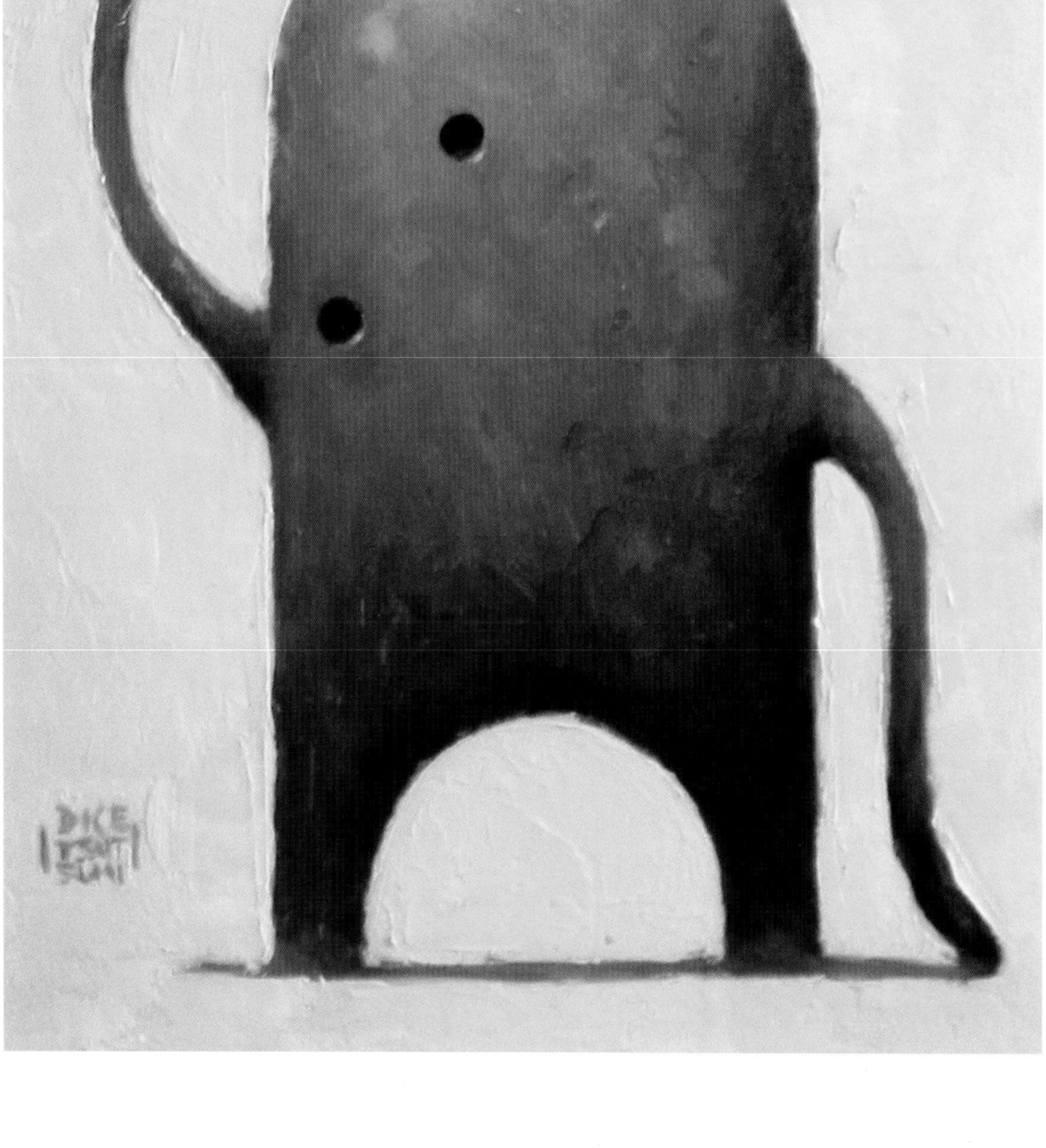
?
DICE
TSUT
SUMI

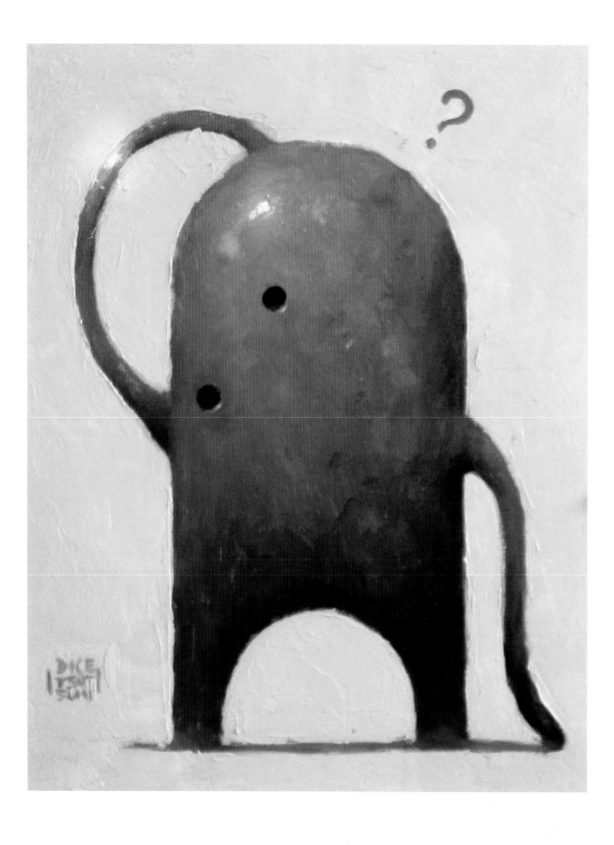

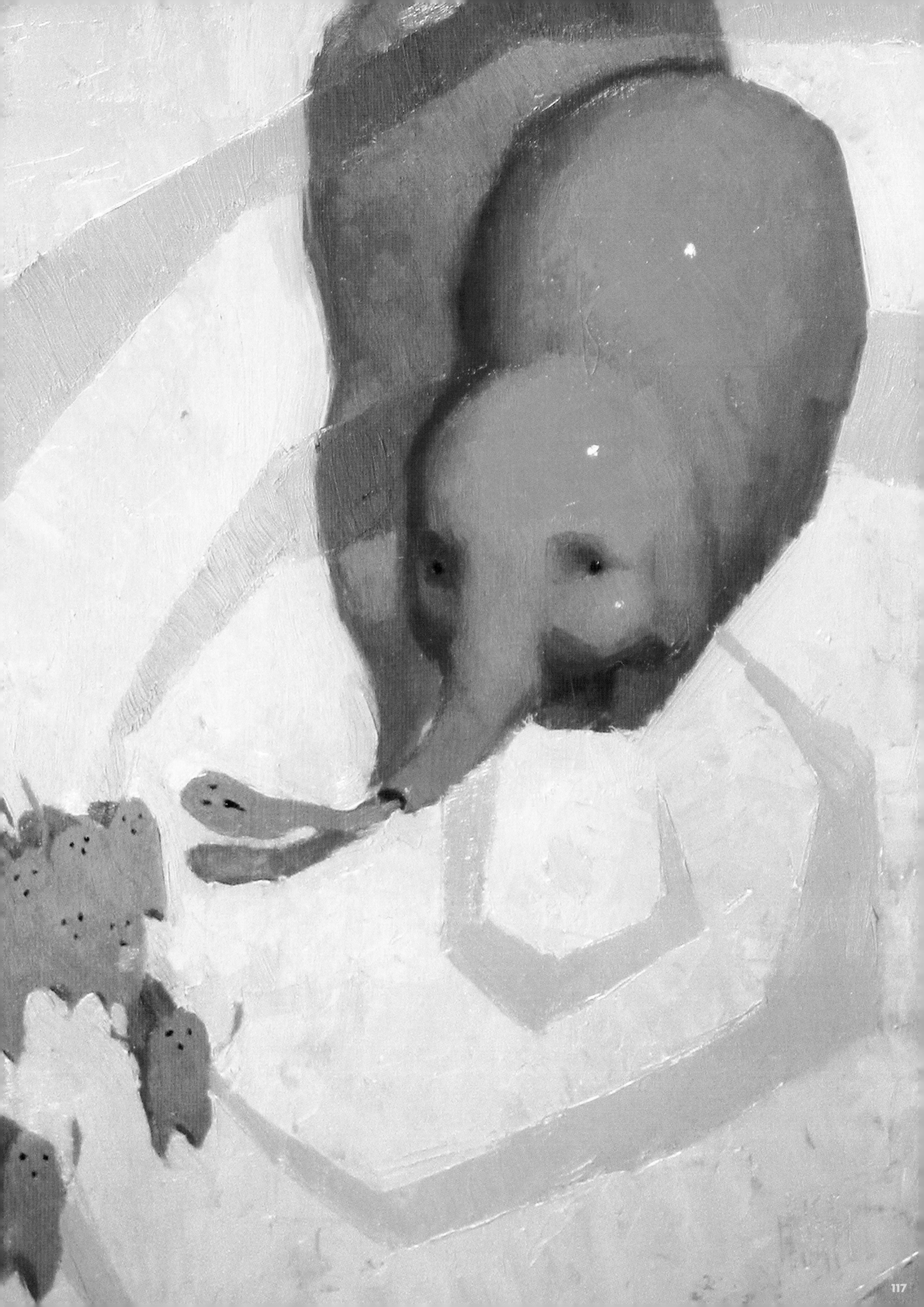

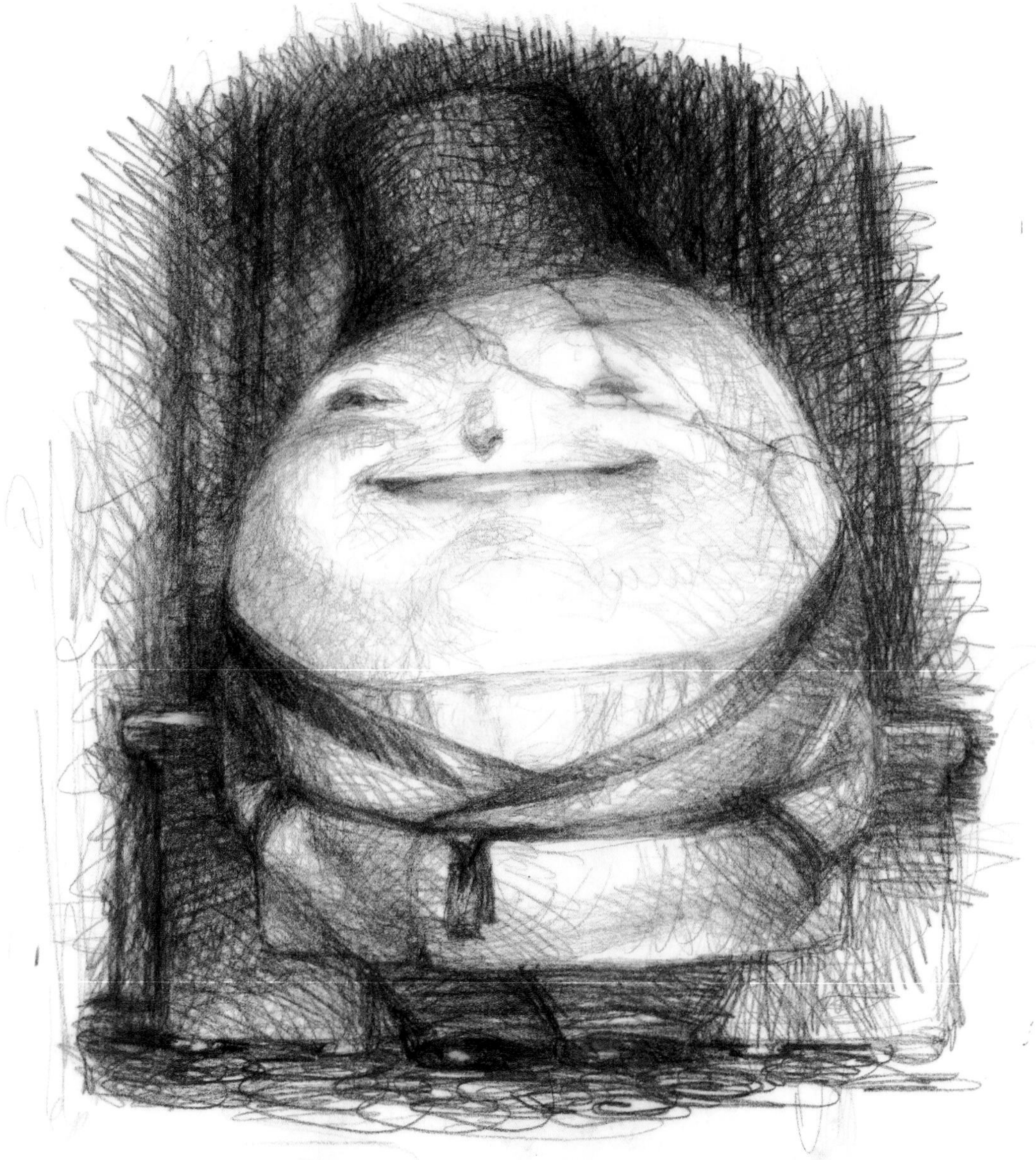

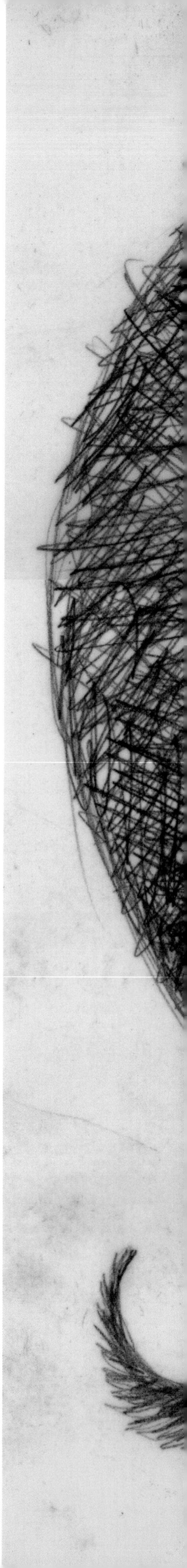

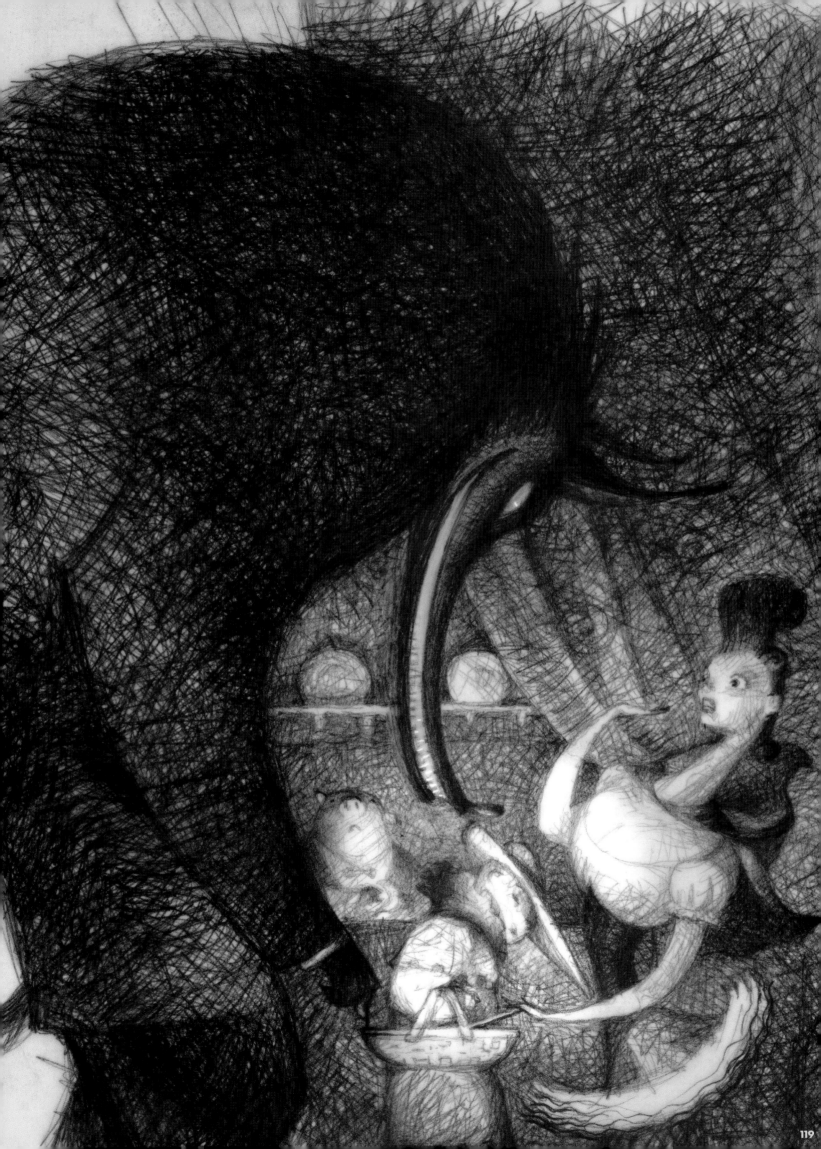

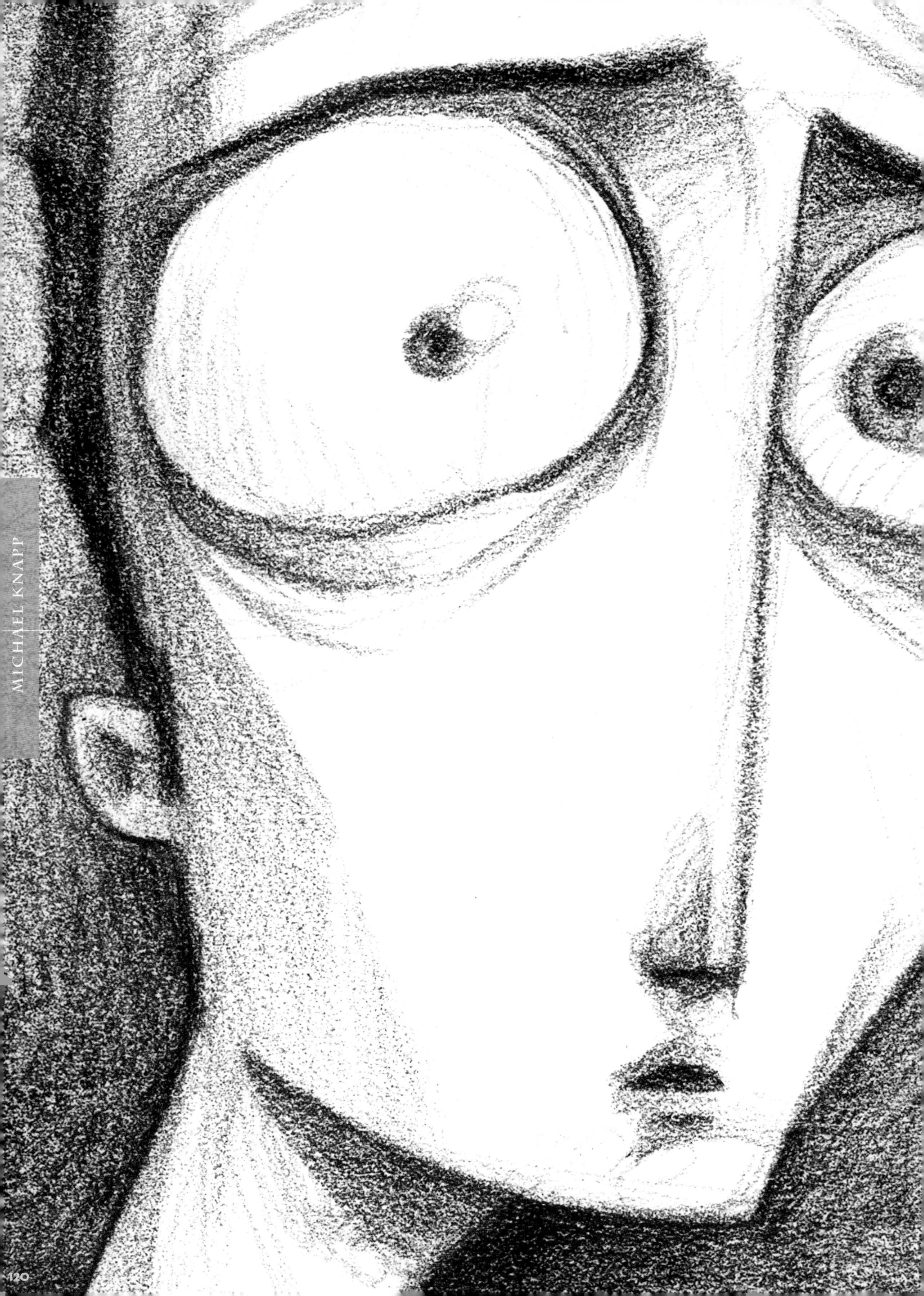

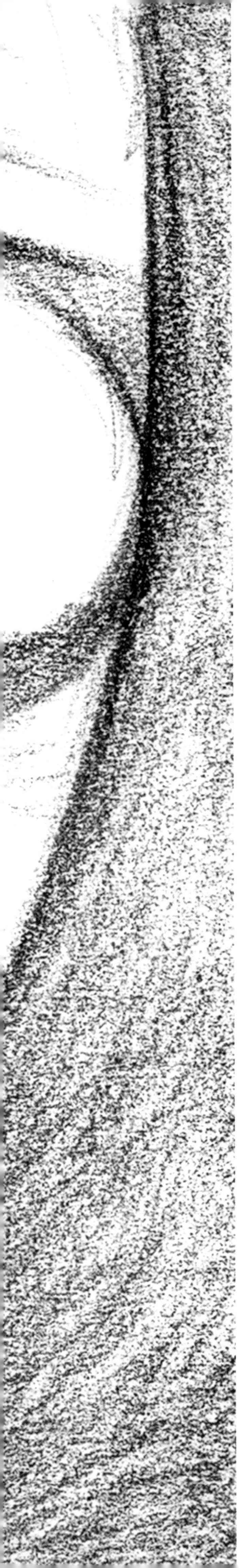

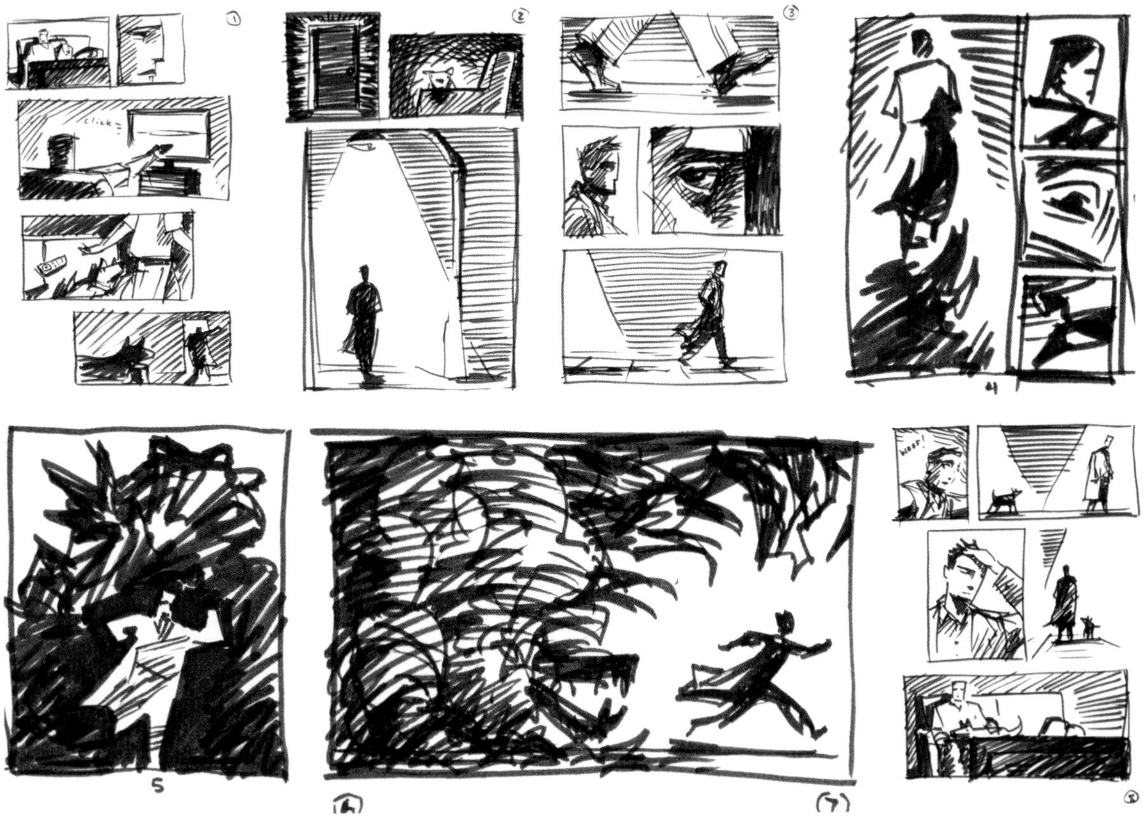

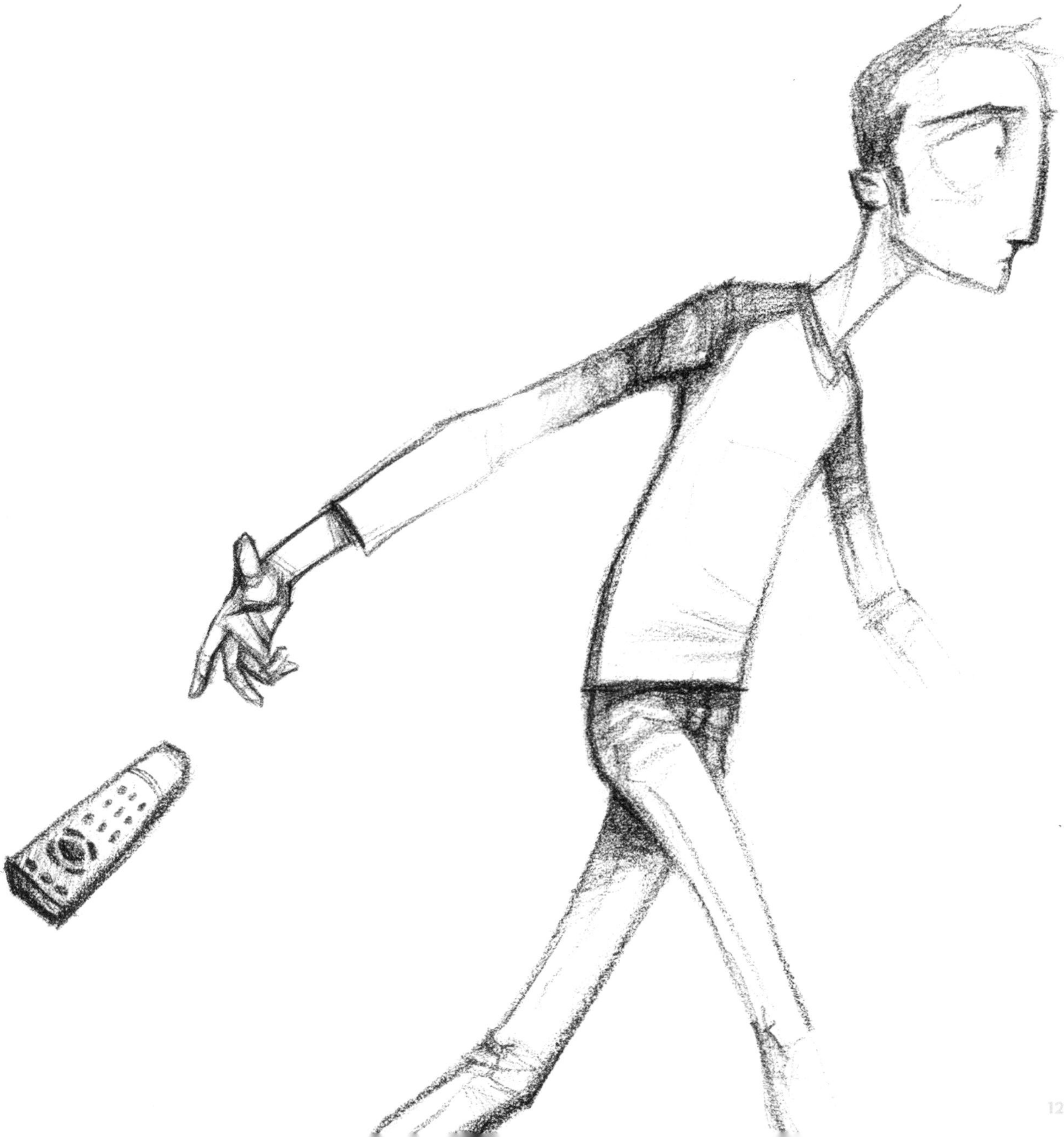

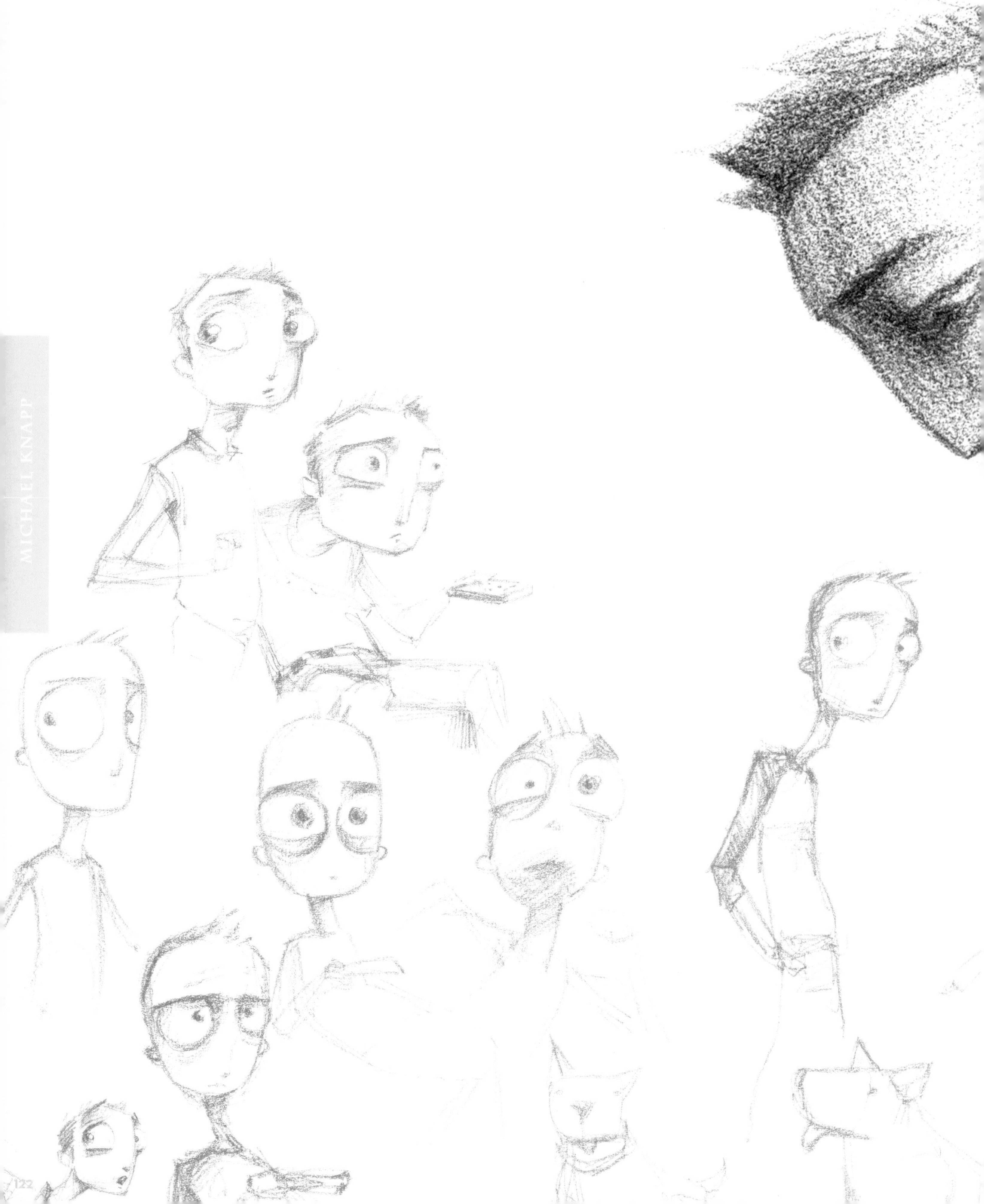

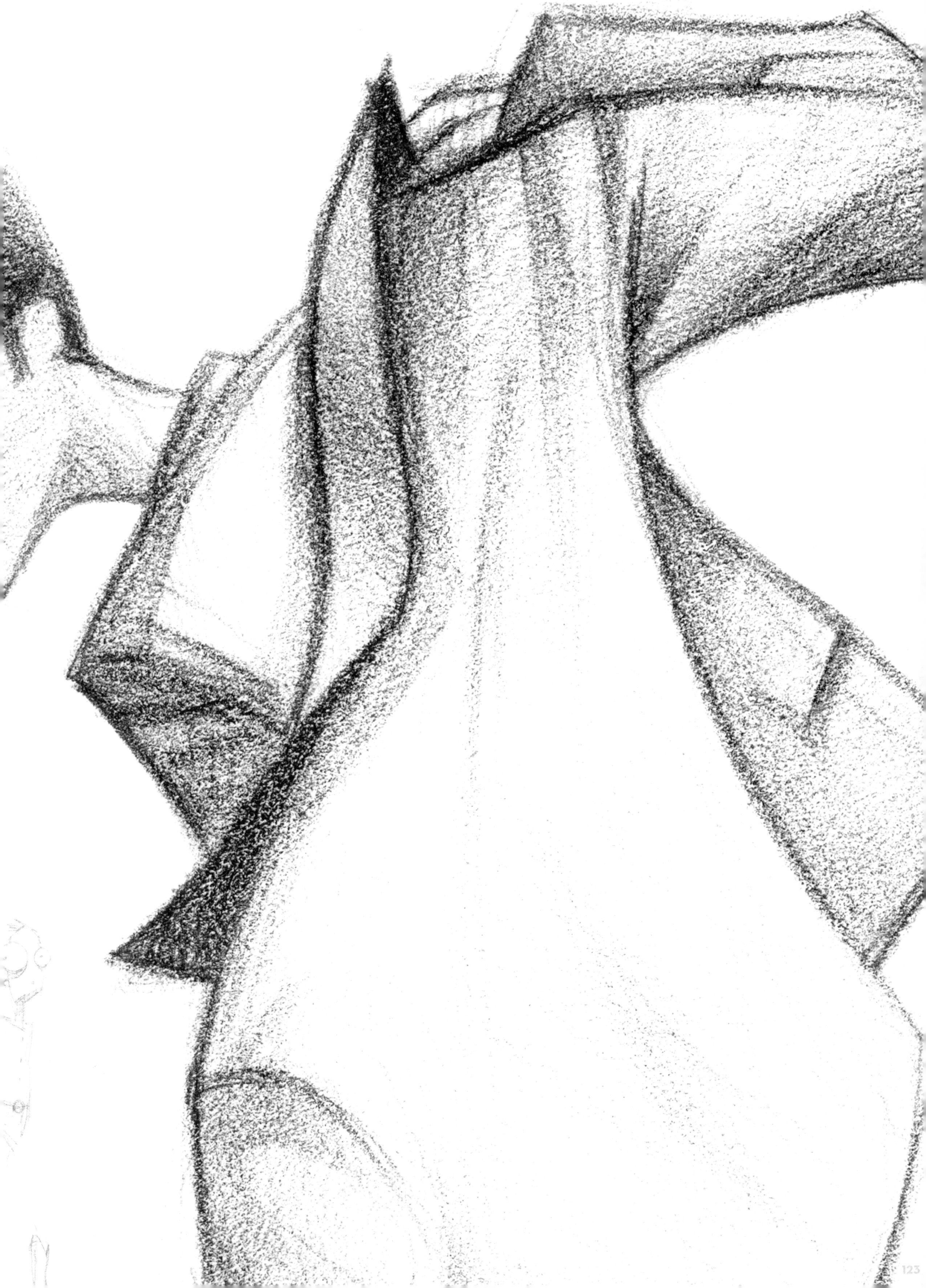

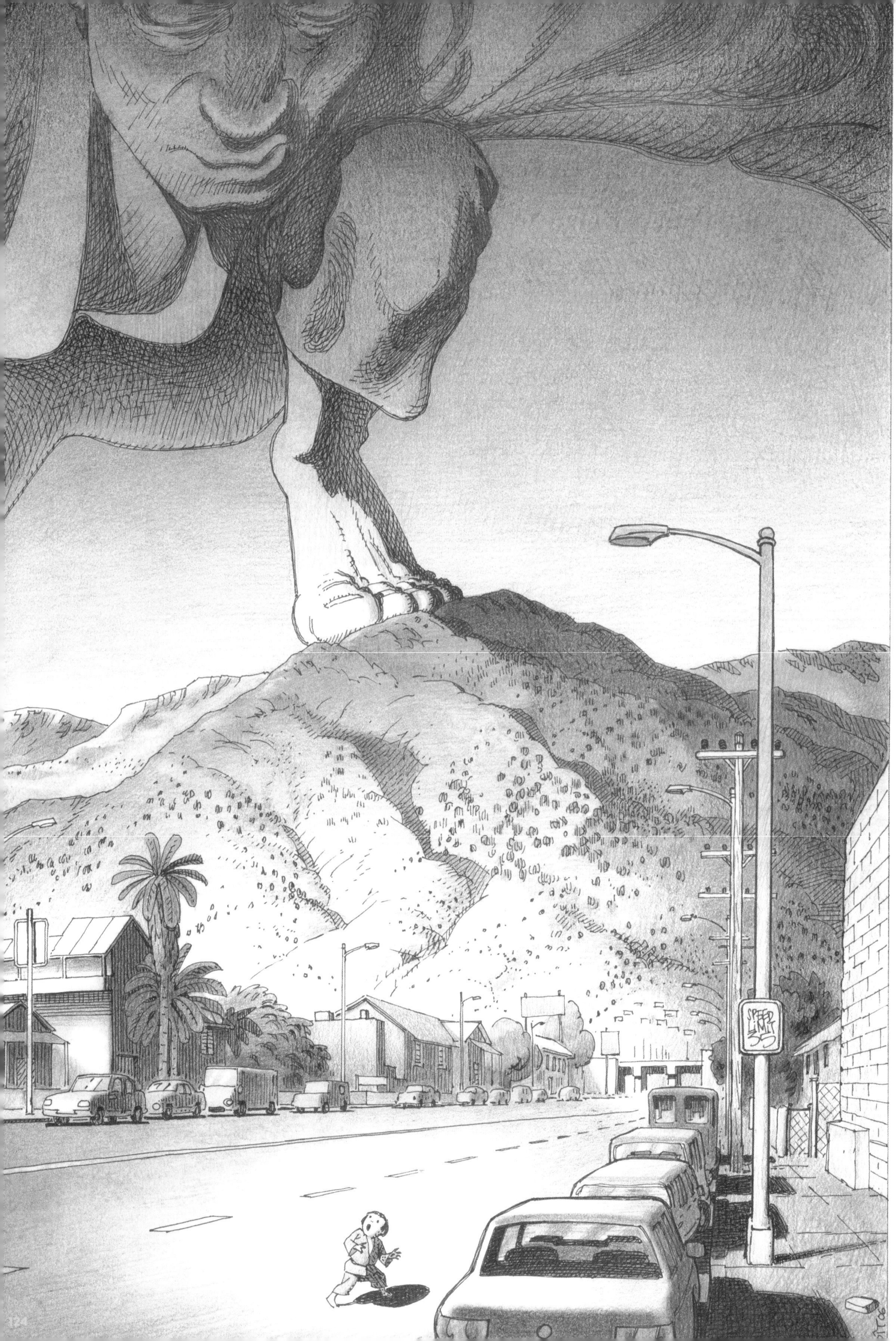
SPEED LIMIT 35

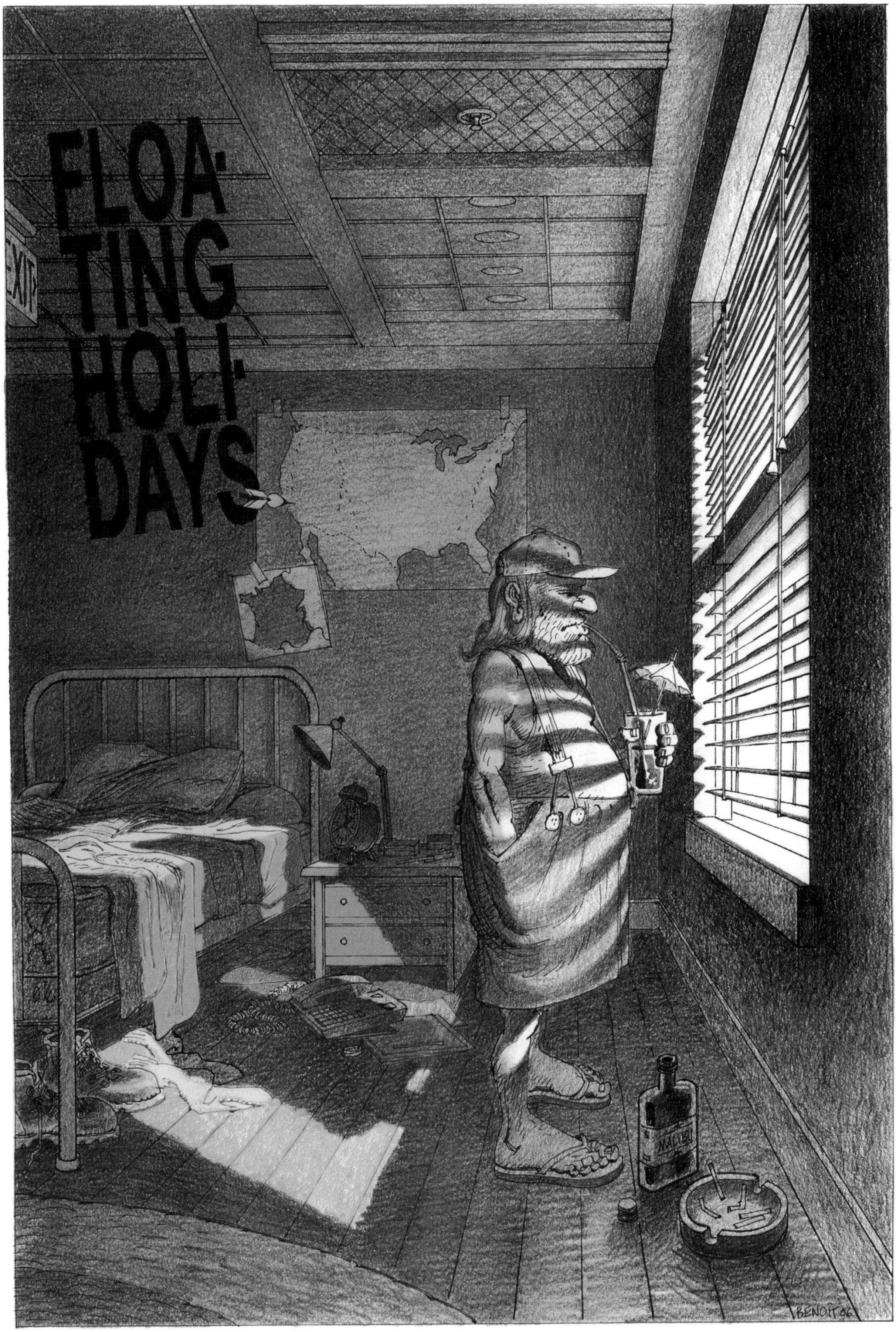

FLOA-
TING
HOLI-
DAYS
EXIT
BENOIT 06

ECHOES
FROM A SILENT
WELL

Of his journey he proclaimed
to have understood
human life from above.
"We are all haunted
by the resonating echoes of our past.
And on their fading ripples

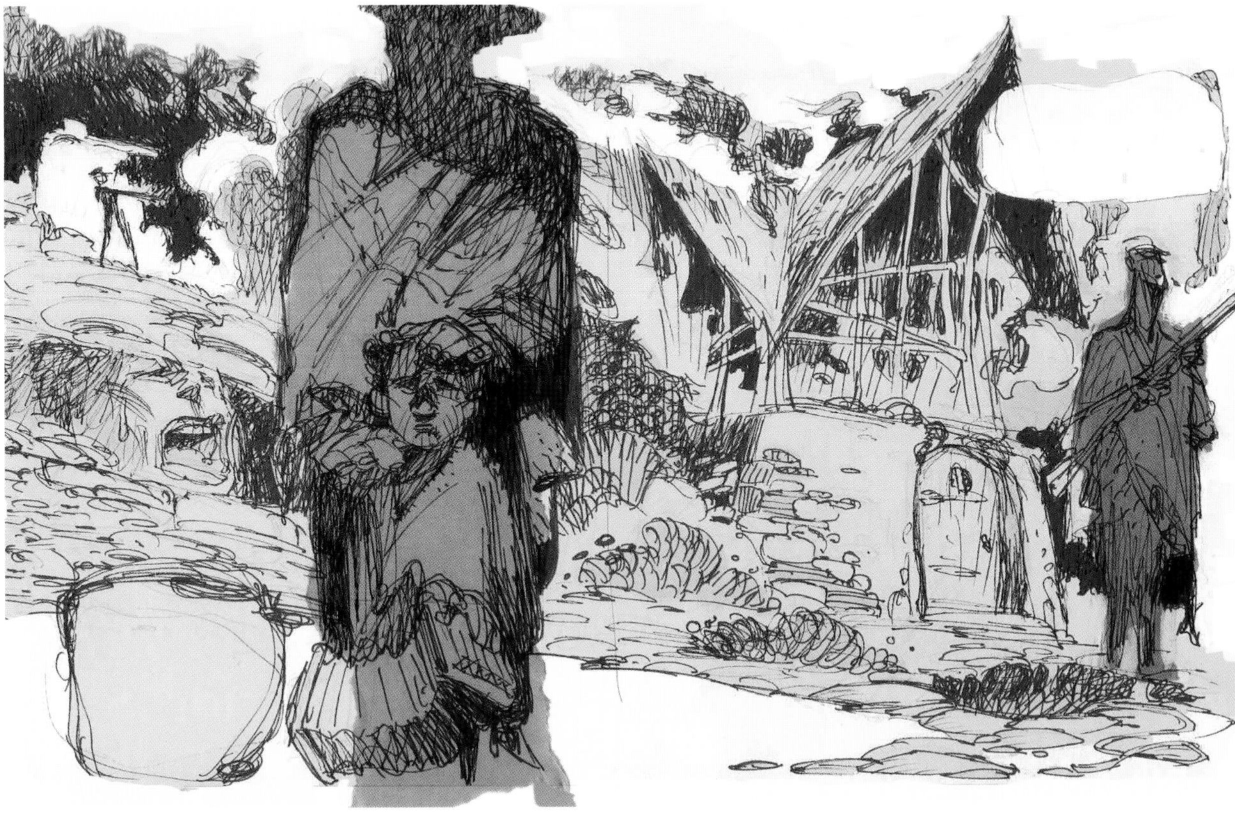

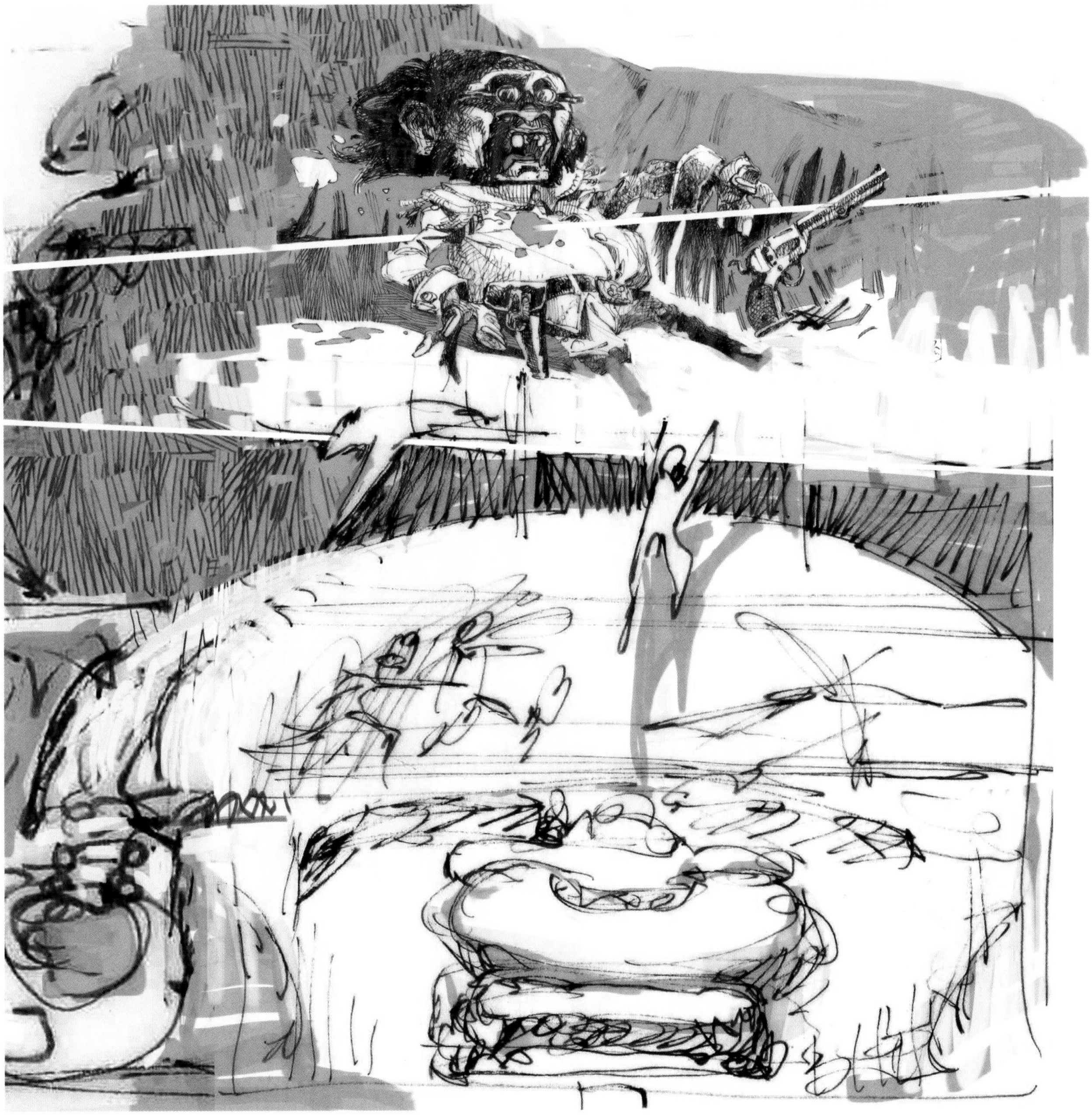

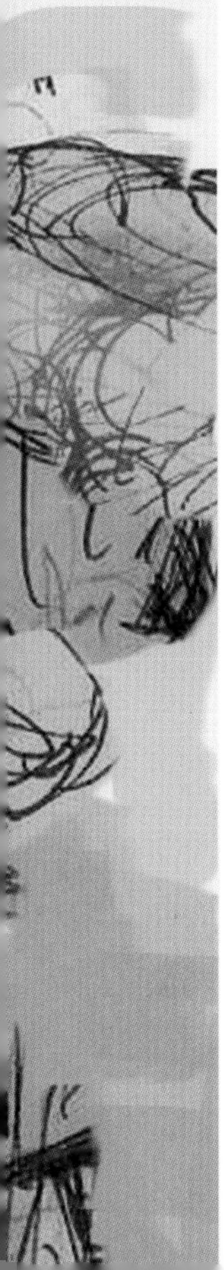

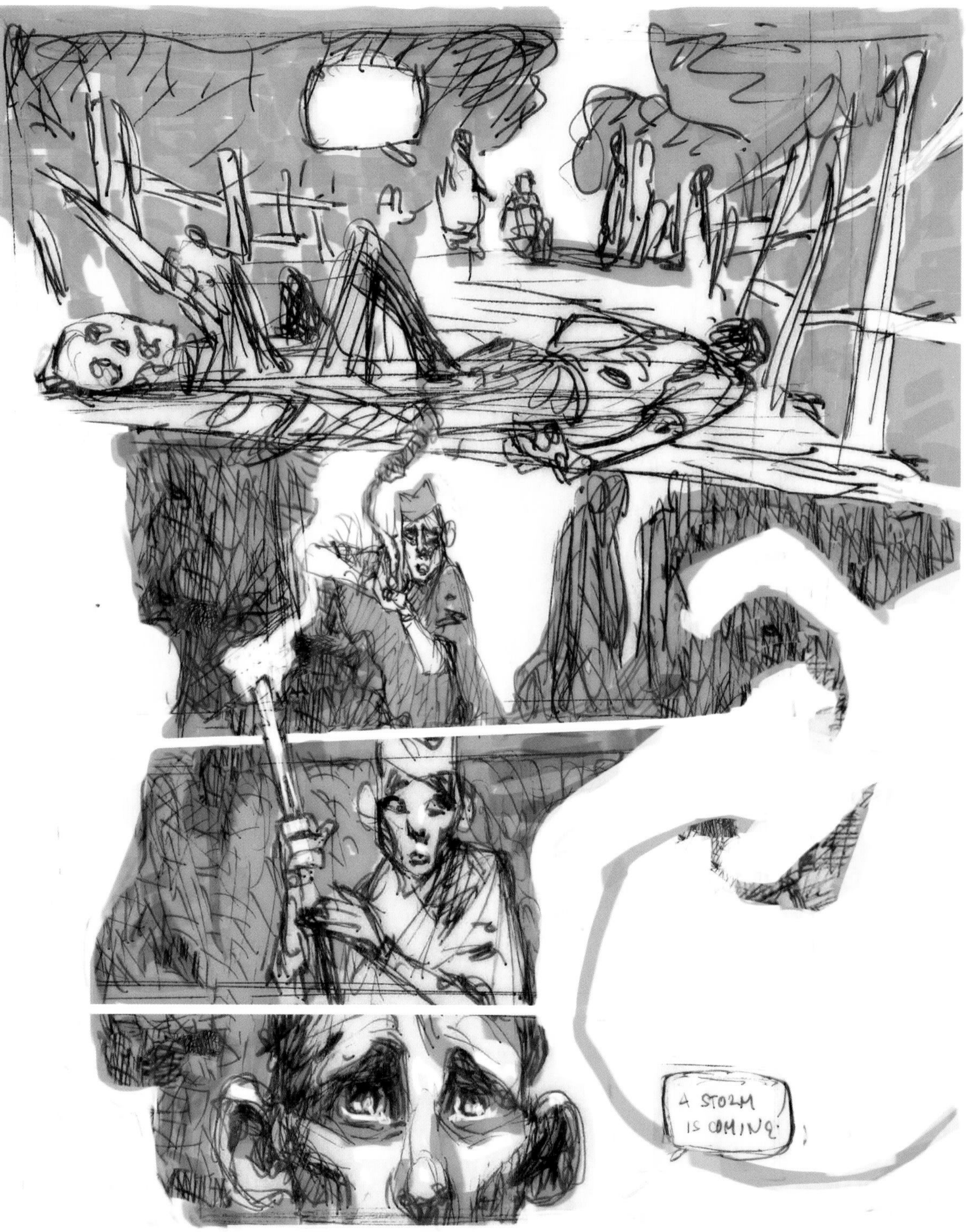
A STORM IS COMING

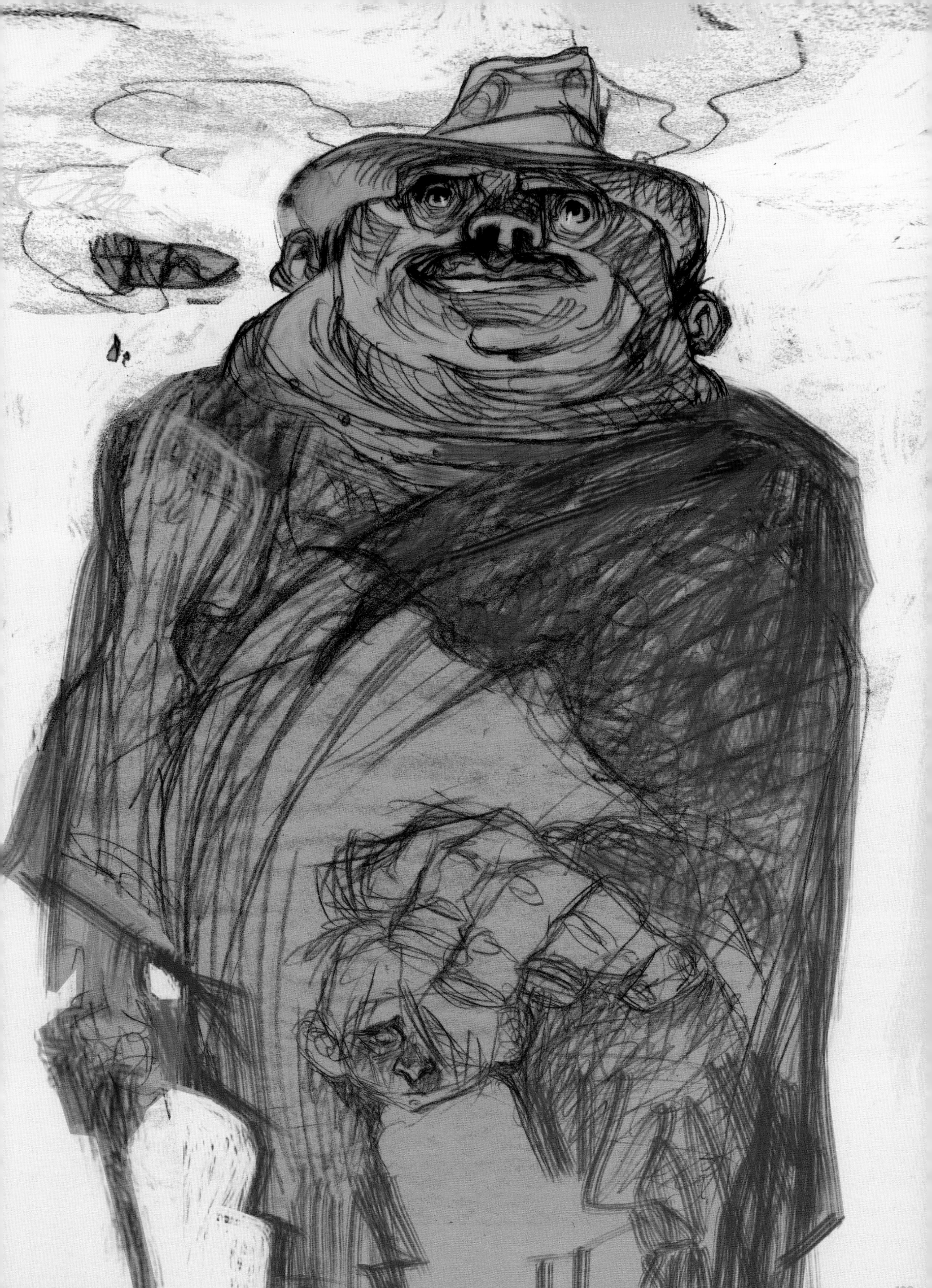

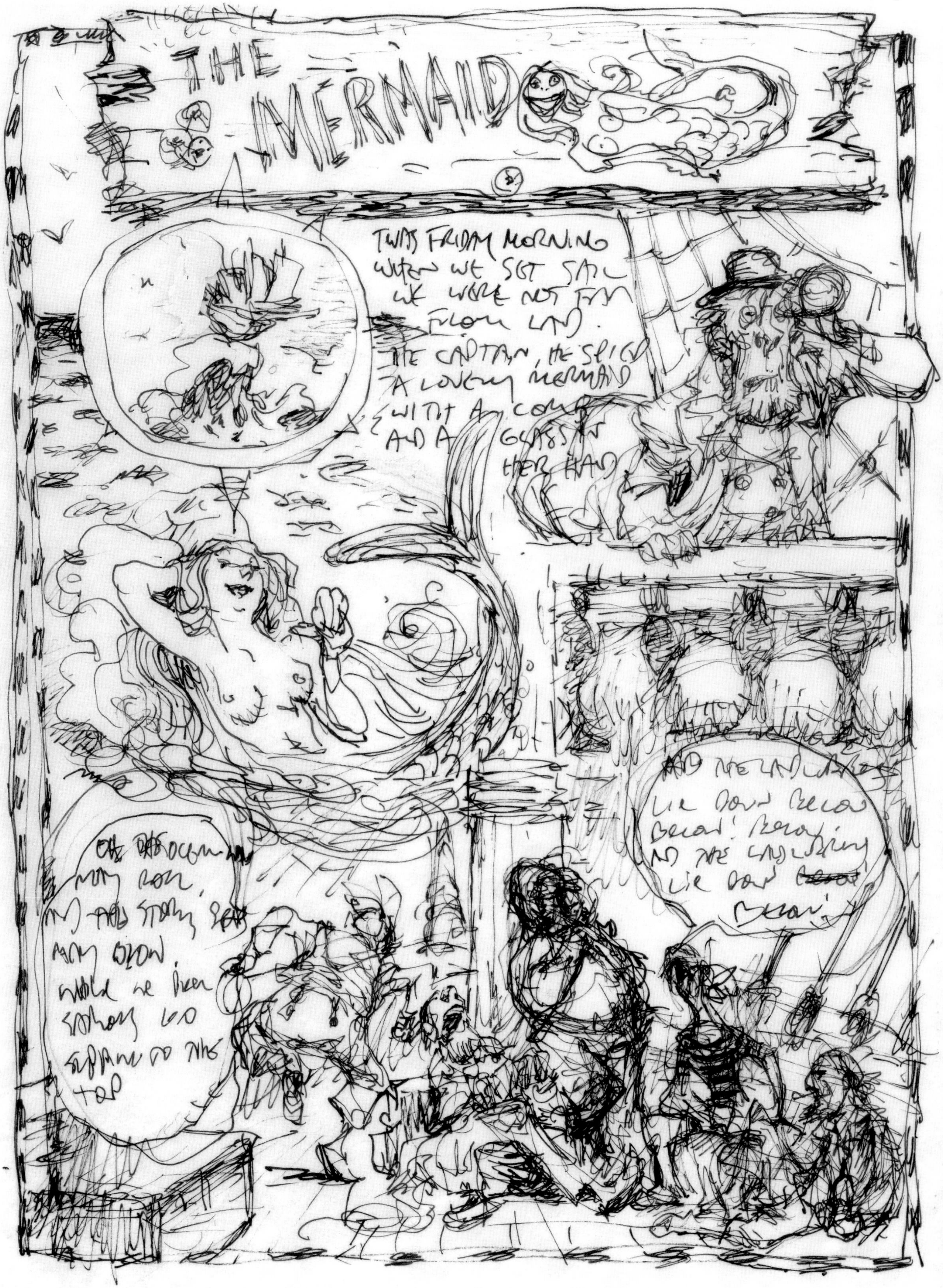
THE MERMAID
TWAS FRIDAY MORNING WHEN WE SET SAIL WE WERE NOT FAR FROM LAND. THE CAPTAIN, HE SPIED A LOVELY MERMAID WITH A COMB AND A GLASS IN HER HAND
LIE DOWN BELOW

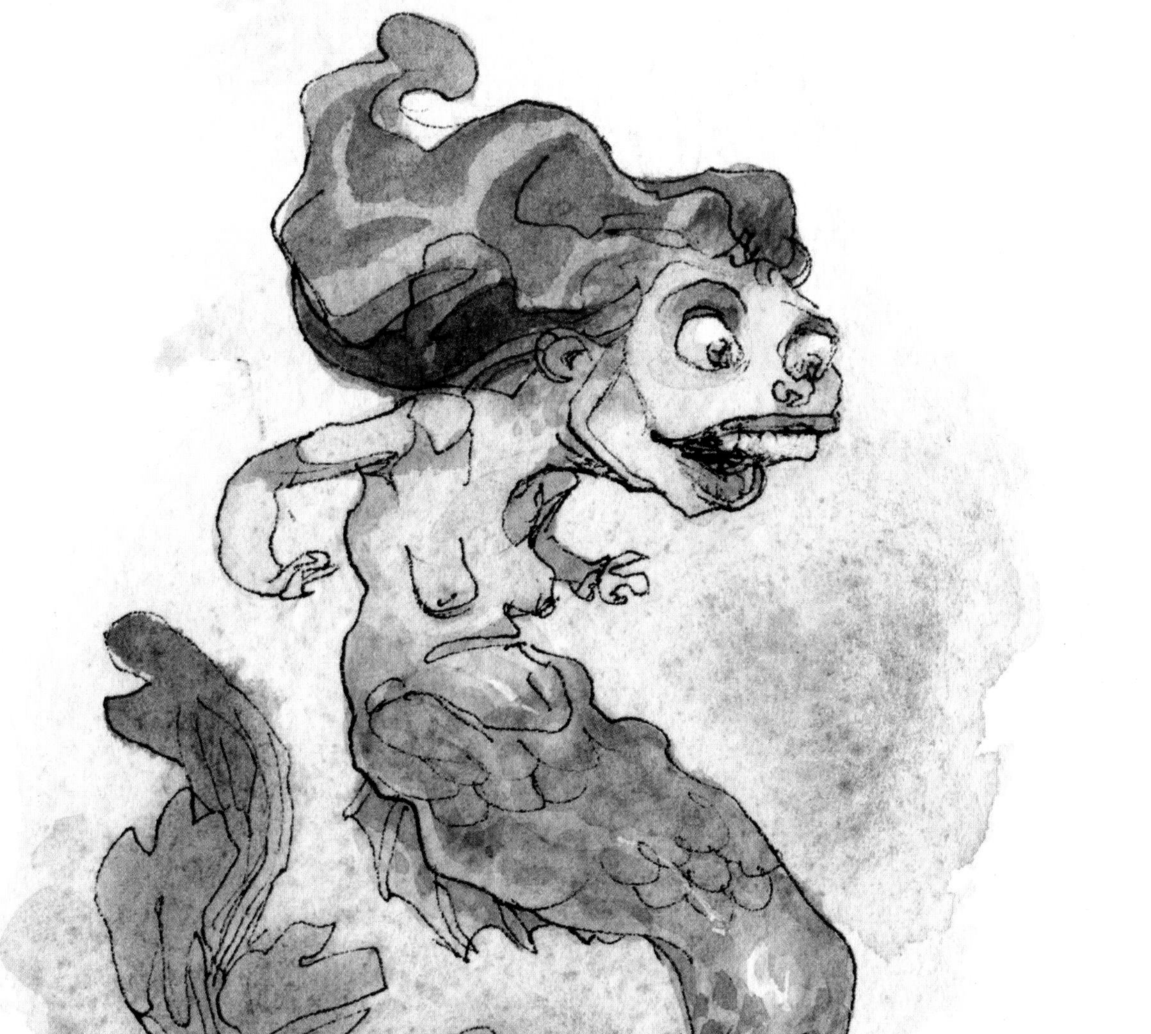

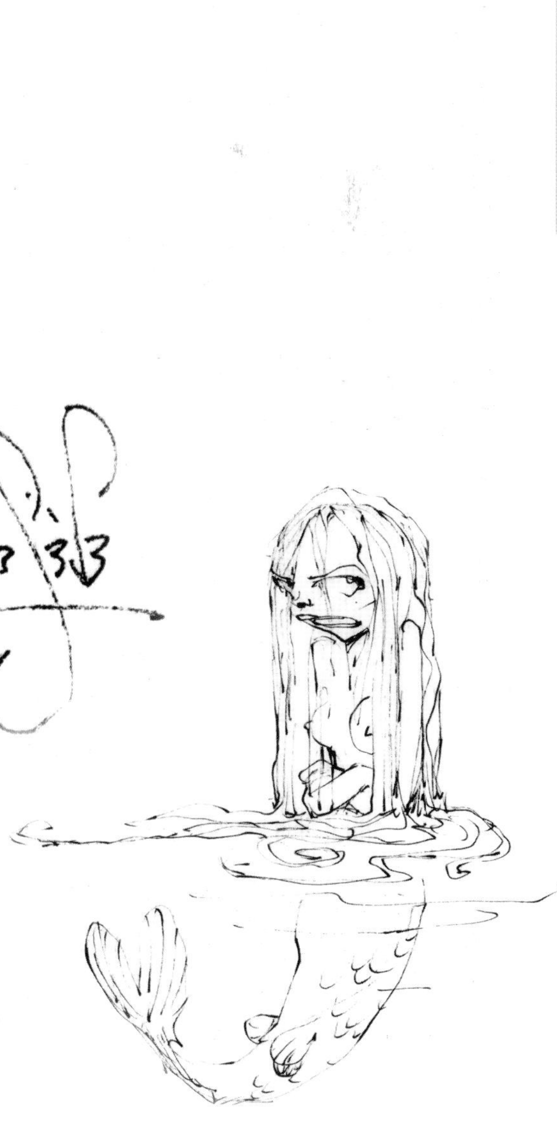

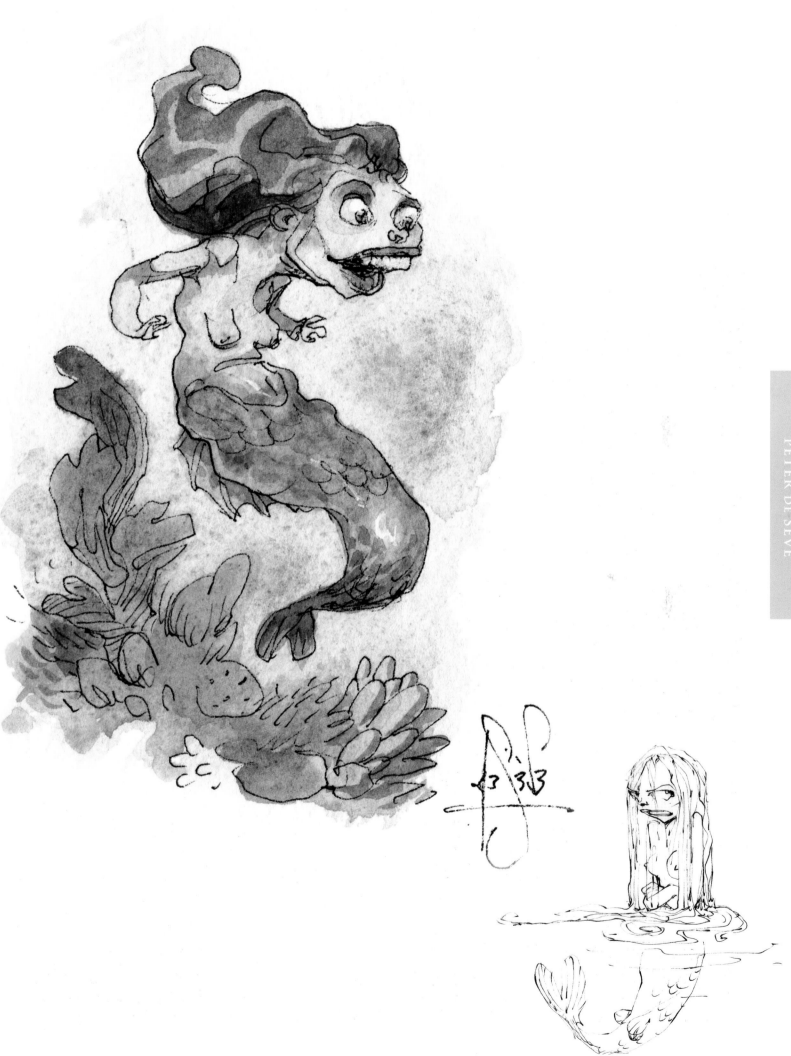

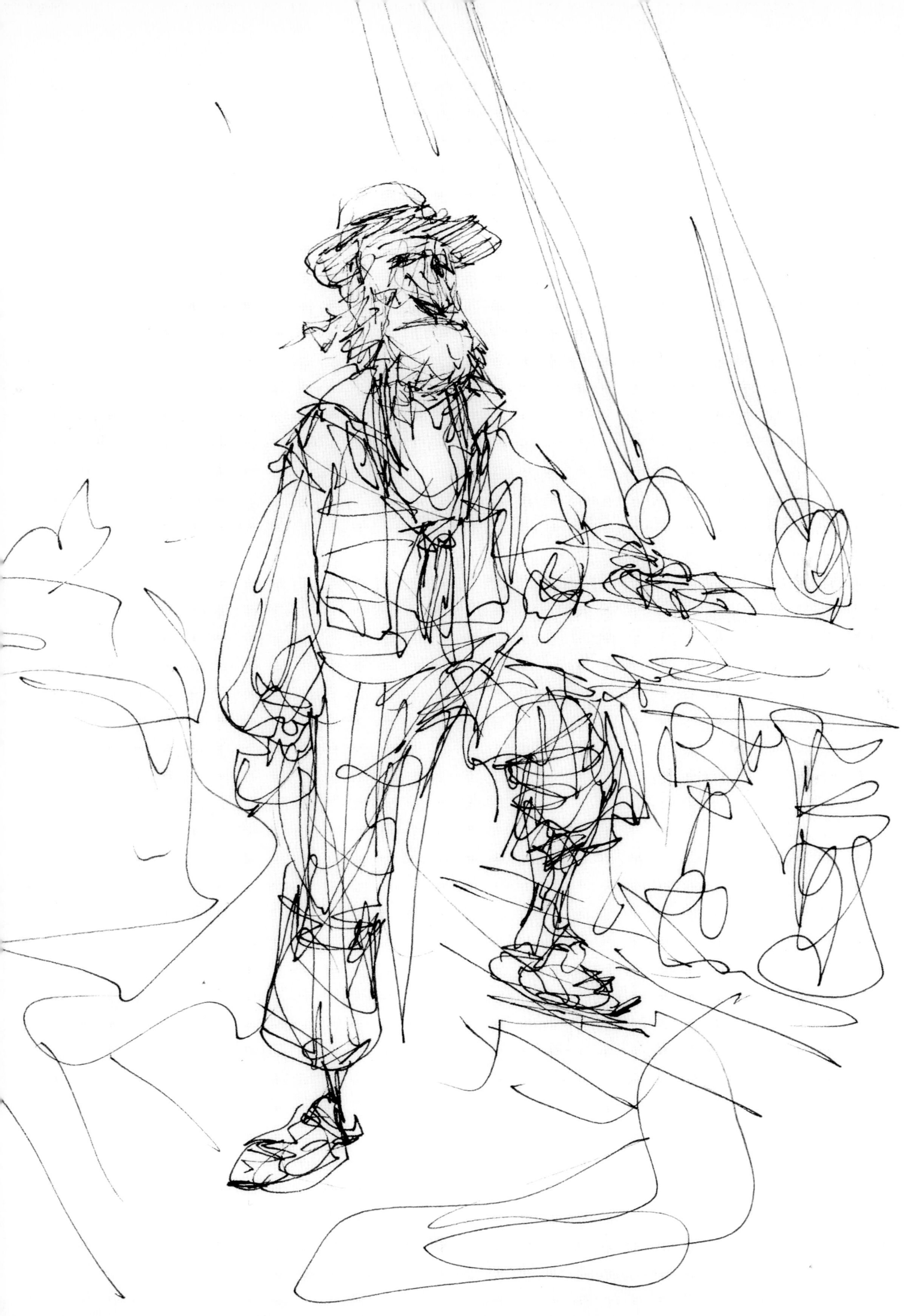

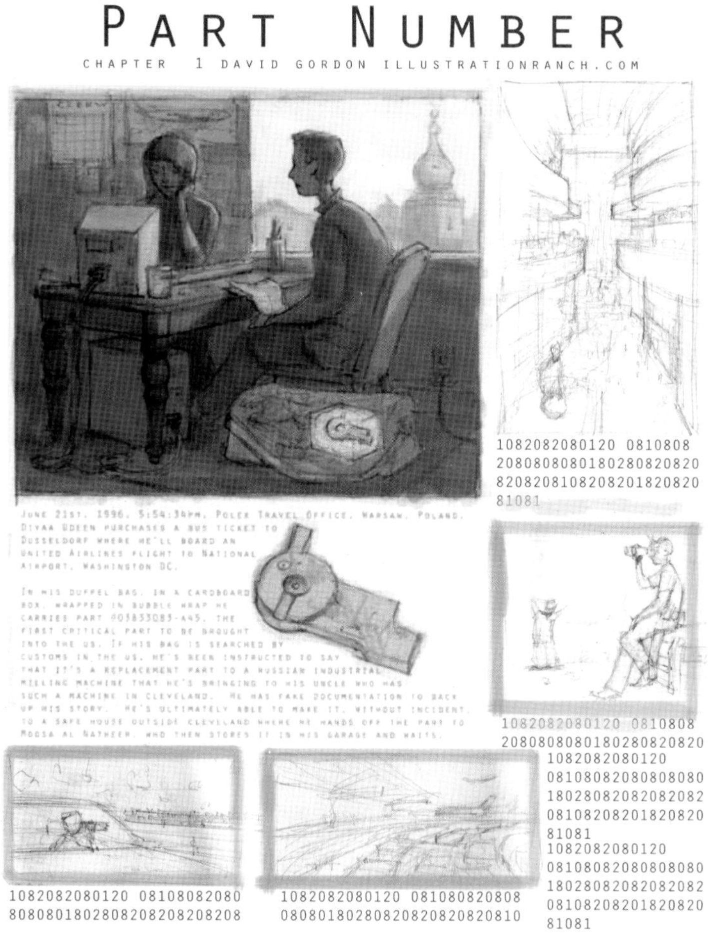

PART NUMBER

1082082080120 0810808
20808080801802808208208
20820820810820201820820
81081

June 21st, 1996, 5:54:34pm, Polex Travel Office, Warsaw, Poland.
Diyaa Udeen purchases a bus ticket to
Dusseldorf where he'll board an
United Airlines flight to National
Airport, Washington DC.

In his duffel bag, in a cardboard
box, wrapped in bubble wrap he
carries part #03833083-445. The
first critical part to be brought
into the US. If his bag is searched by
customs in the US, he's been instructed to say
that it's a replacement part to a Russian industrial
milling machine that he's bringing to his uncle who has
such a machine in Cleveland. He has fake documentation to back
up his story. He's ultimately able to make it, without incident,
to a safe house outside Cleveland where he hands off the part to
Moosa al Natheer, who then stores it in his garage and waits.

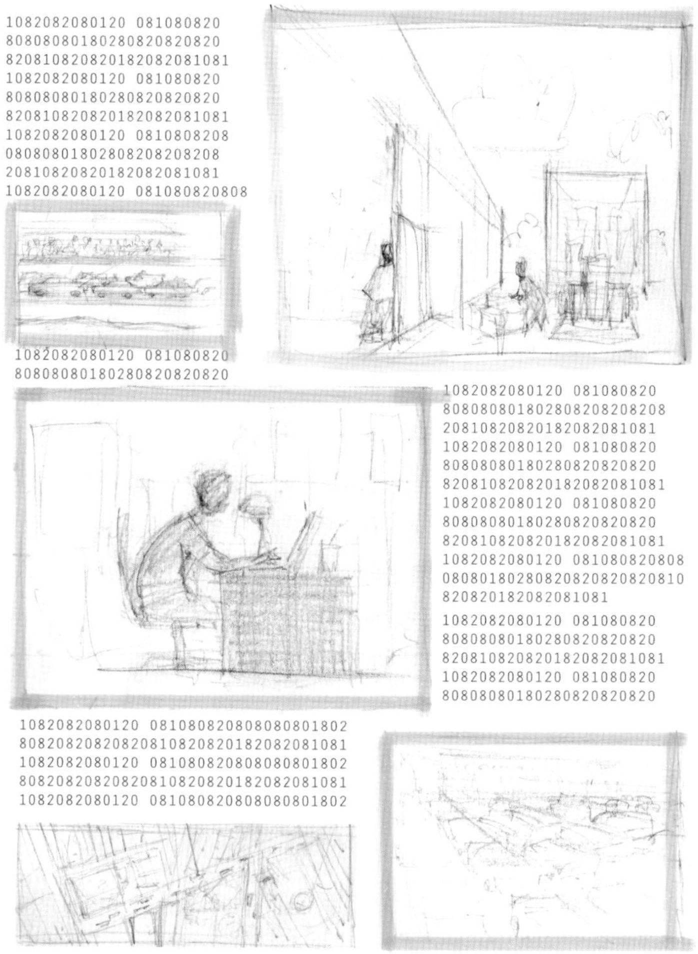

1082082080120 0810808
20808080801802808208208
1082082080120
0810808208080808080
180280820820820820
081082082018208208
1082082080120
0810808208080808080
180280820820820820
08108208201820820
81081

1082082080120 0810808208080808080
80808018028082082082082082082082082
0808018028082082082082082082082081

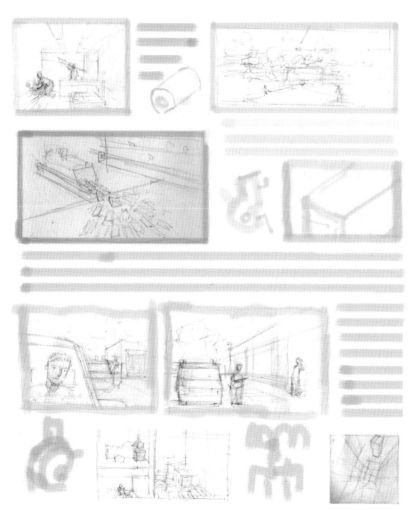

1082082080120 0810808
2080808080180280820820
1082082080120
0810808208080808080
180280820820820820
08108208201820820
81081

1082082080120 081080820
8080808018028082082082082082082
8208108208201820820810810820810
1082082080120 081080820
8080808018028082082082082082082
8208108208201820820810810820810
1082082080120 081080820
8080808018028082082082082082082082080
208108208208201820820810810
1082082080120 081080820808

1082082080120 081080820
80808080180280820820820

1082082080120 081080820
8080808018028082082082082082082082082082082082
208108208208201820820820820810810
1082082080120 081080820
80808080180280820820820820820820
8208108208208201820820810810
1082082080120 081080820
80808080180280820820820820820820
8208108208208201820820810810
1082082080120 081080820808
080801802808208208208208080820810
820820182082081081

1082082080120 081080820
80808080180280820820820
820810820820182082081081
1082082080120 081080820
80808080180280820820820

1082082080120 081080820808080801802
80820820820820810820820182082081081
1082082080120 081080820808080801802
808208208208208018208208201820820810810
1082082080120 081080820808080801802

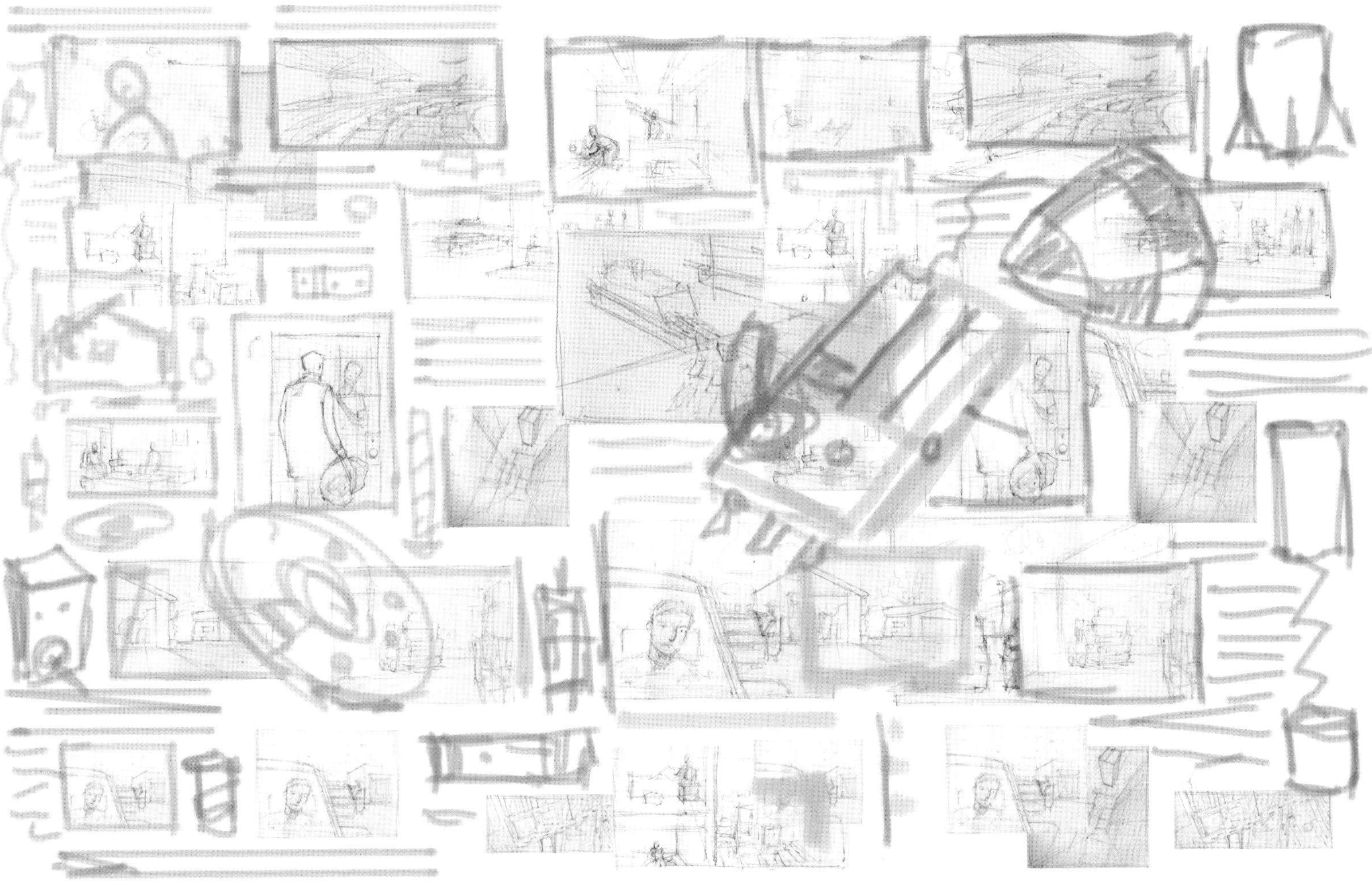

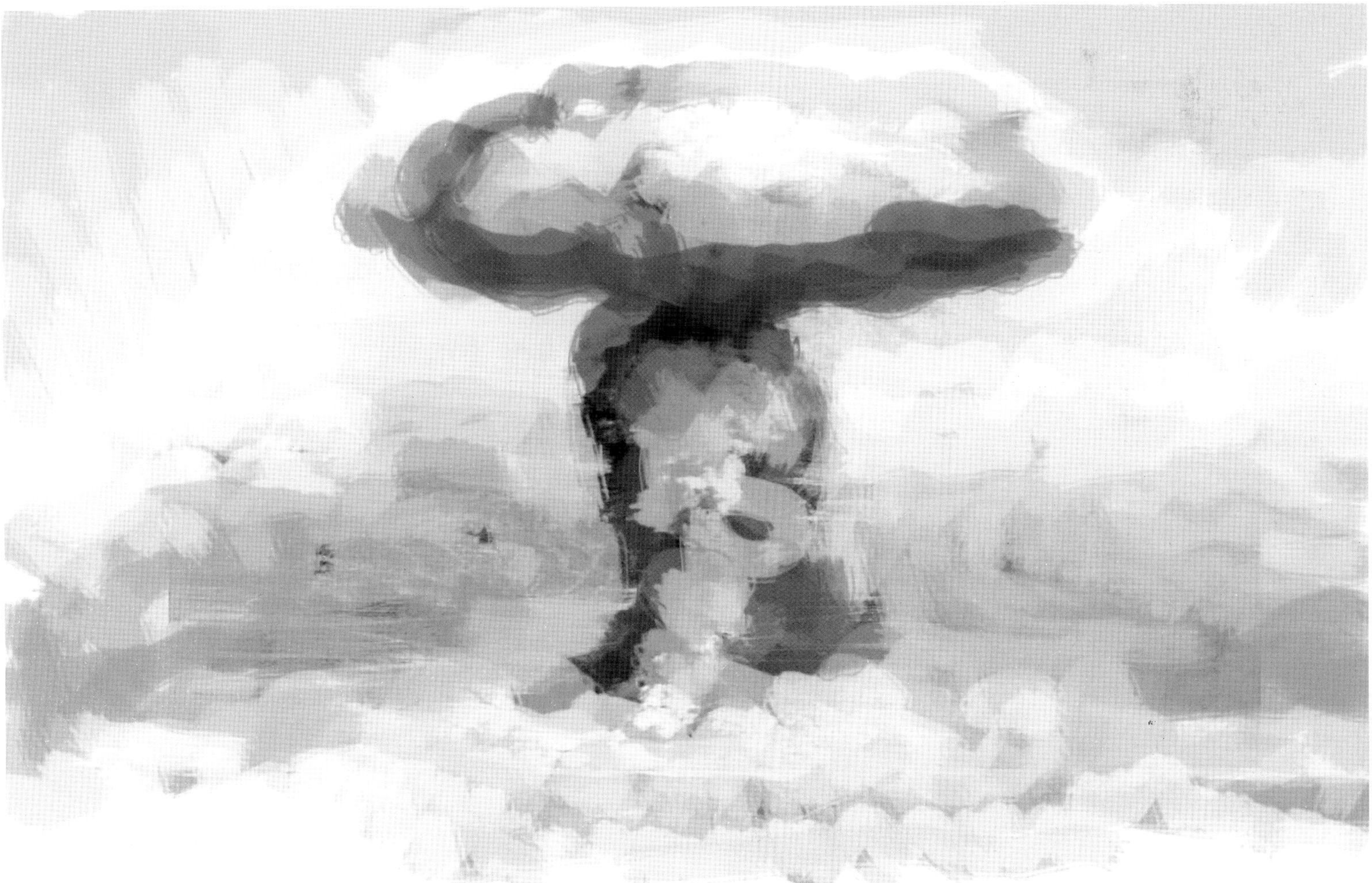

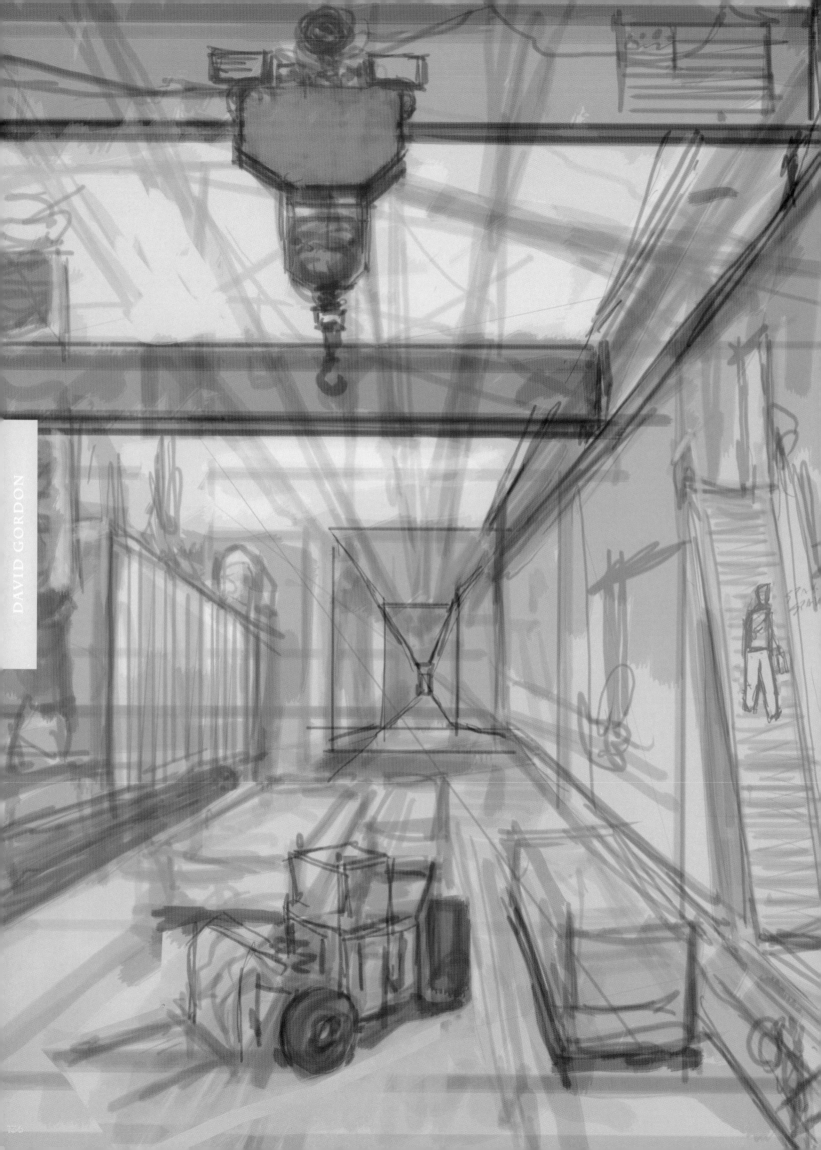

WATCH AND
CLOCK

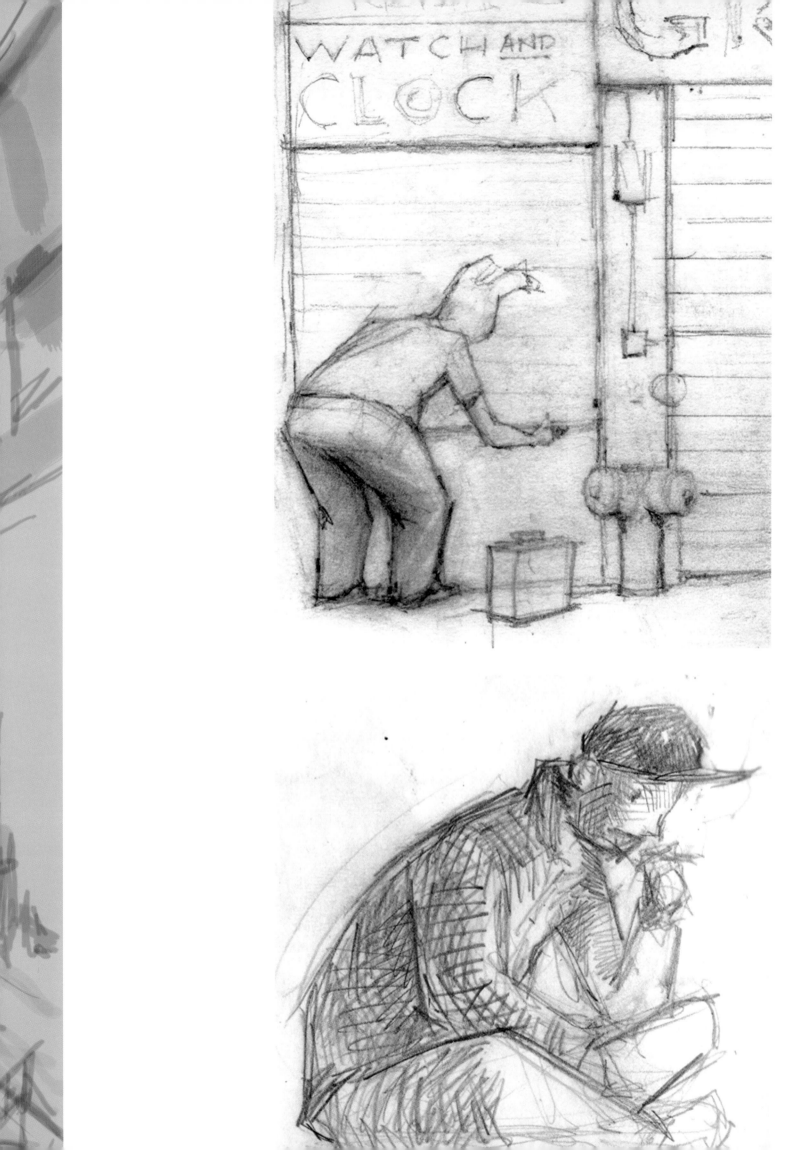

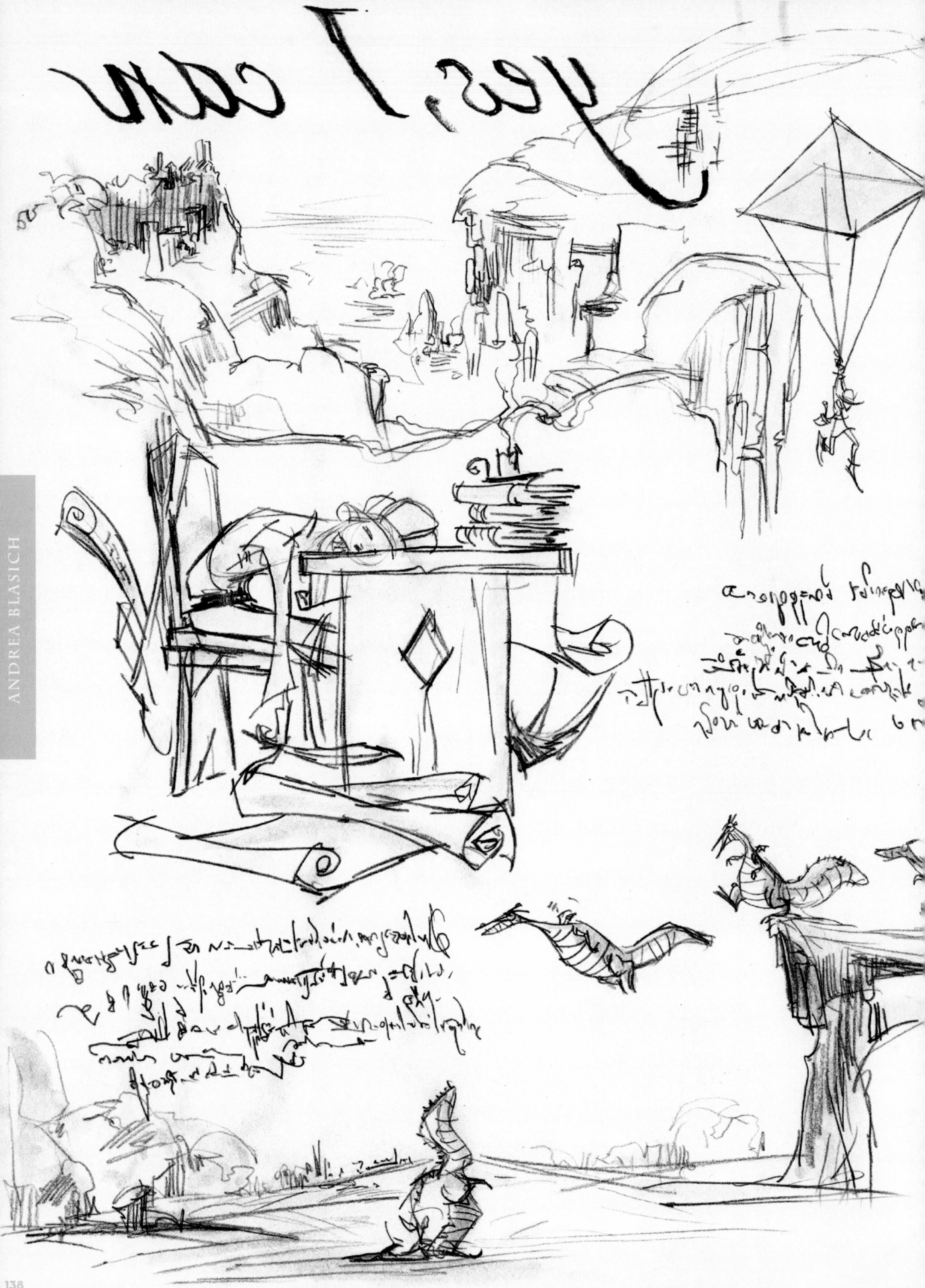

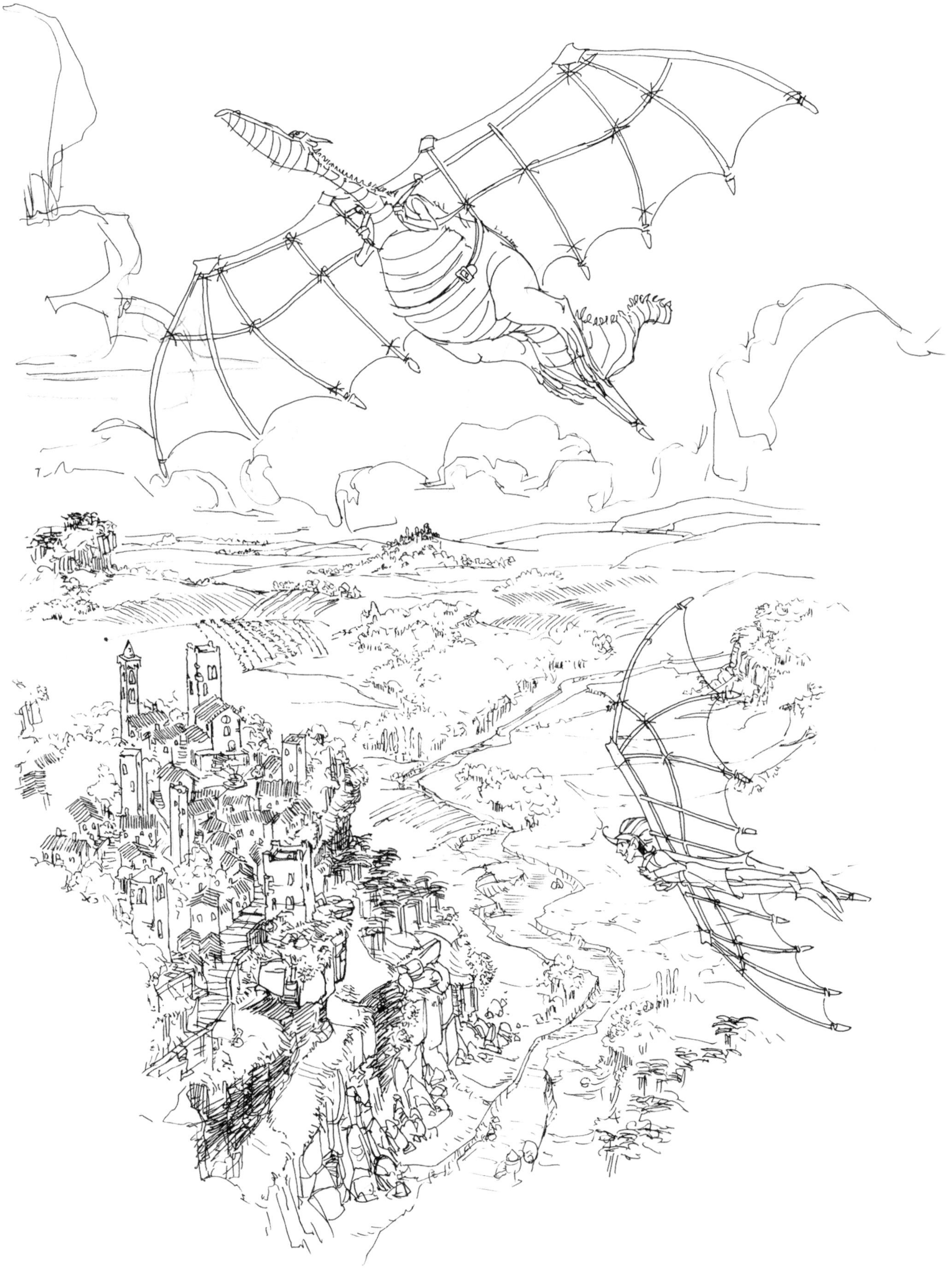

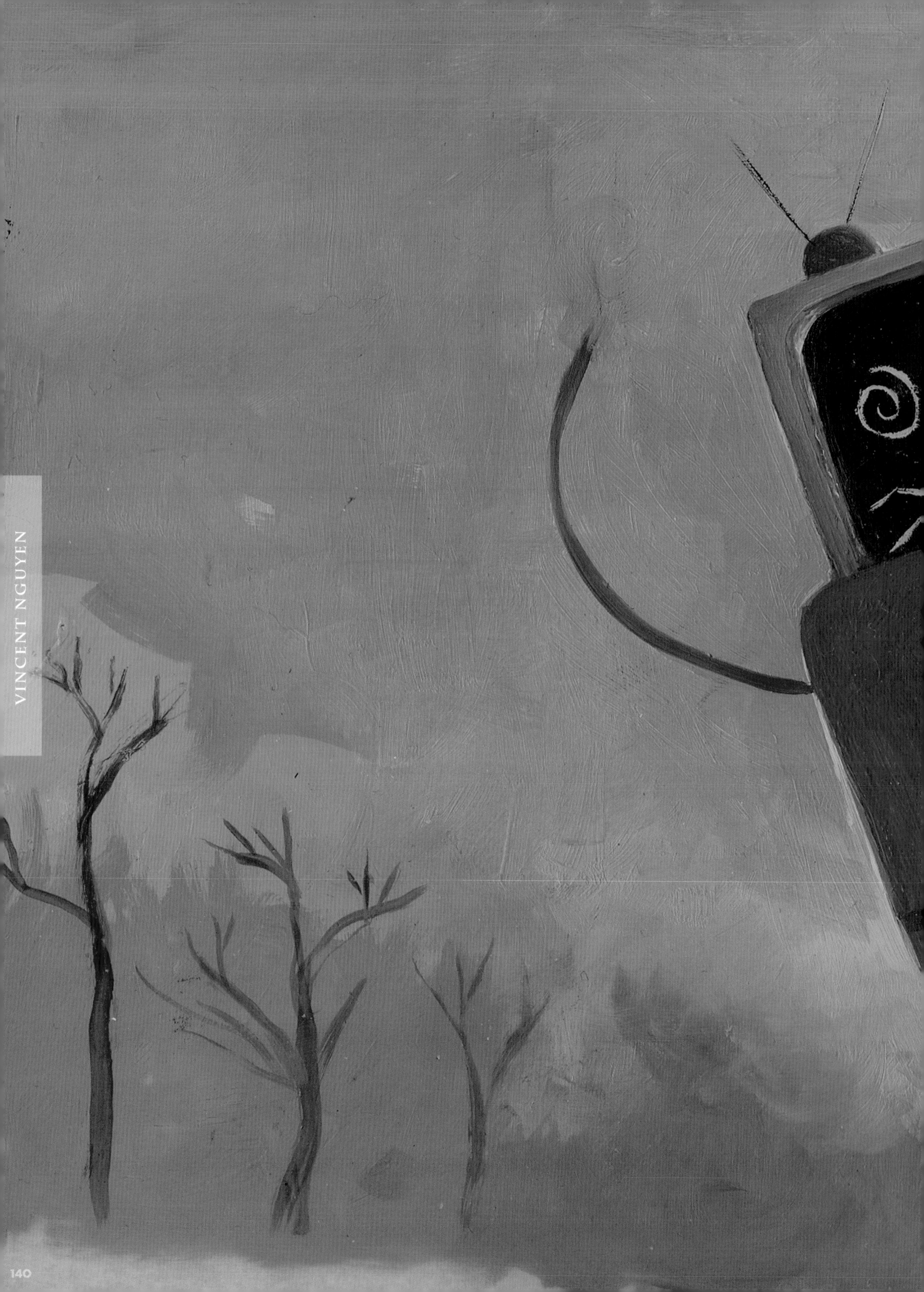

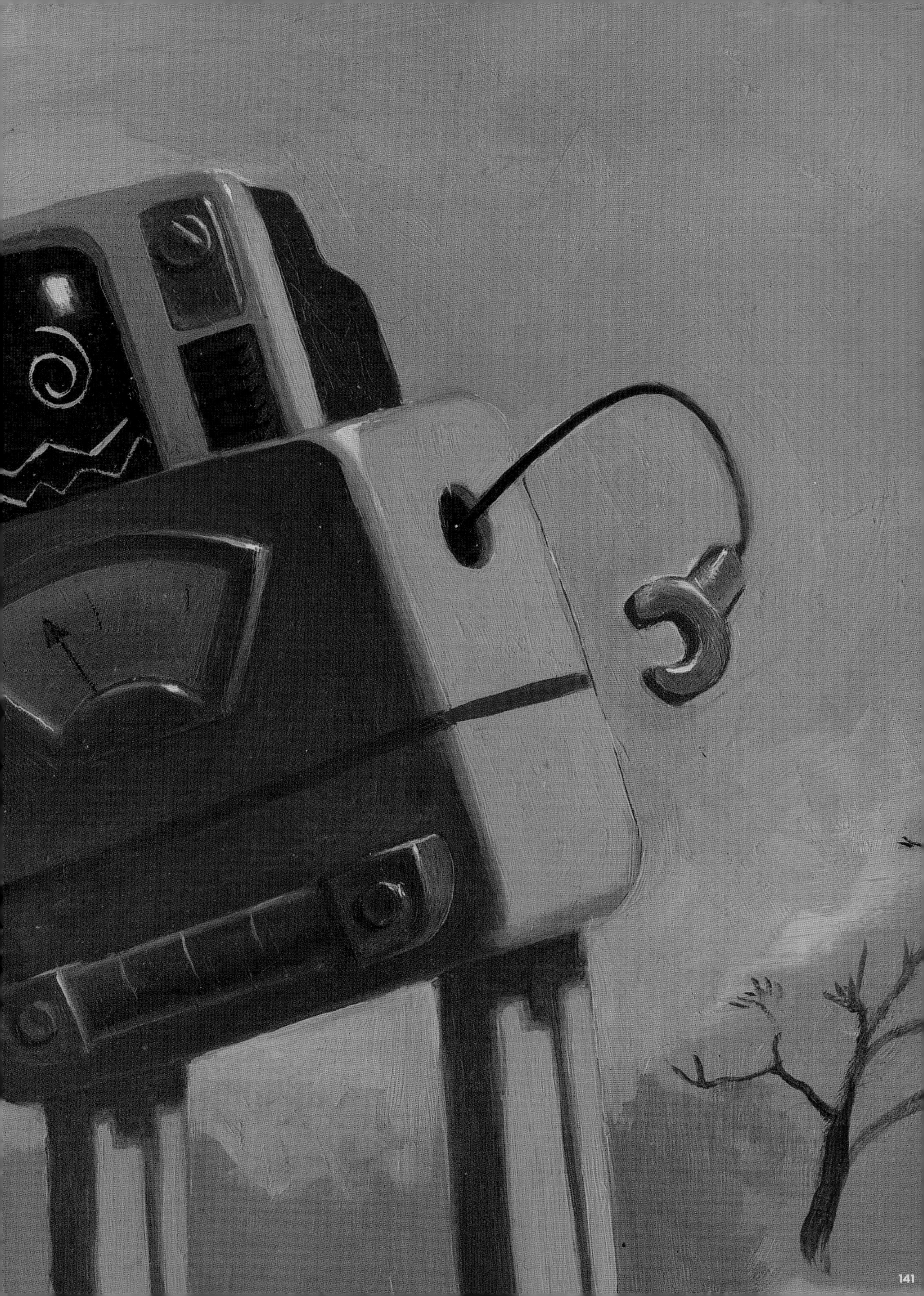

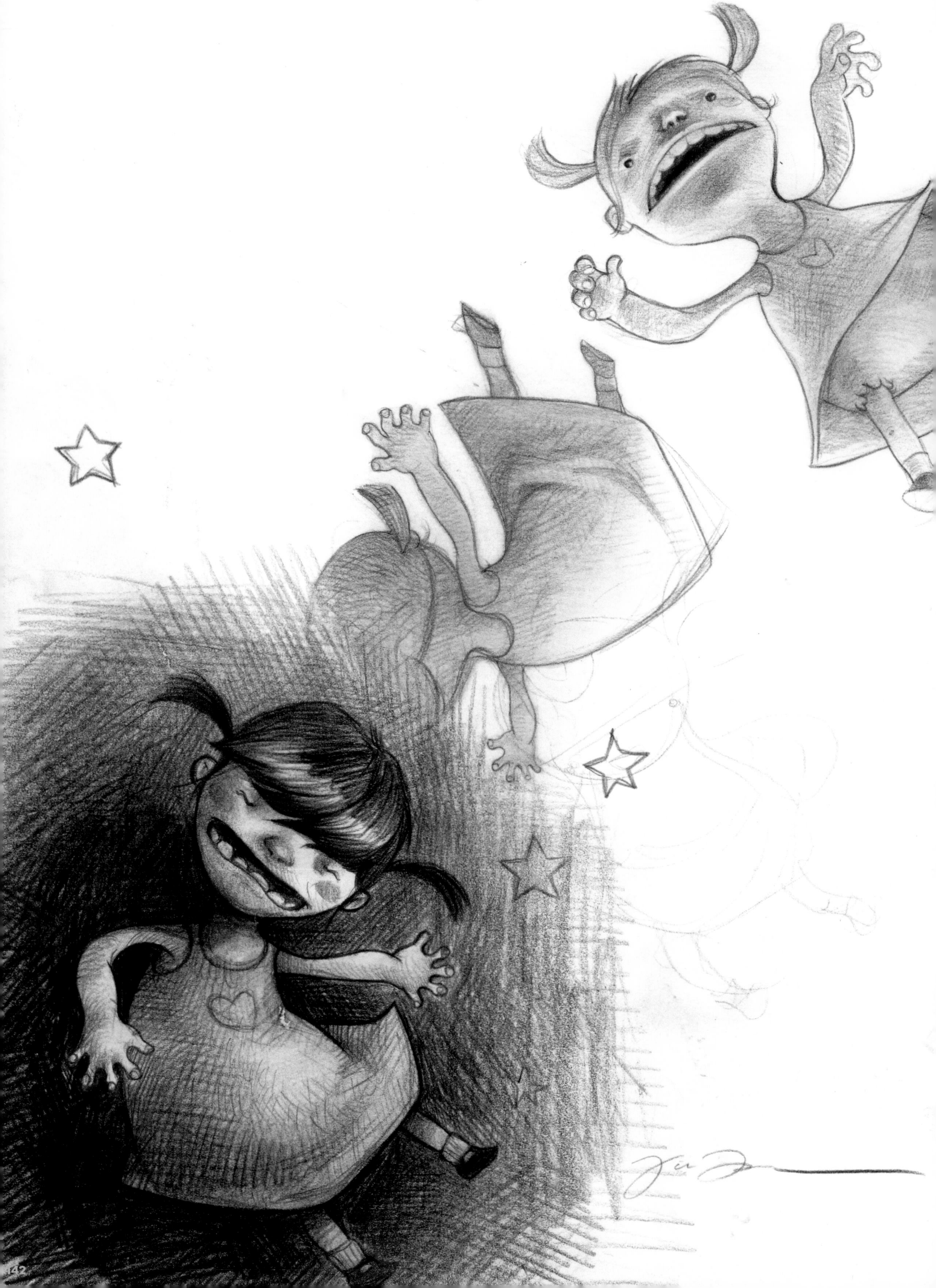

Dolly Driver

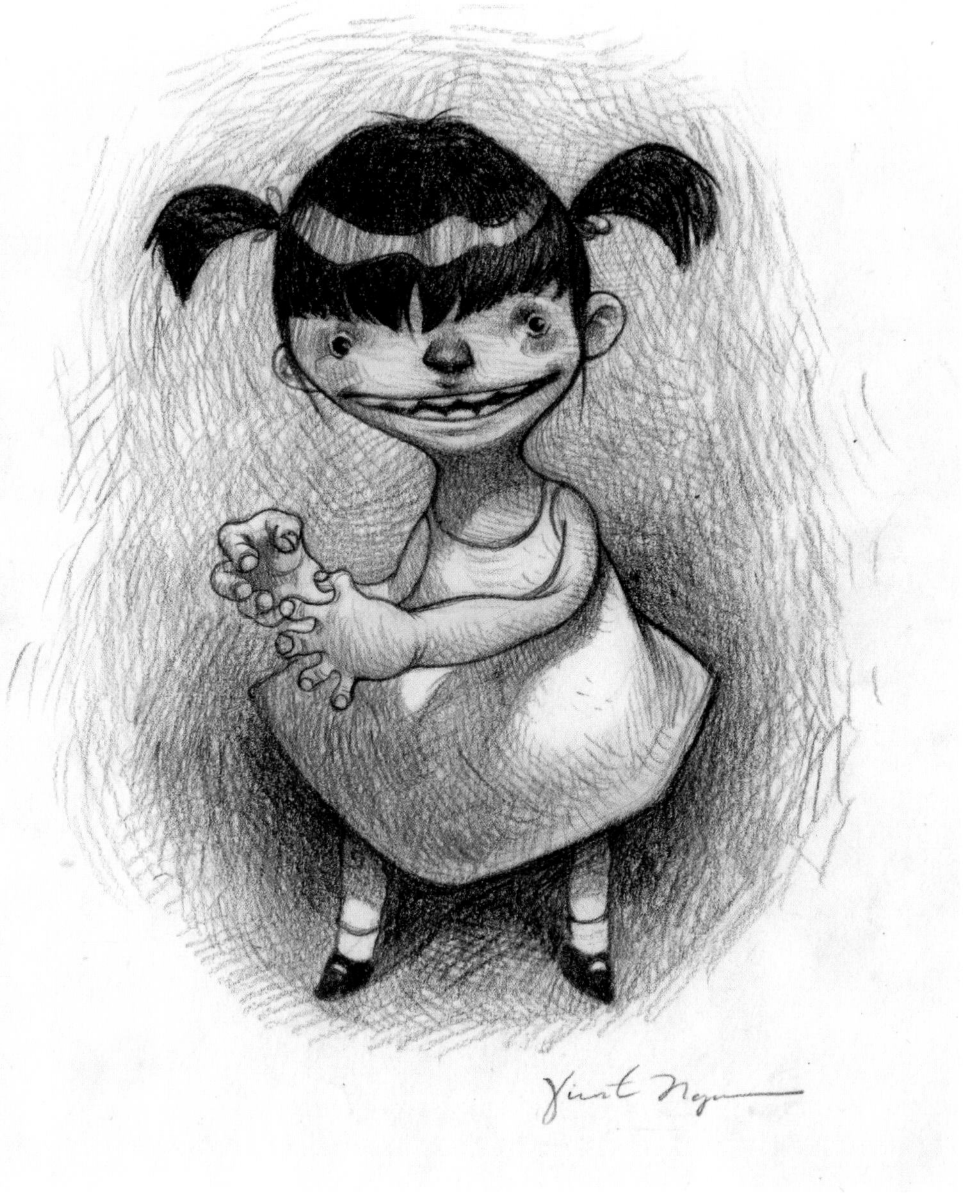

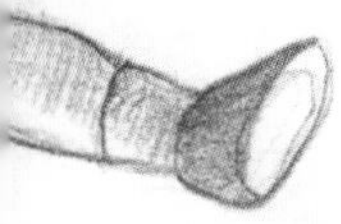

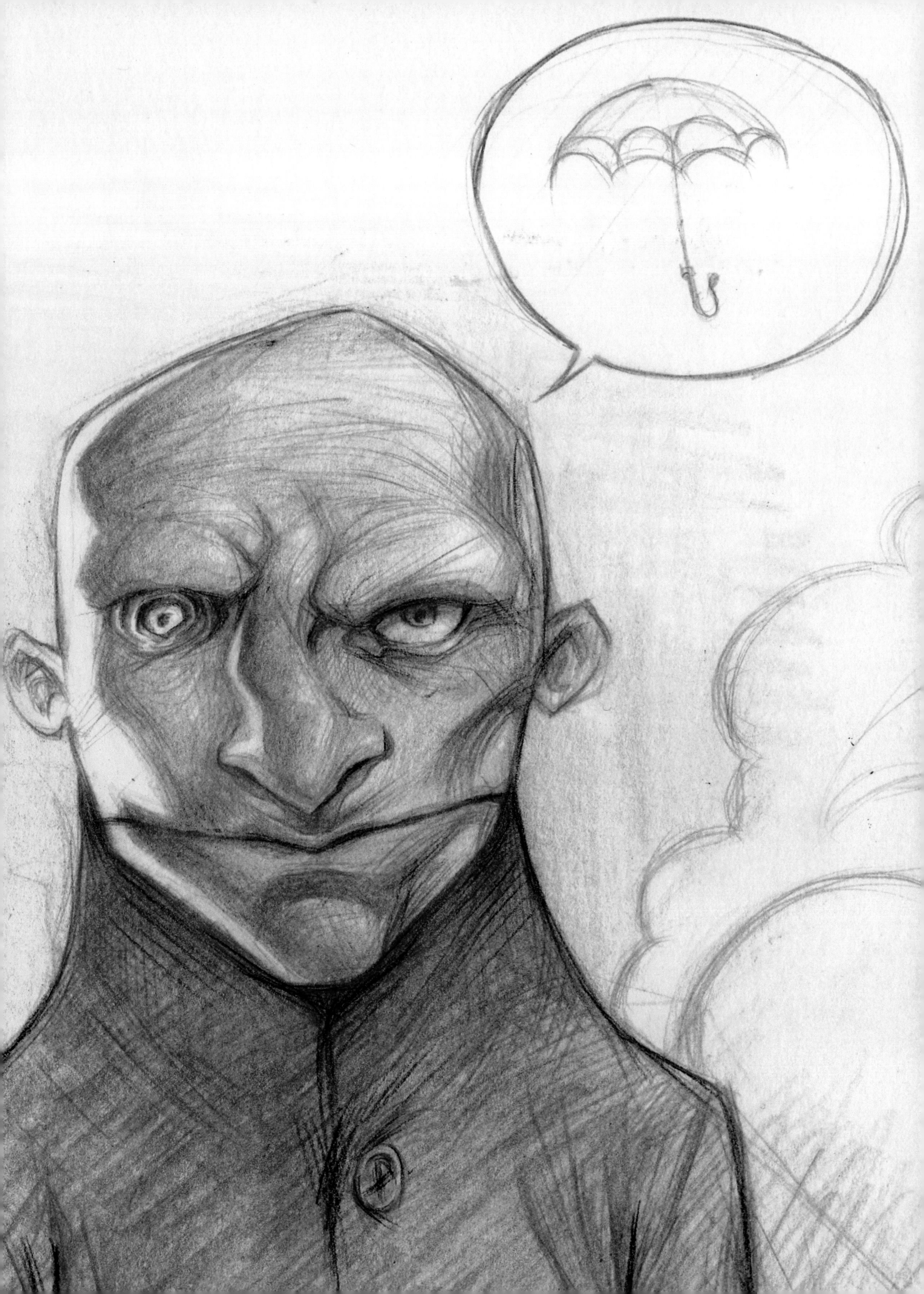

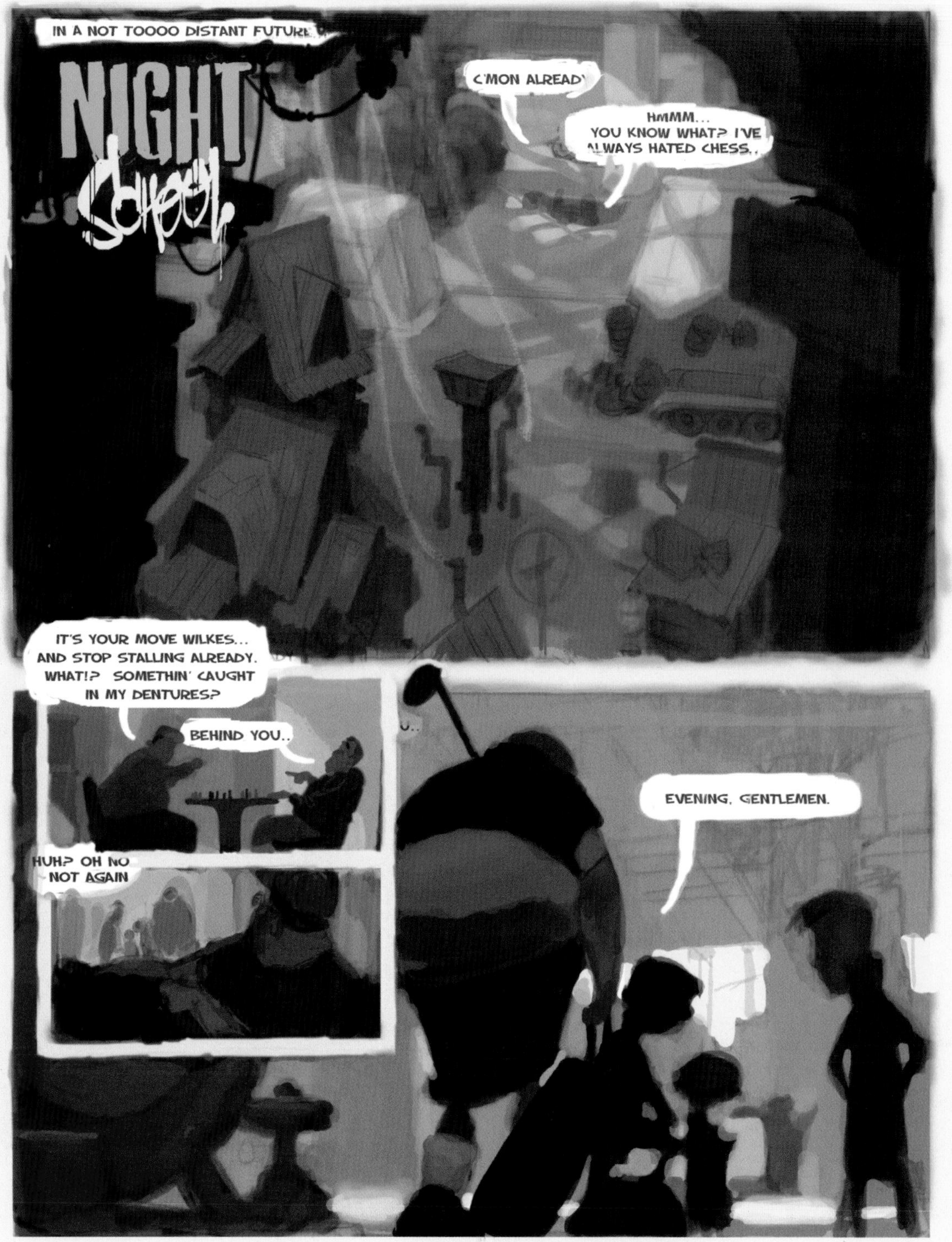

IN A NOT TOOOO DISTANT FUTURE
NIGHT
School
C'MON ALREAD
HMMM...
YOU KNOW WHAT? I'VE
ALWAYS HATED CHESS..
IT'S YOUR MOVE WILKES...
AND STOP STALLING ALREADY.
WHAT!? SOMETHIN' CAUGHT
IN MY DENTURES?
BEHIND YOU..
HUH? OH NO
NOT AGAIN
EVENING, GENTLEMEN.

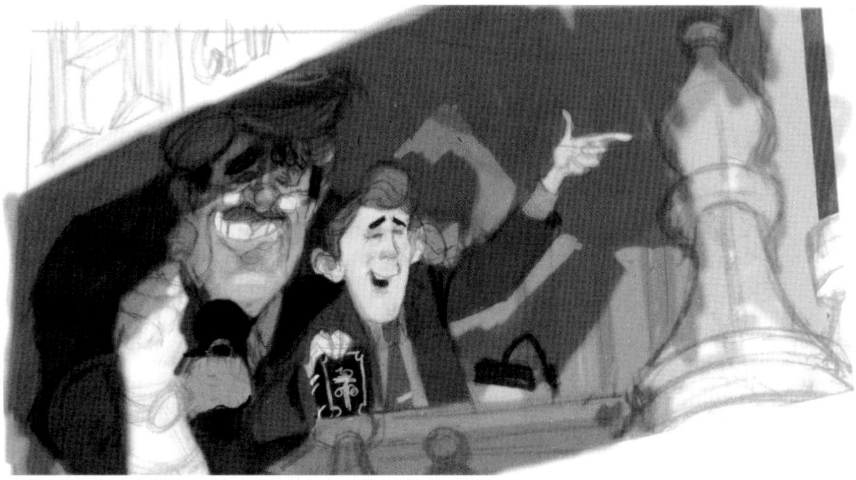

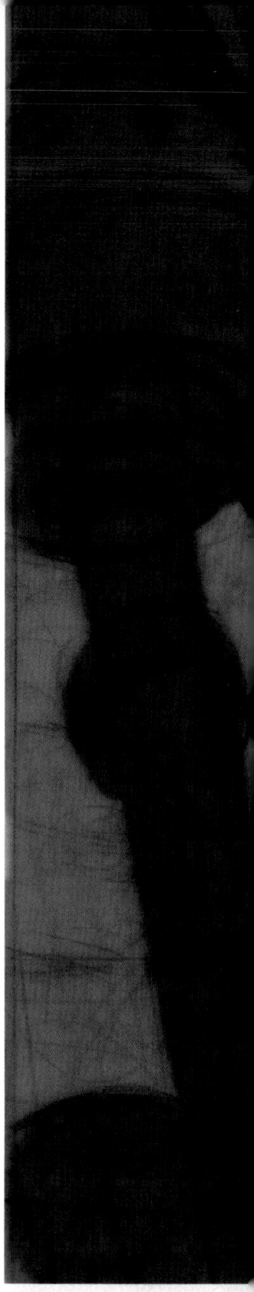

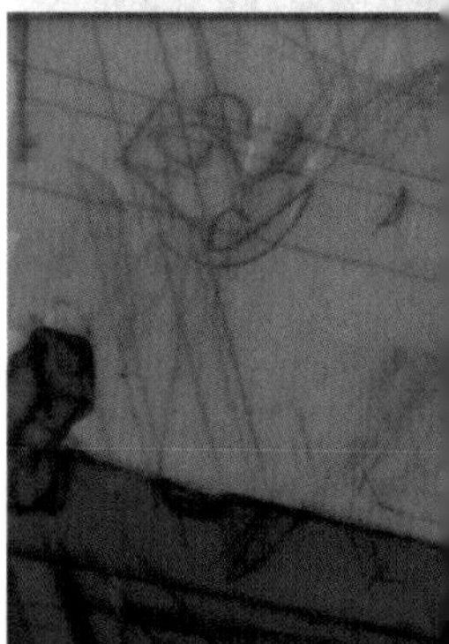

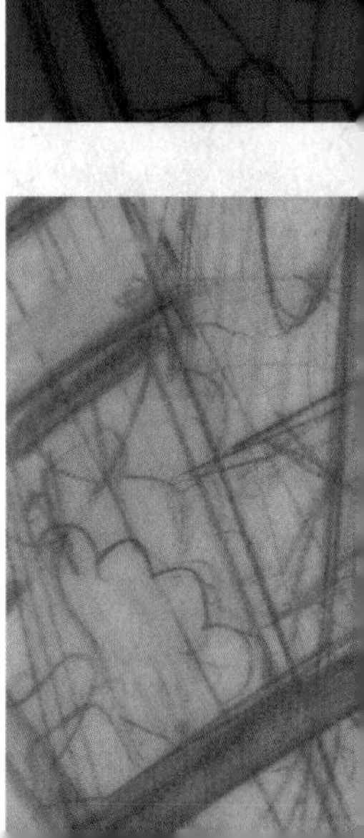

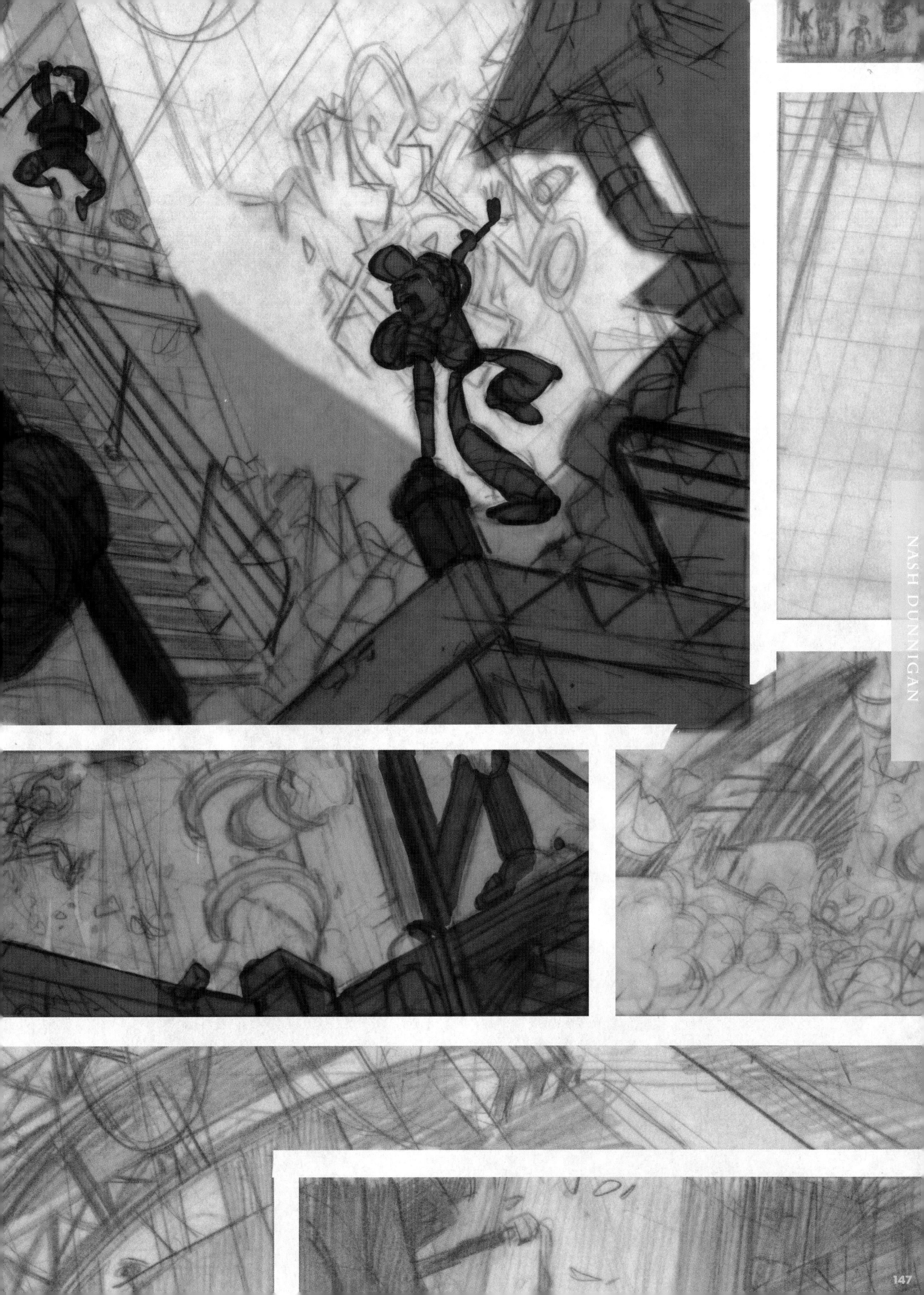

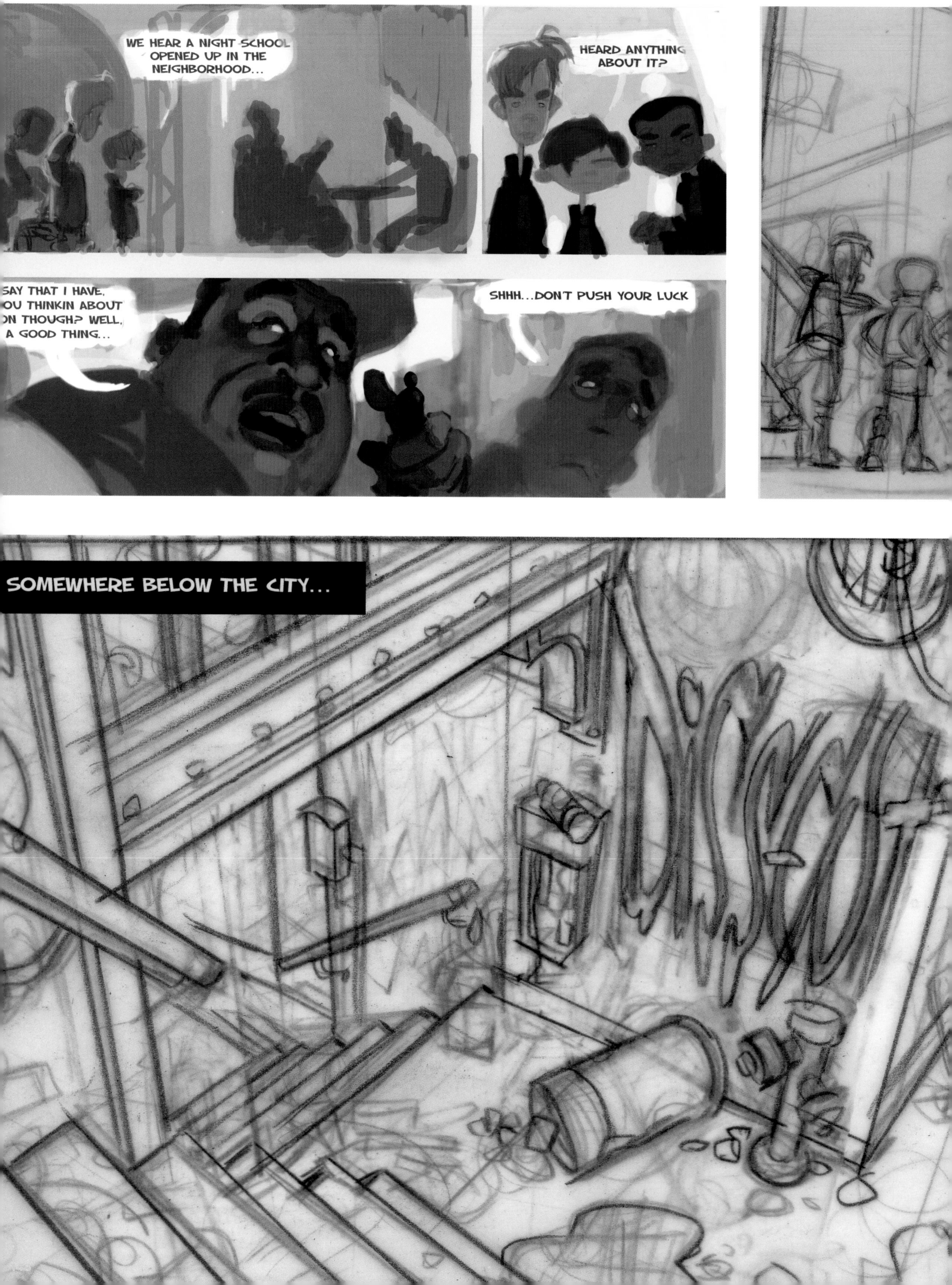
WE HEAR A NIGHT SCHOOL OPENED UP IN THE NEIGHBORHOOD...
HEARD ANYTHING ABOUT IT?
SAY THAT I HAVE, OU THINKIN ABOUT ON THOUGH? WELL, A GOOD THING...
SHHH...DON'T PUSH YOUR LUCK
SOMEWHERE BELOW THE CITY...

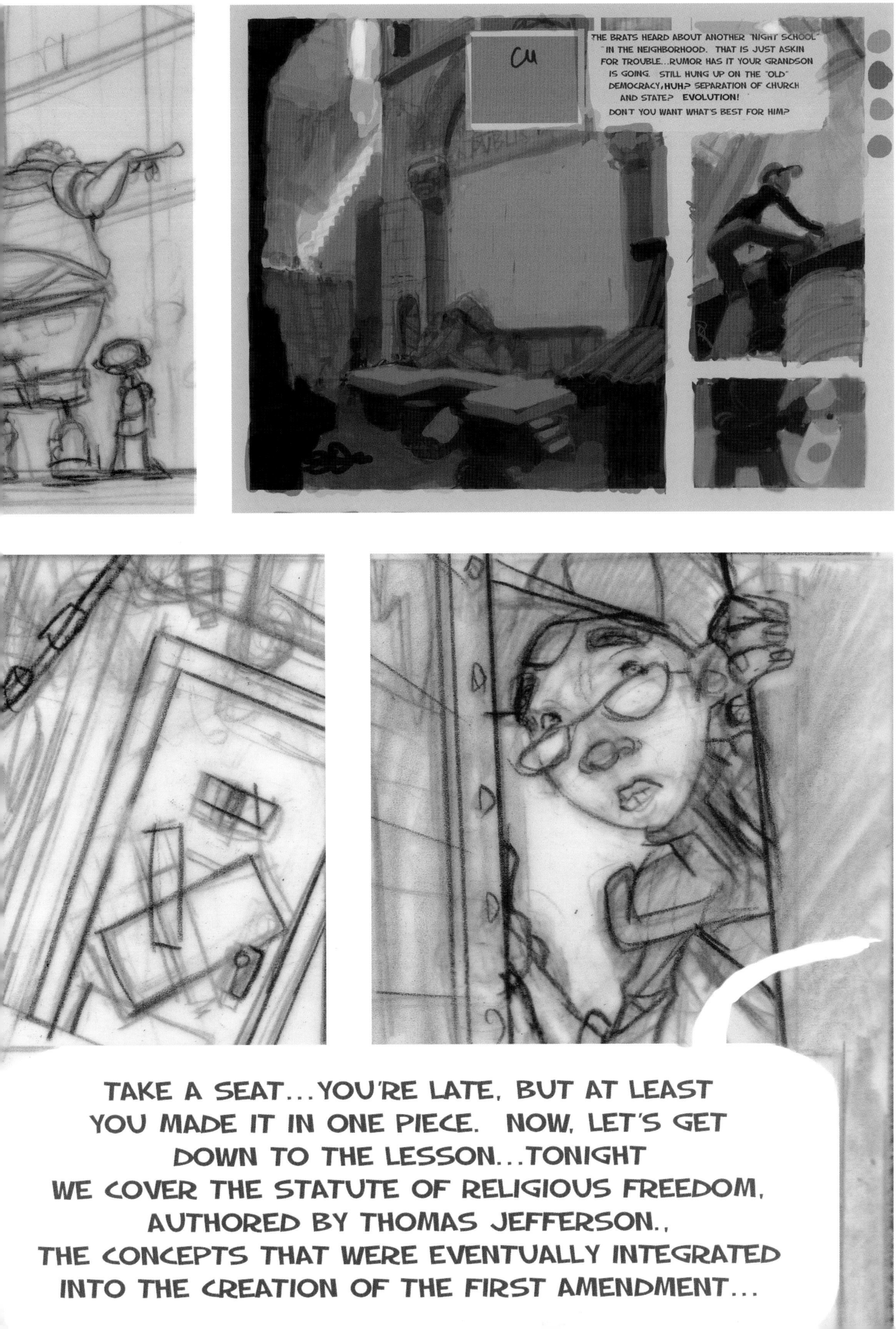
CU
THE BRATS HEARD ABOUT ANOTHER "NIGHT SCHOOL" IN THE NEIGHBORHOOD. THAT IS JUST ASKIN FOR TROUBLE...RUMOR HAS IT YOUR GRANDSON IS GOING. STILL HUNG UP ON THE "OLD" DEMOCRACY, HUH? SEPARATION OF CHURCH AND STATE? EVOLUTION! DON'T YOU WANT WHAT'S BEST FOR HIM?
TAKE A SEAT... YOU'RE LATE, BUT AT LEAST YOU MADE IT IN ONE PIECE. NOW, LET'S GET DOWN TO THE LESSON... TONIGHT WE COVER THE STATUTE OF RELIGIOUS FREEDOM, AUTHORED BY THOMAS JEFFERSON., THE CONCEPTS THAT WERE EVENTUALLY INTEGRATED INTO THE CREATION OF THE FIRST AMENDMENT...

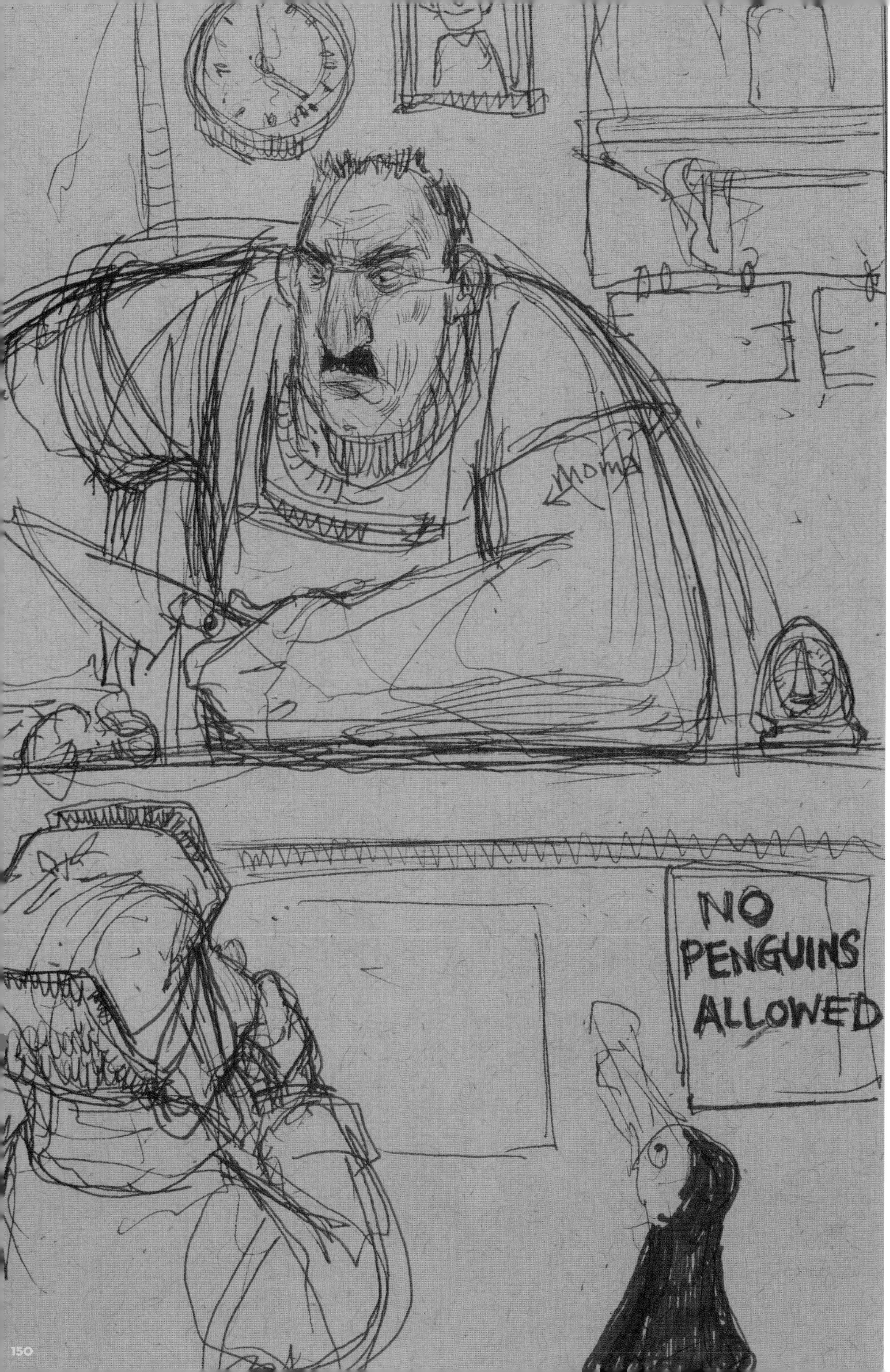
moma
NO PENGUINS ALLOWED

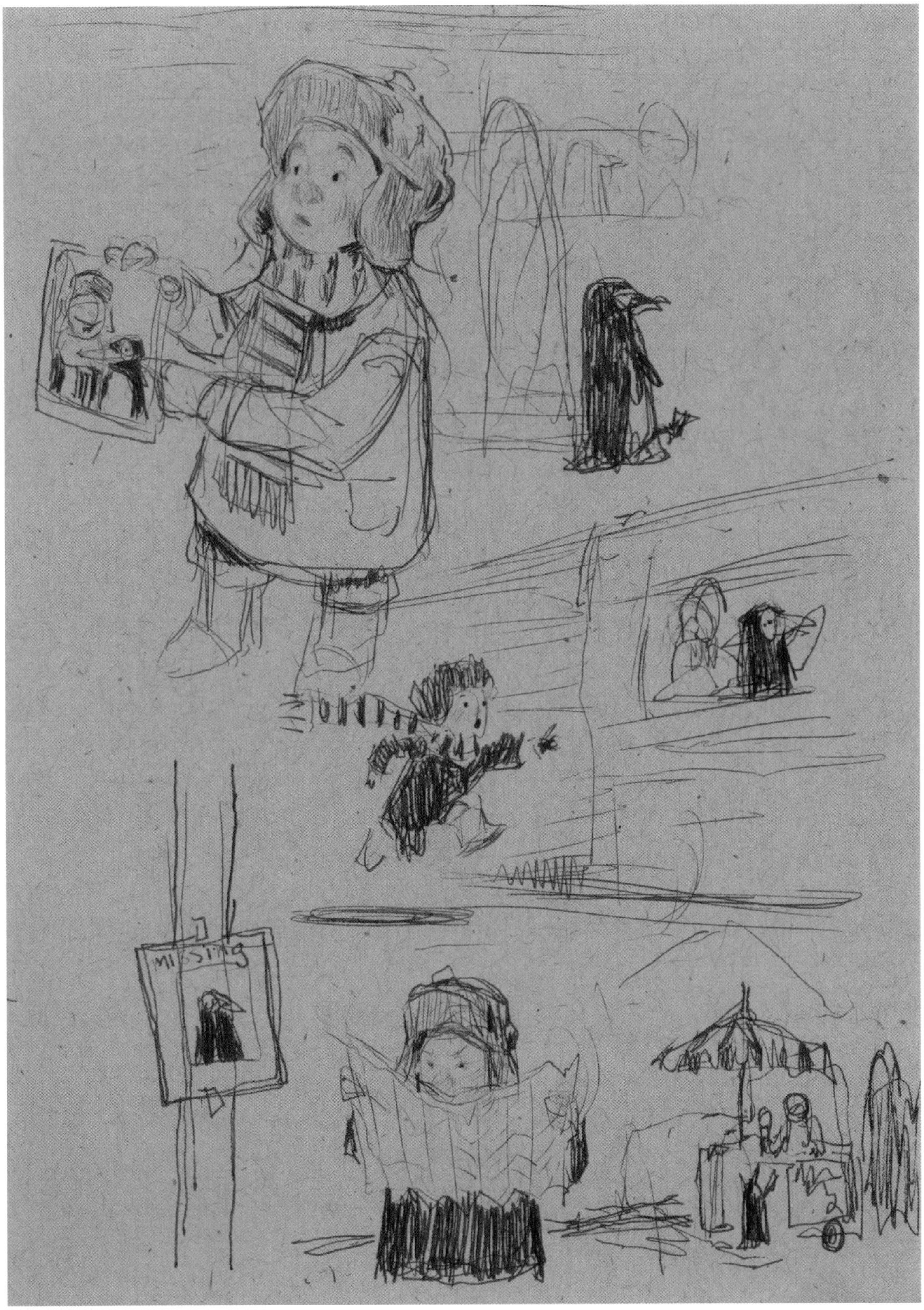
MISSING

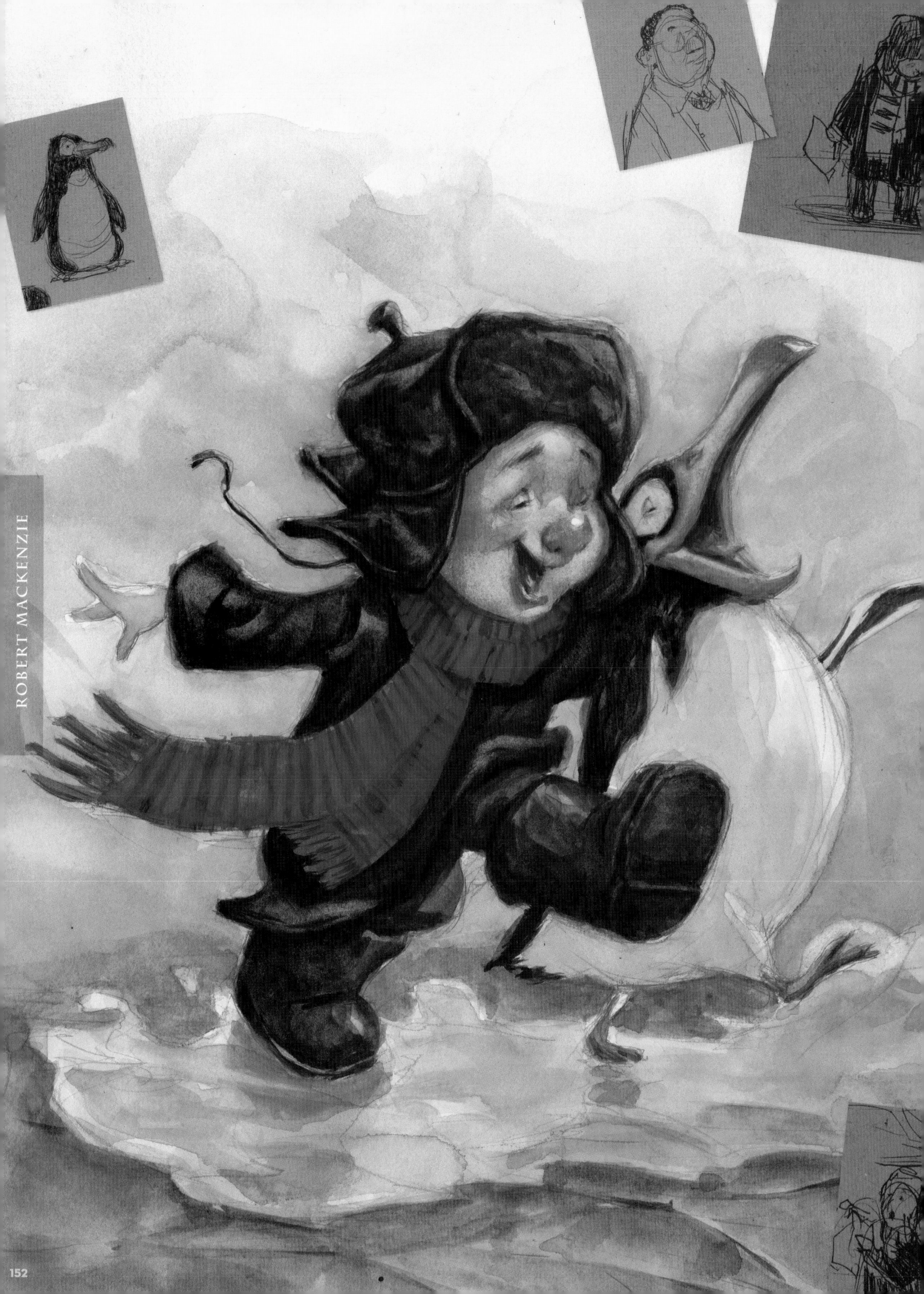

ROBERT MACKENZIE

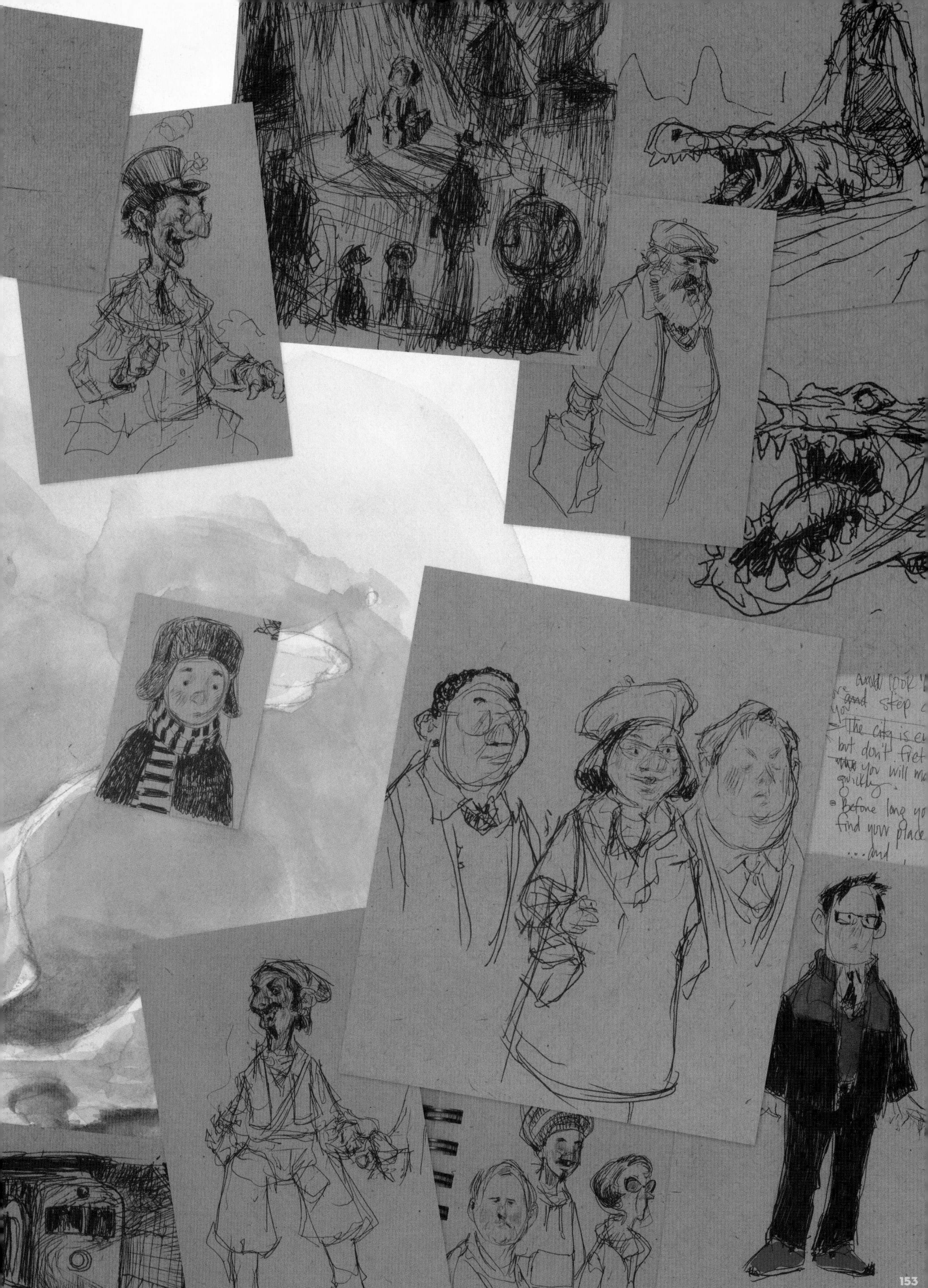
and look
step
The city is
but don't fret
you will
quickly
Before long
find your place
...and

BIOGRAPHIES

ANDREA BLASICH

Born in 1967, Andrea Blasich grew up in Milan, Italy. From an early age he was dedicated to art. His mom still remembers when she found Andrea drawing at three o'clock in the morning. Growing up in Italy certainly influenced Andrea's artistic view greatly. In 1990 at the Academy of Brera, while studying scenography, he discovered a new way of expression that would influence his entire life: animation. This passion led Andrea on a journey around Europe and eventually to the United States. His first "real" job was in Munich, Germany, for Munich Animation. Then he worked in London for Warner Bros until 1997, when he had the opportunity to come to the U.S.A. to work for Dreamworks. The dream had come true. He spent five years working in the art department as a character sculptor, visual development and layout artist for movies such as *The Road to El Dorado, Spirit: Stallion of the Cimarron, Sinbad* and *Shark Tale*. In 2003, he and his family moved to New York, where he worked on *Robots* and *Ice Age 2* at Blue Sky Studios. There he met an incredible group of artists and friends, from whom he learned a lot.

andreablasich.blogspot.com

GREG COUCH

At a very early age, Greg Couch was regaled with stories of the infamous Algonquin Round Table and its habitués. He thus became obsessed with the works of Dorothy Parker and Dashiell Hammett. Sadly, Greg emulated their drawing styles instead of their written works, which left him at a certain disadvantage professionally. Greg has a thirteen-year-old daughter whom he adores. He ate a bug once.

PETER de SÈVE

Peter de Sève has been drawing pictures for a living for the last thirty years and is still trying to get the hang of it. He wants to take the space here to officially thank his Blue Sky pals for inviting him to be a part of this wonderful book and for their limitless patience in waiting for his meager contribution. The story, "The Mermaid," is based on a traditional sea song sung by Dan Zanes, from a terrific collection of shanties called *Sea Music*, published by Festival Five Records.

www.peterdeseve.com

NASH DUNNIGAN

Nash Dunnigan spent much of his youth inside drawing, which would explain his severe allergies to all things natural that he might have encountered outdoors. Pale, tall, and curious, he made his way to art school in 1987, in the moderately sized city of Richmond, Virginia, only to be prematurely ejected after four years and a BFA diploma in 1991. Seeking all the glory and fame that goes with a jet-set illustration career, he moved to New York, and promptly starved. But the artificial climes of a bustling metropolis suited him well, toughened him up, and he eventually clawed his way into the nurturing arms of mother animation. Revived and determined, he landed the enviable position of background/layout designer and art director at many a New York animation studio. Heck, he even helped start one. Ah, life was good. He basked in the glory of seventy-hour work weeks and no overtime pay on the hot granite slab of New York for ten years.... Could it get much better? In 2003, life began again, as not forty miles outside of New York, a studio found him in a humble portfolio thatched from reeds on the banks of the Hudson. They took him in. Their name was Blue Sky, and they called their gangly, wide-eyed bundle "Layout Artist." Here, he grew up among art giants, practiced the art of cinematography on wondrous moving pictures like *Ice Age 2* and *Robots*, and learned many things. They even let him be in their super-cool art book, *Out of Picture*.

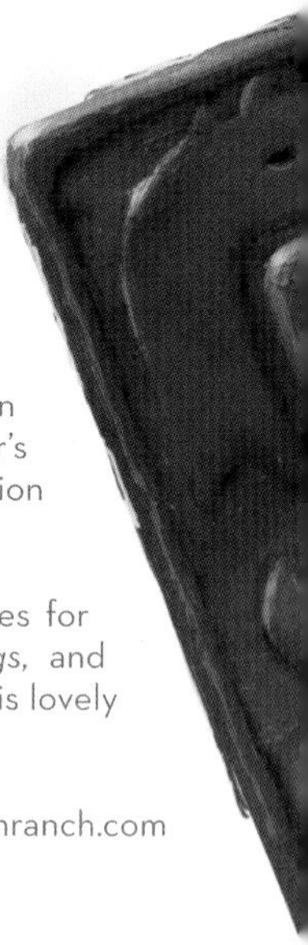

DAVID GORDON

Dave Gordon is a children's book author and illustrator who has a passion for airplanes, trucks, tractors, construction equipment, and other cool heavy machinery. He was born and raised in Colorado and later moved to the big city to attend Parsons School of Design in New York. After graduating, Dave moved out to Northern California, where he created concept art for many of Pixar's films. He also worked on the acclaimed animated television series *SpongeBob SquarePants* and on Blue Sky's *Robots*.

Dave has authored and illustrated three vehicle fairy tales for HarperCollins: *The Ugly Truckling, The Three Little Rigs*, and *Hansel and Diesel*. Dave now lives in New York City with his lovely girlfriend, Susan, and their dog, Subway.

www.illustrationranch.com

MICHAEL KNAPP

Born in 1972, Michael Knapp grew up in Wilkinsburg, Pennsylvania, just outside of Pittsburgh. Inspired by films (mostly *Star Wars*) and many cartoons (*The Jungle Book, The Hobbit*, and *Battle of the Planets*, to name a few). Michael made drawing a manic practice from a very early age. While growing up, he devoted many weekends to art classes at the Carnegie Museum and Carnegie Mellon University before attending Ringling School of Art and Design in Sarasota, Florida. In 1995, with his BFA under his belt, he began his career as a freelance illustrator in Pittsburgh before moving to New York City in 1999, where he now works as a concept artist/designer at Blue Sky Studios. He has designed for *Robots, Ice Age 2*, and also art directed the Scrat short "No Time for Nuts."

www.michaelknapp.com

BENOIT le PENNEC

Born in France in 1962, Benoit was raised mostly on comic books. After studying graphic art in Paris, he gained experience working for both publicity agencies and TV animation studios. He then moved to London to work on the movie *Balto* (a 2D animated feature) for Amblimation. When that company dissolved into Dreamworks California, he moved along with many of his colleagues to the United States, where he had the chance to work on all of Dreamworks 2D movies (from *The Prince of Egypt* to *Sinbad*) as a layout artist. He recently had the opportunity to work at Blue Sky Studios on *Robots* and got to meet the great talents of that neat East Coast studio. Thanks to them!

DANIEL LÓPEZ MUÑOZ

Daniel López Muñoz grew up in Córdova, Spain. At age 5, a wandering pencil falls into his hands. Enchanted by its magic, Daniel never lets it go. The happy pair is now found at Pixar Animation Studios, where their love continues to grow.

daniellopezmunoz.blogspot.com

ROBERT MACKENZIE

Robert Mackenzie grew up in San Mateo, California. At the age of five, he discovered that being either Santa Claus or the Easter Bunny was an unrealistic career goal, so he decided that he wanted to draw cartoons instead. He has been drawing ever since. In 1998, Robert graduated from San Jose State University with a degree in illustration and has worked as a concept, visual development, and color key artist at Lucasfilm, PDI Dreamworks, and Blue Sky Studios. Prior to moving to New York, he was on the faculty of the School of Art and Design at San Jose State.

robert-mackenzie.blogspot.com

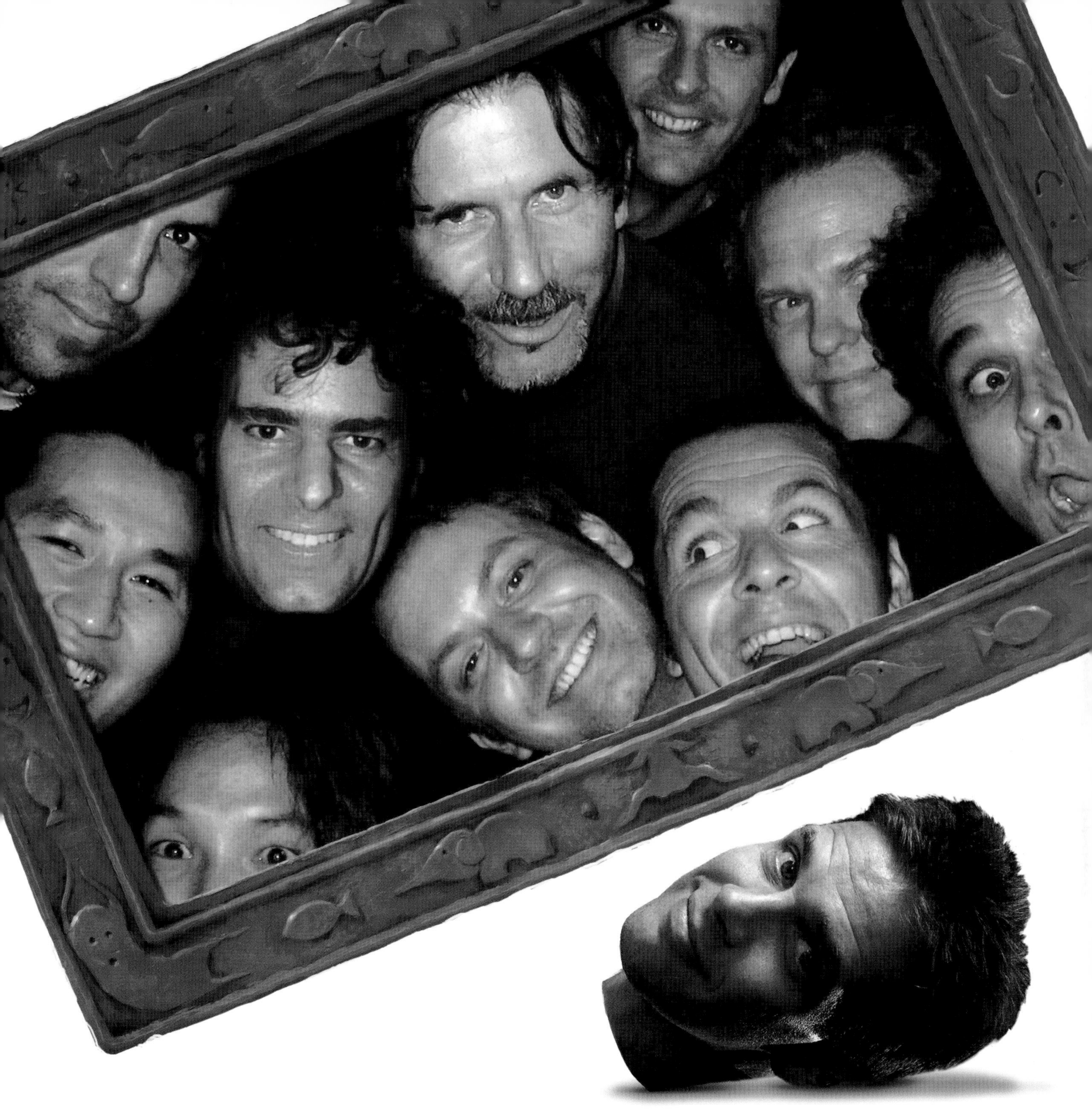

VINCENT NGUYEN

Vincent Nguyen grew up in Houston, Texas, where he began his art career drawing cowboys, monsters, and superheroes. Frustrated by his inability to draw Aquaman riding a six-headed sea horse, he decided to attend the School of Visual Arts in New York, where he earned his BFA in illustration.

A longtime fan of comics and graphic novels, Vincent has always wanted to create sequential art to tell a story of his own. He illustrated children's books for three years before joining the art department at Blue Sky Studios. This book gave him the opportunity to draw and paint all the cool stuff he's always wanted, with the exception of Aquaman riding a six-headed sea horse.

www.vincentdi.com

DAISUKE TSUTSUMI

Born and raised in the beautiful country of anime and karaoke, Daisuke "Dice" Tsutsumi was determined to become a baseball player at an early age. When faced with the reality that he wasn't actually that good, he migrated to America to look for something else to do.

After receiving irresponsible compliments from his nice and old retired classmates at his first painting class in a small community college in New York, he decided to define his American dream as making a living painting pretty pictures. Once he graduated from the School of Visual Arts, he worked for Lucas Learning LTD and now works for Blue Sky Studios painting a lot of pretty pictures .

www.simplestroke.com

Thank YOU for buying this book.

We would all like to express a HUGE thank you to Chris Wedge, who played quite a large role in bringing all of us together.

Also, many thanks go out to our friends and co-workers for their encouragement and interest in this book. They helped keep us motivated while we worked on it for such a long time.

A gigantic thank you to our dear friends in Paris: Gerald, Sophie, Diane, and Jean-Jaçques—we simply can't thank you enough for all you've done for us!

To Pierre and everyone at Paquet Editions—thank you so much for taking us on in the first place and putting out the first edition!

And finally, thank you to Tim, Erich, Judy, and everyone for taking such an interest in our book and helping us do more with it than we ever imagined!!!

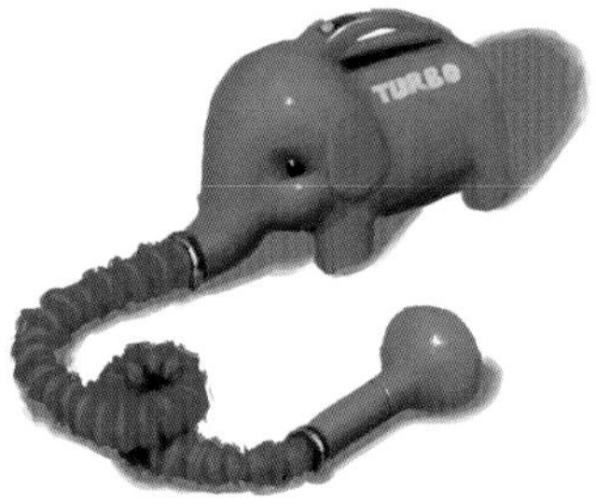
TURBO

Andrea: I want to thank my beautiful wife, Alexandra, and my little daughter, Vanessa, for their patience and love. Thanks to my fellow *Out of Picture* artists and friends, who gave me the opportunity to be part of this amazing book (a big "kiss" to Dice and Mike), and a big thank you to you readers for buying this book. Sounds like the Oscars, doesn't it?

Greg: I'd like to thank Dice, Bob, Vince, Mike, and especially Chris Gilligan for all their help and advice.

Nash would like to thank his artistic compadres for their words of encouragement and cajoling throughout the whole *Out of Picture* endeavor. Huge thanks to mom, Lynda Dunnigan ("world's greatest teacher"), for her conversations on politics and U.S. history. Big thanks also to Brenda Fairbairn at Lafayette High School and Dr. William E. Blake at VCU. Special thanks to Marina Dominis, for her encouragement and support. Lastly, thanks to Dice for his unwavering patience and friendship.

Dave: Thanks, Susie, for all your support.

Mike: Ellie, thanks for being so patient and for being a fresh set of eyes. Thanks to Ryan and all my book-mates for all the advice, crits, and inspiration. And especially my parents, who have always been a bottomless well of encouragement—thank you.

Benoit would like to thank his family and friends.

Daniel would like to thank Daisuke Tsutsumi for his inspiring leadership and Mike Knapp for his unparalleled craft. But most of all, Daniel wants to thank his beloved Kira, for her love and support. I'm sorry we couldn't go to Cape Cod as much as you had wanted while this comic was getting done. I love you.

Bob would like to thank his family for their unconditional support, Alice Fung for her love and encouragement, Carol MacKenzie and Kathryn Otoshi for their advice, and all of his teachers, students, friends, and fellow artists for inspiring him every day.

Vince would like to thank Katherine Nix and Peter Nguyen.

Dice would like to thank Karin Komoto, Mika Tsutsumi, Rosalinda Malibiran, Teresa Shenberger, and Lara Zador.

OUT OF PICTURE

Keep a lookout for

OUT OF PICTURE
VOLUME 2

in 2008!